Makes a change of

Very be

from
Keith

C000051163

A Two Horse Town
50 years in broadcasting

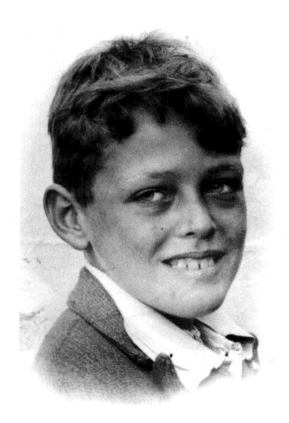

Keith Macklin

London League Publications Ltd

A Two Horse Town
50 years in broadcasting

A CIP catalogue record for this book is available from the British Library.

Published in November 2007 by:
London League Publications Ltd, P.O. Box 10441, London E14 8WR

ISBN:	978-1903659-36-6
Cover design by:	Stephen McCarthy Graphic Design 46, Clarence Road, London N15 5BB
Layout:	Peter Lush
Printed & bound by:	Biddles Ltd King's Lynn, Great Britain

Dedicated to the memory of my daughter

Tracy Elizabeth Macklin

1964-2005

Foreword

In the mid 1950s, I, then a rugby league mad teenager, fought with my grandfather and my dad to be the first to read Keith Macklin's match reports on Widnes, Warrington, Wigan and especially St Helens on a Saturday night in the *Liverpool Echo*. An hour later my mother and my grandmother prepared our evening meal exactly for the time when Keith and his co-commentators presented their *Rugby League Round Up* programme on the BBC's Northern Home Service for just 20 minutes. Yes, just 20 minutes of rugby league comment and news to whet the appetite of families like mine who absorbed and respected Keith's every word on our great game.

How surprising then that Keith should be the first correspondent to interview me after my first game of rugby league against Wakefield Trinity in 1961 following my switching of codes from rugby union and even more surprising that my good friend, having travelled alongside me to France, Australia and New Zealand to cover the XIII-a-side code's most prestigious events in the intervening years, should still be commentating with me for BBC Radio Merseyside in 2007. This is a longevity and service to the game which few can even attempt to match.

Though ever calm and totally unflappable in his approach to his profession - I well recall his delivery of a six o'clock BBC News bulletin from a telephone box in the centre of Brisbane from a few scribblings on the back of an envelope - his sense of humour and civility to all has endeared him to the players, the fans, and his fellow journalists and broadcasters. His wide range of work in rugby league, cricket, and football has provided him with a depth of knowledge on three of our premier team sports and allowed him to build up a fund of humorous stories and incidents which reflect so well the camaraderie and fun behind the scenes, especially in rugby league.

How pleasing to be asked to introduce the autobiography of a man so committed and so dedicated to his chosen sports and one who can reflect on his 50 years plus involvement with both gravity and humour. It is a rare combination which makes Keith Macklin's story all the more enjoyable and rewarding.

Ray French

Ray French was a distinguished rugby player in both codes. He is now one of rugby league's leading journalists, and is BBC Television's rugby league commentator.

Acknowledgements

It is impossible to remember and thank everyone who, however briefly, has helped along the way. Any list, however, should include the following: Mike Latham, Harry Edgar and publishers Peter Lush and Dave Farrar, who persuaded me that the book was worth writing; Raymond Fletcher, David Howes, Neil Dowson and Andy Neild for filling the memory gaps; Ken Spurling, Ray Clegg, Alan Jones and Sheila and Keith Miller for help with the mysteries of computers and the internet; Jean Barton for unravelling my handwriting and corrections to type the script; Michael O'Hare for subediting, Steve McCarthy for designing the cover, the *Warrington Guardian*, the *Lancashire Evening Post*, Action Images, David Williams, Ken Coton and Alex Service for providing photos and the staff of Biddles Ltd for printing the book.

At a personal level Sheila Macklin and my elder daughter Heather for holding the fort during frequent and long professional absences; Kate Thompson; Rickie and Alan Jones; Peg and Graham; David and Susan Mycock; Alf and Ada, Thelma and Grace at Grange-Over-Sands; Ann Lightfoot; Joan and Les; members of St James Methodist Church, Rainhill, and all other friends who have helped me weather the tougher times.

And, of course, all the players, coaches, directors, match officials, backroom staffs, fans and journalistic colleagues who made me welcome in the world of sport in 50 fast-flying years.

Keith Macklin
Blackburn, October 2007

Photographs

Unless otherwise stated, the photographs are from Keith Macklin's private collection. No copyright has been intentionally infringed, if anyone believes this has happened, please contact London League Publications Ltd.

From our sub-editor

When Keith Macklin was commentating on crown green bowls, around 1980, his co-commentator was Stan Kershaw who was the father of two of my school friends. Stan asked Keith if he wouldn't mind talking to me about sports journalism because he knew it's what I wanted to do after leaving school. He was very helpful and talked to me for about 30 minutes after doing his commentary at Spen Victoria Bowling and Cricket club in Cleckheaton, West Yorkshire. And, as a testimony to Keith's dedication in taking time out with a prospective cohort in print, I did indeed become a full-time journalist, finally rising to the point where I have sub-edited his autobiography.

Michael O'Hare

Contents

L

Past books by Keith Macklin

The history of Rugby League Football
(Stanley Paul 1962, new edition 1974)

The Rugby League Game
(Stanley Paul 1967)

Sunday Quiz' Book of World Religions
With Bill Weaver (Stanley Paul 1975)

The story of Rugby League
(Stanley Paul 1984)

1. Early days

Ideally, every life has its share of tales of the unexpected. Dull indeed would be the existence that was yawningly predictable. However, when my journalistic career finally got going after National Service at the age of 20, there would be highs and lows, twists and turns, even dramas that could not have been envisaged: Such as narrowly escaping being trampled to death by horses at a race meeting in New Zealand or steering a German police motor launch within two inches of a stone bridge on a Hamburg lake.

Then there was the radio commentary when my personal choice as man-of-the-match was not even on the field.

There was also the time when the leading citizen of an Australian mining borough wrote to *The Times* complaining that I had called Gympie "a one-horse town".

I have been ordered off a cricket pitch by an England test player, and thrown out of rugby league dressing rooms by club coaches.

Then there was the time when my car went though the plate glass window of a Blackburn shop, and I was nearly arrested for ram-raiding.

There have been good moments too. I suppose there were bound to be some over 50 years, including reporting rugby league Australasian tours and Wembley Challenge Cup finals, an Olympic Games and a football World Cup.

But I am getting ahead of myself.

****

According to Shakespeare's *Hamlet*, a character much quoted in sporting circles: "There is a divinity which shapes our ends". If this be true, then my ends were shaped by guidance from above, by three separate sporting events in early and late childhood. They took place at three famous sports venues: Knowsley Road rugby league ground at St Helens, Old Trafford cricket ground, and the home of Liverpool Football Club, Anfield.

Between them they decided the path my life would take once I left school behind and set out to augment the family income in the great big world outside. At school my favourite lessons, and the only ones I displayed any aptitude for, were English and games. I was hopeless at physics and chemistry, marginally better at maths, and could just about cope with Latin, French, history, geography and scripture. But my spirits were only lifted when I saw on the lessons charts the magic words "English language", "English

1

literature" and "games". I looked forward to them eagerly, and the most miserable afternoons were ones when we looked out of the classroom window in winter to see pouring rain, or snow, or frost and knew that games would be cancelled and we would have two hours in dreaded 'private study'. These were spent in surly adolescent silence bewailing the weather gods' cruel machinations.

It was inevitable, then, that the incidents that stand out from childhood are all connected with sport. The first occurred when I was seven. My father decided I was ready to be taken to a professional rugby league game, so he took me on the trolley bus to Knowsley Road, just a few miles down the road from our village, Rainhill, a small suburb of St Helens. It was 1938, the last year before the outbreak of war.

I do not remember the team Saints were playing, or the result. I spent the game perched on my father's shoulder, as he stood on what was then a mound rather than a terrace, and tried to take an interest in what was happening on the field. It was not easy for a restless seven-year-old, for on the field all that was happening was that a lot of large, hairy men were barging into each other and throwing the ball while they indulged in wrestling bouts on the turf. Smaller men would occasionally scamper off with the ball, but they, too, seemed only too anxious to get rid of it. The only name I heard mentioned, or remember hearing, was that of a chap named Tracey, who was something of a local hero with St Helens. He ran about a lot with the ball and received great cheers from the crowd. When I later asked my father about Mr Tracey, my father said he was something called a 'stand-off', which puzzled me because he had seemed to get involved far more than anyone else.

My father was in those days a Saints fan, because we lived that short bus journey away in Rainhill. However, in later years he became first a fan of Warrington, for a slightly bizarre reason I shall recount later, and then of Widnes when I got married and lived in a house about 300 yards from Naughton Park.

The trip to Knowsley Road did not, at the time, make much impact on me apart from causing a small boy to be impatient and bored.

But the seed had been sown.

****

Seven years later. It was 1945, I was 14 and the Second World War was mercifully over. People had danced in the streets to celebrate VE Day, and children were allowed to stay up late, but to be honest I do not recall being greatly inconvenienced by the war. Mercifully none of my relatives had been killed or injured, though my uncle Les had served in the Royal Navy, and we had been made to put on gas masks and run down into Anderson shelters when the sirens started wailing. The nearest we came to the horrors of war was a night when Liverpool, 12 miles away, was bombed. Although the docks were the ostensible target, large areas of the city were devastated, and many innocent lives were lost, and on that night I remember cowering under the stairs, looking out of the window occasionally to see the hideous firework display amid the crump, crump, crump of exploding bombs. My dad had continued to work at the wire mill at Prescot, unfit to serve - he had lost the sight of one eye in a childhood accident - and my mum, like millions of others, had worked minor miracles with the rationed food and clothing supplies. At junior school neither my younger brother Brian nor I had proved exemplary scholars, but we had done enough to pass the scholarship necessary to enter Prescot Grammar School.

It was a wonderfully hot summer in 1945, befitting V for Victory year, or perhaps in my youthful euphoria it merely seemed so. The sport of cricket blossomed again, as the servicemen and crowds flocked again to all sporting venues. A great event in cricket's revival was the staging of a Victory Test at Old Trafford, home of my county, Lancashire. It was between an England XI and the Royal Australian Air Force, a team heavily sprinkled with Australian Test and state players.

The long school holidays came, and my parents had agreed that I could go to watch all three days of the match, staying overnight with my auntie Janey and uncle Harold and my cousins Audrey and Sylvia, who lived wonderfully conveniently in Chatsworth Road, Stretford, a boy's walking distance from the ground.

In those pre-television years the only way to watch live sport was to be there and after the austerities of war massive crowds flocked to all events. I knew that Old Trafford would be packed, with hundreds of under-16s squatting behind what was then a rope at the boundary edge. So I set off early for the ground, after an eventful evening with my uncle, aunt and cousins which almost brought a premature and messy end to my young life, or at least might have sent me to hospital. I had arrived at Stretford in early afternoon and at one stage had wandered into the garden, amusing myself at the expense of the family's huge St Bernard dog called Bruce. Even now I feel ashamed at my behaviour, which was not excusable even in a youngster of 14 summers. Seeing that Bruce was outside his kennel, but on the end of a long chain which did not reach as far as the garden path, I spent several minutes picking up small pebbles and flicking them at Bruce's head, hitting the target, Bruce's nose, several times and occasioning yelps of mixed pain and anger.

3

The pavilion at Old Trafford – Keith has many fond memories of watching cricket here. (Photo: Peter Lush)

That evening the family sat down to dinner, as they did in those days, and we chatted. Then my cousins Audrey and Sylvia said it was time for Bruce to be allowed to come into the house and be cosseted and petted. We left the table and Bruce lolloped into the house, only to stop dead when he saw me. With one bound he pinned me against the wall, a paw on each shoulder, and was just about to have his supper, starting with my nose, when uncle Harold and auntie Janey leapt to the rescue. They grabbed Bruce's head and collar, and my cousins joined in by getting hold of Bruce's tail. For a few minutes there was a life-or-death tug-of-war before the huge St Bernard, a breed not renowned for fearsome rages, was finally subdued and returned in disgrace and supper-less to his outside kennel.

When I had stopped gibbering with fright I had the good grace to confess all, pleading for mercy for Bruce. I received a lecture from my uncle on the foolishness of antagonising large dogs, and retired to bed offering thanks to the deity that I was still alive and well enough to go to Old Trafford on the morrow.

The evening's traumas were soon forgotten when I arrived at Warwick Road and joined the heaving throng clamouring eagerly for admission. It took an hour to finally get through the turnstile, but at last I was ensconced on the grass behind the rope in my own small space amid the mass of excited youngsters.

It was a bakingly hot summer's day, the sky above Manchester was for once a cloudless blue, as it remained throughout three wonderful days, and I was in a schoolboy's version of heaven.

For the Australians a spectacularly tall and handsome Adonis of a man, Keith Miller, later to become one of the greatest ever Australian test players, clattered the English bowling all round the field with the same cavalier arrogance with which he shot down Messerschmitt fighters with the RAAF; one rasping cover drive sent me and the other fledglings round the rope scattering like pigeons. Another rather less well known Australian batsman, Bob Cristofani, hit a century, while for England two Lancashire bowlers, 't' owd chain horse', as Dick Pollard was known among the Old Trafford faithful, and Eddie Phillipson opened the attack. It was all played in a cheerful, albeit competitive spirit in keeping with the continuing victory celebrations.

It was during these three marvellous days that my ends were further shaped. During a lunch interval I glanced upward after eating the sandwiches made by auntie Janey and saw that immediately above me was the old press box. Inside were journalists of all ages, shapes and sizes, some of them wearing the trilby hat which in those days was a badge of office, all with busy fingers tapping furiously on clattering typewriters.

My immediate thought was born of the deadly sin of envy. How lucky they were to have a privileged vantage point for which they paid nothing and did not have to queue; eventually they would be able to go to the dressing rooms and talk to the demigod Keith Miller and our own Dick Pollard while we, the hoi polloi, sat on benches or on the grass.

Another seed was sown.

****

In 1946 came the apogee of my school career, which, in academic terms, had been no more than adequate. Once again the unworthy attribute of low cunning played a major part as I conned my way into the Prescot Grammar School (PGS) Junior Football XI, an achievement which was to lead all the way to Anfield, home of my favourite football team, Liverpool. Although not the force they are today the Reds had always been first my father's and then my team, and I had stood in the boys' pen and on the Spion Kop to support them during the war years when clubs continued to play patched-together sides from locals and guest players who were not away on the battlefields.

I must return to the start of the 1945-46 school season. The PGS games master, Mr Eyton-Jones, summoned together on the main football pitch all under-16s who wanted a trial for the Junior XI. Around 40 to 50 turned up, which posed a problem for our games supremo, who had only 22 places to offer for a trial match.

He took the sensible course, indeed the only fair one, of saying he would make substitutions throughout the game, and try to fit in as many players as possible. To form his starting teams he asked us to line up in rows corresponding to the positions in which we wanted to play, from goalkeeper to the now old-fashioned position of outside left. This is where cunning came into play. I noticed that there were half-a-dozen would-be centre forwards, and four or five goalkeepers, and at least two for every position. Except one, that of outside right, or right wing as it is called today when it is not buried under the all-purpose title of 'midfielder'. My own favourite position, and the one in which I played for my class team, was yet another 'midfield' role, then known as inside right. However, having spotted just one body in the right wing line-up, I moved forward one pace into that line. Mr Eyton-Jones had no option but to start the game with me, and I must have played reasonably well, for I was only subbed late in the game, and was chosen for the school team in the first inter-school fixture against Quarry Bank High School. Luck was with me in that game, too, for I got an easy tap-in goal early on and, in the absence of anyone better, kept the place.

Along came the cup competition, the Liverpool Secondary Schools Junior Shield, a trophy which Prescot had never won, and for which we were rank outsiders in every sense, geographically as well as in presumed playing ability. We surprised ourselves by beating Quarry Bank again in the first round, and were absolutely elated when we beat the favourites, Alsop High School, on their own pitch in the second. Then followed a win at Liverpool Institute, and, to our utter amazement, a fourth consecutive away tie saw us beat the second favourites St Francis Xavier.

It took a long time for it to sink in. Prescot, the team from out in the sticks, had beaten four Liverpool city schools, and would play a fifth, Holt High School in the final. At Anfield.

Anfield! Surely our luck could not hold out at these schoolboys' theatre of dreams. Mr Eyton-Jones told us we had done far more than expected by reaching the final, and not to expect too much, just be glad we had got there. That was fair enough for me, a Reds fan who throughout the war had watched the likes of Matt Busby, Don Welsh, Jackie Balmer, Willie Fagan and the legendary Billy Liddell do their stuff in the red shirt. I would tread the hallowed ground; might even get a goal, and be able to brag about it for the rest of my life.

When the midweek day arrived I was a bag of nerves, which were hardly calmed when I ran with my teammates down the famous Anfield tunnel, where the intimidating sign 'THIS IS ANFIELD' is now displayed. Running down this tunnel has paralysed nervous systems much more resilient than mine. When we ran out on to the pitch it looked enormous, as massive and overpowering as the occasion.

I will not tell a lie. It got to me from the first minute to the 83rd. My legs felt like jelly and I could do nothing right. I muffed a few attempted shots, sent attempted crosses wide or miles over the top, and at the end of the first half was a lonely figure on the right while my Prescot colleagues attacked down the middle or the left.

This sorry anti-climax continued until the aforementioned 83rd minute, by which time we were trailing Holt HS by two goals to one. Needless to say, I had played no part in the goal, and was resigned to defeat and the humiliating inquest afterwards. Then, out of the blue, the Prescot captain Ian McIntyre, later to go to Oxbridge and become head of BBC Radio 3, decided to give me another chance. He pushed the ball up the right touchline just over the half-way line, and shouted "Go, go Macklin!" This time I went.

Whatever celestial force was with me drove me past two covering defenders. As I neared the corner flag at the Anfield Road End I saw the burly left back, who hitherto had had me in his pocket, tearing across with a look on his face that suggested I was about to be propelled into orbit. Not fancying this I turned inside on my left foot and he roared past me into touch. As I reached the edge of the penalty box another defender clattered into me, but not before I had slid the ball across the area with my left foot. I saw stars and the world went round for a few seconds, and when I pulled myself up I could see our left winger Ronnie Mercer cavorting away from the area with the rest of the team chasing jubilantly after him. He had cracked my cross into the net and it was 2-2.

If this sounds like one of the more far-fetched stories from *Boys' Own Paper*, or the old-time story magazines *Wizard* or *Hotspur*, believe me it is true, and there was more to come. Two minutes from the end our left back Ted Burgham took a free kick on the left hand side of the area. He hit it head-high straight at the goalkeeper who panicked a little and punched it up in the air. As it came down I saw the half chance. The petrified goalkeeper stayed on his line and the other defenders just seemed to stand and watch as the lanky string bean of a Prescot right winger ran in and, seeing the goalie standing with his legs wide open, nutmegged him by heading the ball between the outstretched limbs.

It was my turn to be buried by ecstatic teammates and I remember McIntyre arriving first and shouting in my ear "You took us through". Such is fate.

I had had an absolute stinker for 83 minutes, but two moments when my head and feet actually got themselves together had made me an unlikely, and possibly unworthy, hero. But I had done it, I had scored a goal at Anfield.

The result had pleasant repercussions the following day. I had been due at the headmaster's study during the afternoon to be caned for a misdemeanour in class earlier in the week, and it was a frightening prospect. Six of the best from R. Spencer Briggs, accompanied during each stroke by a mini-lecture on the need to maintain behavioural standards in class, was a salutary experience. Furthermore I knew I deserved it, and to this day I have no truck with the ideological twaddle that is spouted about the effects of corporal punishment on young minds. I felt no bitterness, and have not suffered lifelong psychological damage causing me to become an antisocial psychopath, nor have any of my schoolmates whom I meet regularly at old boys' functions. Indeed, I never repeated whatever misdemeanour it was that landed me in the head's study for a caning.

I had prepared myself, rather deceitfully, by putting on four pairs of football shorts under my long trousers, but they were not needed. As I stood, trying not to quiver, in front of R. Spencer Briggs he delivered one of the most welcome short speeches I have ever heard.

"Macklin, in view of your services to this school's sporting achievements yesterday, I have decided to commute your caning to the lesser punishment of writing 100 lines on the necessity to show respect to your teacher and the privilege of learning in this establishment. You may go back to your class." I nearly fainted with relief, and went to the games changing room to take off my four pairs of football shorts before returning to tell the tale to my astonished classmates.

It was the third of the three boyish experiences that were to steer me in an inevitable direction. One had been in rugby league, one in cricket and one in football. Pure chance or the workings of fate? Who knows? But I knew that a career path had been set. I was not to be a librarian, a novelist, a film critic, or a psychiatrist (a choice born of the fact that I was a neurotic little sod). I was going to be a sports journalist. Little did I know that it would take six more years, and would include spells as a colliery clerk and a reluctant National Serviceman before I finally started the climb from the bottom rungs of the Fourth Estate.

2. National Service

Actually, it all started reasonably promisingly. In the winter of 1946 I applied to several local newspapers for a job as junior reporter, and eventually got what seemed to be an encouraging reply from a now defunct evening paper, the *Liverpool Evening Express*. It was the stable companion of the still extant and thriving *Liverpool Echo* at a time when it was not unusual for a large city to have two evening papers. Because they were owned by the same company there was no competition between the *Echo* and the *Exy*, as they were colloquially known, and between them they sold nearly half a million copies in the post-war glory days of newspapers, with the *Echo* outselling the *Exy* by an average of three copies to one.

The letter was from a Mr D.G. Christie, the news editor, and invited me to an interview in Victoria Street, Liverpool, home of the editorial offices and printing works of the two newspapers. It was for a 'junior position' in the editorial department, and it was with the proverbial and traditional pounding heart that I travelled by train from Rainhill to Lime Street and walked to Victoria Street to the interview which, I fondly imagined, would see me in a couple of years reporting on Liverpool, Everton and possibly St Helens and Warrington as the youngest star reporter and columnist in newspaper history.

Donald Christie turned out to be a small, dapper, fast-talking Scotsman who grilled me on my limited academic background, did not seem overwhelmed by my derring-do at Anfield, and asked if I did shorthand and typewriting, which were apparently de rigueur among journalistic aspirants. Momentarily panic stricken, I told a porky, that I was indeed engaged on an intensive course of the twin subjects, and making excellent progress. This was only a half-truth, because I had enrolled for the subjects with a Rainhill private tutor, Mrs Summerfield, at 10 shillings a week, and was due to start the following Monday.

He nodded, and then told me the welcome news that I could start on the *Express* in a month's time. However, I was not to be a fledgling reporter. The vacancy was for a copy-typist, a job which involved sitting at a typewriter, putting on a pair of headphones, and taking copy from real journalists. I swallowed my disappointment, saw it as a stepping stone to greatness, shook his proffered hand, and resolved to take extra typing lessons from Mrs Summerfield.

This I did, applying myself with such intensity of concentration that a month later, when I seated myself in the copy room of the

9

Evening Express on my opening day I was up to a reasonable 50 to 60 words per minute.

Being a copy-typist was not quite like being a journalist, but it was a start, plus the fact that I was typing out court cases, crimes, accidents and oases of sport including cricket scores from Old Trafford, dog racing results, and, best of all, Don Kendall's column.

Taking the Kendall column was both a privilege and a responsibility and I was flattered after several months in the copy room to be assigned to the duty. Don Kendall was one of the gods on the Merseyside sporting planet. He was 'Pilot' in the days when many journalists adopted noms-de-plume instead of using their proper names, and he covered all Liverpool games - to me at that tender age this was a job made in heaven.

There was, however, a drawback. Pilot rarely bothered to come into the office, choosing to work from home and from there to matches. In order to get his daily Anfield column or match report into the first edition of the paper - for those were the days when big evening papers ran off several editions a day - he had to be awakened by a phone call at 7.30am prompt. He would then dictate his literary pearls before, presumably, going back to sleep.

For his 16-year-old copy-typist it meant travelling into Lime Street from Rainhill on the 6.00am workmen's special train, but it was worth it to sit at the feet of Don Kendall, even if he had a dictating habit which made life a bit hard and tortuous.

He never wrote his column. He dictated it from memory or from a few notes scribbled on scraps of paper, or both, which was all right when his sleepy voice, punctuated by frequent yawns, gave off fluent sentences. However, when occasionally he lost his thread, he would say "Scrub that last bit and start again". A 500-word column could be up to an hour to take and correct, before an irate early-morning sub-editor would snatch the finished product from me and scribble headings on it before handing it to the printer.

After about a year in the copy room I finally caught the eye of the sports editor, I think his name was Shaw, and when I declared my ambitions he asked me if I knew anything about rugby league. I told him I was a lifelong, well, 10-years supporter of St Helens, and he assigned me to do a 200-word report for the Saturday *Sporting Pink* on Liverpool Stanley versus Bramley.

It was not exactly Wigan versus Saints, but it was the pathway thereto, and on a wet Saturday I arrived at the press box at the Stanley Greyhound Track at Knotty Ash, not far from the house where an unknown young comedian, Ken Dodd, was polishing up his first act.

The older denizens of the press area gave me a few scowls and curt nods, a traditional journalistic welcome to newcomers, and I made copious notes on a brand-new notebook with a brand-new fountain pen. Where I got the notes from I do not know, for it was a dull game, played in rain on a muddy pitch, and I forget the score.

At the end of the match I composed what I thought were 200 words of sharp, penetrating analysis and flowing prose, picked up the *Express* telephone and, at last on the right end of the reporting operation, dictated it to the woman who came in on Saturday afternoons especially to take match reports. I then ran out of the stadium, boarded a bus to Liverpool, and went post-haste to the *Express* offices to watch the presses roll as they carried a moment of history.

When the grinning overseer finally handed me a copy it was a minor anti-climax. My piece, anonymous with no by-line attached, was tucked away near the bottom of an inside page, and had been cut to half its original length. I caught the train home a chastened young man, refusing to be cheered up by my dear mother's quotation of the proverb "From little acorns giant oak trees grow". My first masterpiece was no more than a bent twig, and to make matters worse no one, least of all the sports editor, mentioned it on Monday morning.

If that was bad enough, much worse was to come. Not long after my evening paper journalistic baptism all the male copy typists under the age of 18 - I think there were four of us - were summoned to Don Christie's office. We had no idea what was in store, but were soon left in no doubt that our careers were to be ended before they had really begun. In his most terse Scottish vernacular the no-nonsense news editor told us that because we would be eligible for National Service at the age of 18, and according to law would have to be reinstated by our employers on completion of military duty, we were all to be given one month's notice, ensuring that our next employers, if any, would be forced to carry the burden.

It was a devastating blow, and I deliberately missed two trains home from Lime Street while I tried to pull myself together and work out how to tell my parents. When I did so my father, as ever the soul of practical philosophy, said the comforting words: "Never mind, Tommy Cunliffe will get you a job down the pit".

Tommy Cunliffe was a jovial family friend who throughout the war had worked at the nearby Burtonwood air base of the United States Air Force. Because the Yanks did not have rationing, and were liberal with their generosity to Limey employees, Tommy had frequently brought home chocolates and other treats from the airmen's canteen. He was something of a fixer in local circles, having won widespread friendships for his Burtonwood-fed generosity, and he had contacts at the local colliery near the village of Cronton. When Tommy was consulted he duly reported that there was, indeed, a junior clerkship going in the training officer's department at Cronton and when he broke the news I recall that my head sank and my jaw dropped with gratitude.

However, there was nothing I could do about it. I had failed to get a job anywhere, and not just in journalism, because of impending National Service. Furthermore, as Tommy Cunliffe told my gleeful parents, people in the mines were providing fuel to drive the nation's factories in the post-war revival, and were, therefore, exempt from National Service.

The die was cast and it was with a heavy but resigned heart that one late autumn morning in 1948 I cycled the two miles from Rainhill to the nearby village of Cronton just outside Widnes. I turned right into the colliery gates to be confronted by the high towers of the pithead winding engines endlessly drawing up the huge metal tubs filled with newly hewn coal. A long concrete yard led to the red brick office blocks and behind them were the pithead baths whence issued the newly scrubbed miners up from their shift, weary and with blue-black rings around their eyes.

It was a culture shock of the first magnitude. I had read and heard of the privations and hard lives of miners, but had never dreamt that one day I would work among them against the continual clonk and rattle of the winding engines and the rumble of the cages bringing the black-faced colliers up from the bowels of the earth.

From day one I was the proverbial fish out of water, or square peg in a round hole. Instead of sitting in a grandstand press box with notebook and telephone watching rugby, soccer and cricket, I was condemned to spend the rest of my life totting up miners' shift payments and tonnages of coal, and occasionally, on dreaded days, going down into the blackness in a cage to take messages to the managers of pit numbers 1, 2, and 3.

Weekends were an oasis of relief from boredom and depression. The *Express* had given me a tiny lifeline commissioning 100-word reports on amateur rugby league at 10 shillings a time, about £5.00 in today's currency.

I could keep my ambitions barely alive watching encounters between UGB St Helens, Vine Tavern, British Sidac and Blackbrook in the St Helens Amateur Rugby League. The matches were played on bumpy, unfenced grounds, and the players changed at the local pubs.

I stuck it out at the colliery for about a year with my mother convinced that I would, one day, do her proud and enable her to brag to the neighbours by reaching the heights of colliery manager.

But finally I had had enough. Despite the entreaties of an angry father, a tearful mother and an indignant Tommy Cunliffe I handed in my notice to the colliery training officer, Alf Taylor, and shook the coal dust off my feet for the last time. Even the rigours of National Service could not be worse than the bleak, grinding boredom of the mines. I knew I was behaving in a "soft as muck" manner but my mind was made up.

****

In mid-1949 I enlisted into the service of my country at RAF Padgate near Warrington, the main British recruit entry camp. Like most of the rest of the freshly-washed besuited lads from all over Britain it was to be my first experience of living away from home, and it hit me hard.

From the start it was made clear to we smooth-chinned innocent mummy's boys, as the drill instructors insisted we were, that we were entering into a stage in our lives that would involve acute discomfort and rigid discipline. All, of course, for our own good and for the security of the country.

The following morning, after a fitful night's sleep in the bleak barrack room with its iron bedsteads, basic sheets and blankets we were rudely aroused by barked commands of "Wakey, wakey, you lazy lot, and get yourselves on parade!"

After a shivering wash in cold water we hurriedly threw on our clothes and stumbled out of the billet to be lined up and marched in ragged formation down through rows of more wooden billets to a long, high wooden storeroom where we exchanged our civilian clothes for plain blue RAF uniforms, blue shirts and black shoes.

The next stop for the still-yawning gaggle of youths was another, slightly smaller, hut where the station barbers had their headquarters. After sarcastically asking us whether we preferred a light trim or a short back and sides, they proceeded, without ceremony, to give us what was known in the services as The Lawnmower Cut, and we came out looking like a gang of trainee nightclub bouncers.

We were now kitted out, and the next stage was square bashing at RAF Bridgnorth in Shropshire.

The next eight weeks were not the happiest in the lives of 18 year olds who had left behind the warm bosom of the family for the rigours of a concrete and timber open prison. There was some small relief at weekends when twice daily drills were suspended, and although we were not allowed home leave, we would potter about the camp and visit the NAAFI canteen, the library or the camp's Astra Cinema.

On weekdays, however, our sensitive souls got some idea of what life must have been like in Sing Sing or Alcatraz, the notorious prisons for American lifers. The DIs, as the drill instructors were known and feared, drove us, shouted at us and humiliated us, and all, as we were to realise later in life, for our own good.

Their acts were well rehearsed and honed to perfection. The scripts followed a pattern of fierce discipline, ritual humiliation and demoralising brutal dialogue.

For instance, anyone standing over six-feet tall, into which category my parents' genes had combined to place me, was automatically called, somewhat contemptuously, 'Lofty', and one particular piece of dialogue went like this, with the drill instructor speaking two inches away from my right ear.

DI: Lofty!!
Me: Yes, Corporal
DI: Louder, Lofty!!
Me: YES, CORPORAL!
DI: You are a stupid airman, Lofty. What are you?
Me: A stupid airman, Corporal.
DI: I can't hear you.
Me: A STUPID AIRMAN, CORPORAL.
DI: You are. And if you offend me again, Lofty, I will tear your right arm clean off at the roots and beat you about the head with the soggy end. Do you understand me, Lofty?
Me (gulping): YES, CORPORAL.

Punishments for being sloppy in dress or posture on parade, or having an unmade bed, allegedly dusty bed space, or untidy locker were often bizarre in their unpleasantness: like running around the parade ground several times clad in full battle dress with fully laden personal pack on one's back, or going to the coal store and painting a prescribed number of coals with white paint. Punishments were always carried out under the ruthless supervision of a DI.

It all sounds too pointlessly cruel to be believable but it happened. And it worked. After eight weeks of this Spartan discipline, along with early bedtimes and arousals, simple but wholesome meals and regular mealtimes, we were all upright young men, fit as young bulls, spick and span in our new uniforms and shoes polished like mirrors, and filled with the team ethic. Homesickness was not entirely banished but it seemed an eternity away. Our horizons had shrunk to the boundaries of RAF Bridgnorth, and our world was, momentarily, the billets, the barrack square, the dining mess, the NAAFI and the Astra cinema.

I recall not doing too badly in my square bashing test, but nowhere near good enough to be a pilot, which was not open to me anyway. The climax of square-bashing was the passing out parade on the big parade square with hundreds of proud parents watching the oafish youths to whom they had waved tearful goodbyes two months earlier striding smartly and purposefully past to the strains of a military band playing the RAF *March Past*. That night brought the happiest nights sleep for ages. Not only was the gruelling torture over, but in the closing days the end-shaping divinity had again been hard at work aided by another piece of cunning and another piece of luck.

During the long weeks of initial training the times of boredom had been relieved by occasional trips to the small library and educational section, where recruits escaped briefly from parade ground, mess and billet for occasional general knowledge talks on historical and literary figures. I had struck up an acquaintance with one of the permanent staff, a young corporal who demonstrated the fact that not all NCOs were hard-nosed drill instructors.

He asked me whether I had chosen the trade I would follow for the remainder of my time in the service, because in the closing days of initial training one had to fill in a form stating three trade choices in order of preference. Because my eyesight was not A1, I could not be a pilot, so there was to be no officer training school for me.

"Why not go for personnel selection assessor?" he asked. These were the people who, either as regulars or National Servicemen, gave written and oral tests in the closing weeks of training to assess potential skills and aptitudes. He was one of them.

What he said next clinched it, and ensured that I would not apply for a clerical job, or pay clerk, or, heaven forbid, an airframe mechanic. He told me PSAs were automatically promoted to the rank of corporal.

It was first on my list - no one else in my section knew about the availability of a job which carried stripes - and I got the placement. My posting was to RAF Hornchurch, near Romford in Essex, one of the bases from which Spitfire pilots took off for the Battle of Britain.

In the immediate post-war years it was the training base for personnel selection assessors, and my six weeks there were blissful in the extreme, and the start of what became as comfortable and enjoyable a lifestyle as a young man in uniform could possibly expect. After the hell of Bridgnorth, Hornchurch seemed like heaven.

No more rude awakenings by bellowing DIs throwing off the bedclothes. No more washing and shaving in cold water. No more

15

drills, parades and punishment duties. No more ritual humiliations. And, in the dining halls, the food was varied, plentiful and edible.

We were treated like human beings, and shown courtesy by NCOs and officers provided we toed a comfortable line and didn't try to be uppity. It was like being in the Upper Sixth at school, with interesting lessons and, delight of delights, mechanical toys to play with in the form of teaching aids.

The job of a PSA was to give tests to airmen to discover their general knowledge, their technical aptitudes and, if they wanted to be aircrew, their abilities in the aforementioned mechanical gadgets.

The dullards, or to be kinder and more politically correct, less gifted recruits, would end up as orderlies doing the more menial tasks around RAF bases. Those with technical skills or experience would become airframe mechanics. Those with clerical or bookish interests would go to desk or teaching jobs, mathematicians would settle in pay accounts. The high fliers, literally and metaphorically, would become pilots or aircrew and go before Officer Selection Boards.

At Hornchurch we were trained in the art of explaining the tests in front of a class of airmen candidates, invigilating, and finally marking them. Marking was easy because most questions were multiple choice and all we had to do was put a master sheet over the answer papers. This sheet had holes in it which revealed the correct answers: underlined was correct, untouched by pen was incorrect.

The real fun, later to provide hours of entertainment for staff, when testing periods were over, was monitoring the technical machinery tests. These took place in a simulated aeroplane cockpit, and our favourite was the CVT; controlled velocity test. This involved steering a sensitive needle over a speedily rotating drum containing a winding snake-like track of electro-sensitive metal dots. Every dot touched clocked a point on the meter, and, of course, airmen who wanted to actually fly as air crew had to get high scores on this and the other cockpit tests.

The six weeks of training simply flew by, and the icing on the cake was the fact that, after lessons in the art of testing, we were free to leave camp on local leave, provided we checked in at the guardroom before midnight. I have not been back to Romford since, but in the late 1940s it was a pleasant little town with an excellent cinema and one or two nice restaurants and was within walking distance of the camp.

All too soon the Hornchurch idyll came to an end, and there were 14 months remaining in my stint serving His Majesty King George VI. I had received a couple of chevrons stitched onto my

RAF blue tunic, but was no nearer becoming a journalist. Or so I thought.

The next move was a posting to the personnel selection staff of a recruit training centre, of which there was one - West Kirby on the Wirral - handily placed for 48-hour passes and even overnights at home in Rainhill. Dame Fortune smiled on me again. There was a personnel selection (PS) vacancy at West Kirby, and I got it, and with it the passport to my first sports contributions to a national newspaper. I regret to say that those were the results of a gigantic con trick, or scam, as it would have been described today, perpetuated on the sadly now defunct *News Chronicle*.

It happened after I had been a few months at West Kirby RAF Camp, which was actually near a village called Meols, not far from the small seaside town of Hoylake. The PS section lads had settled down to a congenial routine of testing, using the CVT machine, playing football, rugby and basketball, going to the NAAFI, and listening to a gramophone record of the songs from the hit musical show of the day, *Oklahoma*. Plus frequent social visits across the Mersey to watch Liverpool FC and nip home for the Saturday night dance at Miss Webb's Dancing Academy in Rainhill. It was a distinctly unheroic form of National Service.

While perusing the morning papers in the library one afternoon I noticed that the *News Chronicle*, a pleasantly middle-of-the-road broadsheet which did not deserve to die, had launched an initiative aimed at sports fans. Supporters with a literary bent were invited to send in letters of not more than 100 words in length, extolling their support for, and the outstanding qualities of, their favourite football teams. The best efforts would be printed on the inside back page, and a prize of one guinea would be awarded to the senders. The letters would be printed in alphabetical order of teams throughout the Football League over several weeks.

I evolved a devious and potentially lucrative scheme. I would speak to my colleagues, and other staff personnel at West Kirby who had become my friends, discover which team they supported and write a short letter to the paper in literate and knowledgeable prose, using their names. One or two efforts might just manage to get printed and we would have a few bob between us to spend at the NAAFI or the pictures.

The scheme, or scam, worked a treat. I sent in 15 letters, all typed on the orderly room typewriter, all ostensibly written by the person who appended his name and home address. All 15 were printed in the paper, and each of my colleagues at RAF West Kirby, from various sections of the camp, received a guinea - one pound and one shilling - which they duly halved with the true author. I cannot recall every fan whose team was researched and written up by me, but I remember George Young from Nottingham, Alan Partington from Southport, Ernie Woodacre from Blackburn Rovers, Jack Dixon from Everton, Ted Deasey from Rochdale, the camp librarian who supported Tranmere Rovers, and two colleagues whose names I forget who followed Stoke City and Birmingham City respectively. I was elated, while wondering how the *News Chronicle* sports staff had not noticed the similarity in typewriter print and identical postmarks.

Looking back I feel rather guilty about my deviousness, but I tried to make the letters, including my own on Liverpool, readable and authoritative. And I have to admit to a perverse pride at being among a select number of journalists who have appeared in a national newspaper under 15 different noms-de-plume.

I must here admit that, in other activities, I did not always get away with it, and occasionally fell foul of Air Council Regulations, resulting in the process known as being put on a charge or, as it was colloquially known, a fizzer.

One escapade caused great hilarity. Members of the PS section had a strict rota for going to the NAAFI for cakes to eat with their morning and afternoon tea breaks. One afternoon, when it was my turn, I decided to treat my colleagues to jam doughnuts. I collected and paid for a dozen raspberry doughnuts, but failed to ask for a bag and started walking back to the section offices with both arms cradling doughnuts.

Then, horror of horrors, I saw an officer, a Flight Lieutenant, approaching.

I tried to pretend that I was preoccupied in deep thought, because it is a cardinal offence to pass an officer without saluting him. He wasn't having any nonsense, and there came the dreaded bellow:

"Corporal!"

"Yes, sir?"

"Are you aware that when you pass an officer you salute?"

"Y-yes sir."

"Then do so!"

The moment I had fought to avoid had arrived. My right arm went up in brisk salute, and a dozen doughnuts went bouncing over the path like tennis balls. As a result, I was put on a charge, was confined to camp for two days, and when I reported back to the section everyone fell about laughing before ordering me back for more doughnuts - in a bag this time.

In 1950 there was to be another helpful breakthrough, one which made tolerable the painful experience for those in my age group of having our time in the RAF extended by six months to two years because of the outbreak of the Korean War, just when we were looking forward to demobilisation. The education officer accepted an idea put forward by another lad with journalistic ambitions, Harry Meikle from Liverpool, that the station produce its own monthly magazine. Harry edited it and did drawings of events on camp, and I wrote articles under the corny generic term 'Our Roving Reporter'.

The Korean War extension did its best to scupper my chances of getting a job on a newspaper. I had been offered a junior reporting post by the editor of *The St Helens Reporter* but, when the extra six months for the Korean War was added, he wrote saying the vacancy would not wait - a sickening blow. However, another intervention of fate repaired the damage. I sent out more letters, grossly exaggerating my contributions to the *Evening Express* and various service magazines and was at last given an opportunity not too far from home by Reg Thompson, editor of the *Warrington Guardian*. Like St Helens, Warrington was a rugby league town and that suited me fine.

Keith on the left with his parents Arthur and Jessie
and brother Brian, probably around 1945.

Prescot Grammar School Junior Football XI 1945-46.
Winners – Liverpool Secondary Schools Junior Shield
Back: Mr E. Eyton-Jones, R.J. Lomax, G. Stevenson, J.E. Brown,
G. Winfield, J.D. Burgham; front: Keith Macklin, R.W. Benton,
N.W. Saville, I.J. McIntyre (c), D.R. Brereton, R. Mercer.

Left: With two colleagues from the RAF, at Padgate RAF station in 1949.

Below:
Nine Flight,
Hut 3,
11 July 1949.
Keith is in the back row, third from the left.

Frank Carlton scoring for St Helens against Halifax in the 1956 Challenge Cup Final at Wembley. This was the first Final that Keith covered as a commentator. (Photo: Courtesy Alex Service)

Left: George Young, Keith's friend from the RAF who always joined him on his trips to Wembley in the 1950s.

3. Warrington and Barrow

My tour of duty ended on a summer day in May, 1951. I was demobbed not from West Kirkby, where I spent most of my time frittering away the King's shilling, but at RAF Weeton near Blackpool, a camp to which I was transferred, though for what reason I cannot remember. The only thing I can recall about my few weeks at Weeton is being put on a charge, though again my selective memory fails me as to the reason for it. What makes it memorable to me is that the officer to whom I was ordered to report was a dapper young Pilot Officer named Corbett, who did not seem at all happy about having to administer a severe dressing-down, and merely gave me a light ticking off and an official reprimand. In later life he has become quite well known as Ronnie Corbett, a member of the *Two Ronnies* of television fame, and, unlike me, he probably has no memory of the incident.

It was a long and slightly harrowing day, because I was due to become a civilian again at 9.00am, but my clearance documents had not arrived from GHQ, and it was 4.45pm before a relieved former airman finally bolted past the guardroom and ran to the bus stop which would start my journey back into civvy street. After a rapturous and somewhat tearful homecoming to Chatsworth Road, Rainhill, I rapidly readjusted myself to civilian life and, while I cannot pretend to have enjoyed every moment in uniform, it is only fair to say that, and here comes another cliché, I went in a naïve and gawky adolescent and came out carrying some trappings of manhood. You can, therefore, put me among those reactionary codgers who think that National Service would work better than ASBOs in sorting out today's thugs, hoodies and malcontents.

At 9.00am on a morning in late May 1951, in newly bought dark suit and tie, I presented myself at the three-storey building in Sankey Street, Warrington to meet my new employer and mentor, Reg Thompson, editor-in-chief of the *Warrington Guardian* series of weekly newspapers.

To give the building its full title it was the headquarters of Mackie and Co., who owned a chain of weeklies in towns in Lancashire and Cheshire including Earlestown and Newton, Cadishead and Irlam, Altrincham, Sale, Runcorn, Knutsford, Northwich, Nantwich and Winsford.

The view across the road from the front window of the editorial offices was an imposing one: the gleaming, gilded entrance gates opening onto the well-kept lawns and floral borders that led up to the Georgian town hall, an impressive piece of architecture by any standards and the former country house home of Lord

Winmarleigh. It was to be the place where I wrote my first ever story as a staff journalist rather than a penny-a-line freelance.

Reg Thompson, a smallish man who chain-smoked and constantly flicked cigarette ash off his coat and shirt collars, had obviously been taken in by my slightly exaggerated CV. I was dispatched across the road and up the floral pathways to report the civic event of the year, the Mayoral inauguration ceremony. I was extremely apprehensive having been thrust into real journalistic responsibility so early but mercifully it worked out fine. An order of ceremonial proceedings had been printed, and there were also copies of speeches, as the new Mayor of Warrington, Councillor Caldwell was installed with civic pomp while nothing untoward or sensational happened.

When I got back to the office to type up a report I was taken in hand by the chief reporter, Les Senescall, who was to become a great mentor and friend, and we worked through the story with the aid of the printed copies and the Pitman's shorthand I had assiduously learned with Mrs Summerfield. When Friday came there was my description of the 1951 Mayoral inauguration, with photographs by a staff photographer, as right-hand lead story on the front page.

It was a happy beginning to four happy years on the *Guardian*, and although I got few chances to report on Warrington's fine rugby league team, including the wing wonder, Brian Bevan, and powerful Australian forward Harry Bath, I watched them frequently from a free seat in the press box as the schoolboy dream came true. The reports were written by Jack Steel, aka Cyril Briggs, a veteran *Guardian* reporter whose weekly comment and gossip column about 'The Wire' was obligatory reading among the local population. He occasionally let me cover the 'A' team – reserves - but Warrington's first team were his empire, and his alone.

I recall two other special moments from my time in Sankey Street in those far off days when newspapers were printed from typed copy, sub-edited and titled by pen or pencil. They were printed by hot metal poured into letter moulds, cooled and solidified as linotype by compositors, and formed into iron sheets fed into the printing machine.

The first memorable moment may seem trivial, but it has amusingly lodged in my mind. On a weekly newspaper, then as now, reporters covered everything from major local crimes and tragedies to the meetings of Women's Institutes and Townswomen's Guilds, the darts and dominoes leagues, and funerals of notables such as lady grandee Frances, Lady Daresbury, where junior reporters collected the names of mourners at the church gates.

One Saturday afternoon Les Senescall dispatched me to a local church hall to cover the annual show of the Warrington and District Cage Bird Society. In an attempt to produce something different from the usual laundry list of prize winners I decided to get away from the inevitable budgies and canaries, and look for more exotic or less well-known species of cage birds. After much touring of cages I came up with an opening line which referred to the church hall being "filled with the cacophony of twittering twites and sibilant siskins". To my joy Les Senescall liked the alliteration and made it the headline, hardly an earth-shattering piece of journalism but one of my favourite faded cuttings.

The other incident concerns not me, but a young colleague, Alan Thomas, who was a junior member of the sports staff under Cyril Briggs, and was for many years until recently the rugby league correspondent of the *Daily Express*. The experience provided a salutary lesson to Alan and all other cocky would-be sports writers who open their mouths or express their opinions with more impudence than authority.

As a member of the genuine sports staff Alan was granted the occasional attendance at a Warrington game as reporter in Cyril Briggs's unavoidable absence. I cannot recall precisely what young upstart Thomas had said or written in a match report or contribution to the Jack Steel column but, in some way, seriously or jocularly, he had made a disparaging remark about Harry Bath, the Australian forward of fearsome reputation.

The comment appeared to have passed uneventfully until, at a charity event at the Wilderspool ground, a mixture of rugby league pressmen and players provided two teams for a light-hearted game to amuse the spectators.

Light-hearted? Up to a point. The point when Alan Thomas caught a pass and a grinning Harry Bath moved in to tackle.

The next thing Alan remembers is waking up dazedly on a bed in a dressing room an hour or so later, not so seriously hurt and with a headache which was not life-threatening but which persuaded the future *Daily Express* correspondent not to blur the boundaries between player and reporter. I have never made that mistake, even if a few feathers have been ruffled along the way, notably that of Ellery Hanley. More of that brief contretemps later.

My four years with the *Guardian* ended in 1955, when the itchy feet which have, for better or for worse, been an integral part of my professional life, persuaded me that it was time to move on from local weekly to regional evening paper, and to look for more frequent rugby league and general sports reporting.

After weeks of trawling the trade paper *World's Press News* I came across the small ad in the Situations Vacant column that seemed just right. It was for a senior reporter at "a North-West evening paper". The name of the paper was not given, and because the North-West was, and is, a large area it could have been anywhere from the Cumbrian border to South Cheshire and East Lancashire. I posted my application and, a few days later, received a reply on notepaper headed *North-Western Evening Mail*, Barrow-in-Furness.

Barrow-in-Furness... I looked at the map and it seemed the back of beyond, out on a peninsula limb. But ambition burned, I replied accepting an interview at the Barrow offices and, despite my misgivings and those of my parents, set off by train from Warrington. It was the train journey which sold the job to me before I even got to Barrow. My limited travelling had taken me only to air bases at Padgate, Hednesford, Hornchurch, West Kirkby and Weeton, plus the odd holiday here and there. Now the prospect of a permanent move to the Lancashire, or these days the Cumbrian, coast, washed by the Irish Sea and the idyllic countryside which opened up new horizons beyond Lancaster, made me feel excited and anxious to accept, if I got the job.

The train meandered through open countryside, coastline and across viaducts through the stations of Carnforth, Silverdale, Kents Bank, Grange-over-Sands, Cark and Cartmel, Ulverston, Dalton and on to Barrow. An hour later, after a brief chat with Fred Wilson, the slight, smartly dressed and gently mannered editor of the *Evening Mail* I took a job, during the tenure of which, exciting horizons opened up.

The offices were in the centre of town on the main road coming in past the historic Furness Abbey. Barrow was then a compact town almost entirely dependent on its long-established Vickers Armstrong shipyard and the big events were the launches which were frequent red-letter days. It had other smaller industries, including the iron and steelworks. It was pleasantly parochial and self-contained, because the only route in was by a road which wound tortuously to the tip of the peninsula. Its sporting outlets and interests were Barrow RLFC and Barrow AFC, then in the lower divisions of the Football League.

The townspeople were fiercely loyal to both, and the tabloid *Mail* devoted plenty of back page and inside back page coverage to both. This included a Saturday night sports final, on the streets at teatime with full running reports of the two senior sides and other rugby league and soccer clubs in semi-professional and amateur leagues.

Those were the days in newspapers. One of the saddest features of the late 20th and early 21st centuries has seen economic circumstances and irresistible competition from television and local radio, advertising free sheets and the internet forcing the slow deaths of so many weeklies, evenings and sports finals. In 1955 this decline lay, happily, decades ahead.

In the brief three years to 1958 I followed Barrow RLFC through to two Wembley Challenge Cup Finals, and, out of the blue and still exciting and bewildering to me after more than half a century, my sudden and dramatic entry into broadcasting.

I joined the *Evening Mail* as a general reporter covering the local courts and town and district councils, but within months my enthusiasm for sport, and particularly rugby league, resulted in a move to the sports desk as rugby league reporter. Tom Clark, the veteran chief reporter who had hitherto followed Barrow, was happy to hand over the job to concentrate on his enthusiasm for trains and railways which eventually brought him a public relations post with British Rail.

Barrow, now in the lower tiers of rugby league, were then one of the top sides despite the remote geographical position which discouraged many players from joining the club because they would be faced with long round trips from their homes in other parts of Lancashire and from Yorkshire.

They were led by Barrow's own idol, Willie Horne, a local lad who won Great Britain caps at stand-off half and was the Craven Park side's attacking inspiration though, sadly, his career was drawing to a close. They also had other internationals in second-row forward Jack Grundy and centre Phil Jackson, and had built around them a side with a great team ethic and local pride. I followed them everywhere, home and away, on the team coach and shared in the obligatory post-match meal of ham, eggs and chips, always at a pub near Garstang in North Lancashire. Every Saturday my job was to use a telephone at the ground, and send a report down the line to a copy telephonist who had it rushed to the composing room to be set in type and printed as the top story in the teatime *Sports Final*. Although I was unaware of it at the time this was great training for commentary, because I dictated from rough shorthand and longhand notes, translated into newspaper English without a weekend to reflect.

In 1955 Barrow reached the Challenge Cup Final at Wembley in a far North-West derby against the Cumbrian post-war newcomers, Workington Town. It was a huge thrill for me reporting on a final, rather than watching as a spectator as I had done when St Helens were beaten by Huddersfield in 1953. In the 1950s and for decades thereafter, Wembley was the high point of the season for rugby league fans and their families, looked forward to and eagerly anticipated in the weeks following the semi-finals. Whole families applied for tickets, or queued for the local club's allocation. They then booked the dozens of special trains and hundreds of coaches, because only the minority owned their own cars, or cadged lifts with other fans. Many saved up to make a weekend of it, booking a Friday night hotel and a London show for Saturday. In those less sophisticated times before air travel opened up the resorts of Europe and Asia, Wembley weekend was an annual mini-holiday for the fans. Attendances were huge in the 1950s and 1960s. With fewer safety restrictions or controls Wembley could fill its seats and terraces to sardine-can capacity. Crowds of more than 90,000 were recorded at 15 finals between 1948 and 1987, the highest being the 98,536 capacity attendance when St Helens beat Wigan 21-2 in, ironically, a one-sided contest in 1966. They were good humoured crowds, too, cheerfully happy in victory; cheerfully resigned in defeat. After the game fans of both sides poured down the steps from the stadium to the coaches and tube trains engaging in banter and good-natured insults. Crowd trouble was unknown and largely remained so in Wembley's post-war heyday.

Many such happy annual outings were ahead of me and Wembley was an exciting new adventure when I made my first pilgrimage there as the *Evening Mail's* fledgling rugby league reporter in 1955. I was 24, as yet unmarried, and living in comfortable digs with two mature single sisters, the Misses Thompson, who spoilt rotten both me and my digs-mate and friend, John Taylor and brought us breakfast in bed at the terraced house in Settle Street, Barrow.

It was the first of many pleasant weekends I would spend at the home of my friend from RAF West Kirby, Corporal George Young and his wife, Sheila at Melville Road, Sidcup in Kent. The drill was always the same: I would catch the train, which in 1955 was crowded with blue and white-favoured Barrow supporters, to London. Then it was out to Sidcup on the British Rail line. George would meet me at the station and it was a 10-minute walk to Melville Road for an evening take-away Chinese meal and chats about the good old days of National Service life, patiently endured by a smilingly indulgent Sheila.

I had brought with me a ground ticket for George, and after breakfast on Saturday we took the train from Sidcup to London and thence to Wembley Park station. We walked together with the crowds up Wembley Way and parted company at the top, George to go to his vantage point, myself to take the lift, flight of stairs and final ladder to the old press box. The 14-year-old boy who looked up and daydreamed at Old Trafford cricket ground 10 years earlier had made it at last.

4. Radio days

It all went splendidly, at least for me and that proportion of the 67,000 crowd who were shouting Barrow to their first Challenge Cup victory. My telephone 'commentary', down the line to the typist, and then to hot-metal print, went perfectly and would be read over their evening meal by those who had stayed behind in Barrow.

Barrow beat Workington 20-12 and once the after-match interviews were over I met George outside the ground, amid the littered detritus of discarded fish, chips, burgers and sausage wrappers, and we made our way back to Wembley Park Station. There we would perpetrate what became a regular dodge in the shape of queue-jumping. In yet another example of chicanery and unworthy behaviour which I hope to have ironed out in more mature years, we managed to sidle into the front rows of the extremely long queues which would take normally an hour or so to shift. We would do it by tying our shoelaces or pausing to pick up an imaginary object from the ground, then standing up again into the nearest row of the queue. That way we got a train into the centre of London early enough to grab another Chinese meal, which was then quite a luxury and a novelty, and a cinema or theatre show before catching the train to Sidcup.

On Sunday I caught the long, laborious train back to Barrow and on Monday morning hastened down from Settle Street to grab a copy of Saturday's *Mail* with my report and by-line spread across the front and back pages. Weekends have not come any better than that one more than half a century ago.

Except, perhaps, for the one which was to arrive less than a year later in March 1956. It came as the result of an impulse following a bout of daydreaming at a particularly tedious council meeting. I had occasionally thought, in similar idle moments, that I would like to exchange the role of written journalist for that of a broadcaster, having seen them in action behind their microphones at Wembley, and having enjoyed the pleasures of ad-libbing and thinking on my feet when dictating stories over the telephone without consulting notes.

It was time to employ once more the lateral thinking which had got me into the school football team. Just as the shortage of outside-rights had opened the way on that occasion, the shortage of rugby league commentators could open another door. After all there were more than enough skilled journalists and enthusiasts anxious to commentate on soccer, rugby union and cricket, but not too many challenging Alan Dixon and Harry Sunderland on the XIII-a-side code. Dixon was a popular all-round broadcaster with his own music show for whom rugby league was a pleasant sideline, while Sunderland was a chirpy little former Australian rugby league tour manager who had stayed in England and in his later years turned to commentary.

I wrote off a letter of application, enclosing my youthful CV, emphasising rugby league coverage for the *Liverpool Evening Express*, *Warrington Guardian* and currently *North Western Evening Mail*. To my surprise and delight I got a reply within days from Robert Hudson, head of outside broadcasts, BBC North Region in Manchester, inviting me to an audition. It was to be held at Swinton's Station Road ground on a Saturday in January 1956 at an actual game, Swinton versus St Helens.

It was a very nervous young man who arrived at Swinton's ground, just a few miles from Manchester off the East Lancashire Road at lunchtime on that grey afternoon. For once, I was really wondering if this time I had bitten off more than I could chew.

There were seven of us from a variety of professions, from clerks to manual workers, and I felt slightly dismayed to discover in conversation that most of the others had gathered experience by doing commentaries on hospital radio. I had not thought of that. I was one down already.

Robert Hudson, tall, well-built and with the clear and precise diction of an Oxbridge don, a BBC stereotype of the time, addressed us in the grandstand where microphones and earphones had been assembled.

We would each draw a numbered ticket out of a hat, ranging from 1 to 7. In the order in which we drew our ticket we would do 10 minutes of live commentary before handing over to the next in line. I drew number 1. This meant that while the others sat back, calmed their nerves, and learned by my mistakes I would have no time to do any of these things. However, almost rendered speechless by nervous tension, I set off into the microphone. In those first 10 minutes no tries and no goals were scored, and I had the additional problem of having to identify the players from scratch.

At the end of my stint I handed over the microphone to the holder of ticket number 2 and sat back glumly in my seat convinced that my future was, after all, in newspaper journalism. On the long, winding rail journey back to Barrow I consoled myself with the entirely correct and rational thought that there was still an excellent career and lifestyle to be earned and lived in the thriving written sector of journalism.

Four days later another letter arrived in a headed BBC envelope. As my stomach sank into my shoes I had to read the opening sentence four or five times, and then pinch myself, for it to sink in. The letter, signed by Robert Hudson, said that my audition had been successful and, wonder of wonders, I was invited to do the radio commentary on Workington Town versus Featherstone Rovers in mid-February. The game was in a fortnight's time, and for the next 14 days I was in a frenzy of nervous excitement, mugging up every statistic I could find about the teams; studying photographs of team members and, to the Misses Thompson, my landladies, behaving in a most bizarre manner.

At various times during the evenings, after a day at the *Mail*, they would catch me standing on the landing, gazing alternatively at a photograph and then talking, or rather enunciating, names loudly into a mirror. Eventually the two middle-aged ladies had to be taken into my confidence, and they rubbed their hands with glee. I also had to tell John, my digs-mate and friend, who was deputy librarian at Barrow, about the forthcoming audition, for he too, had found my behaviour odd and edgy.

Came the Friday night before the game, which would be played just up the Cumbrian coast at Workington. Since rugby league correspondent for the *Mail* was not a full-time role and I doubled up as a news reporter, I attended in a professional capacity a Gilbert and Sullivan concert at Her Majesty's Theatre, Barrow, sadly now long defunct. The star performer was Thomas Round, the Barrow-born tenor, and, as a keen G & S fan, then and now, I was looking forward to a pleasant prelude to my broadcasting debut on the morrow.

It was an extremely cold February night, so cold that a few snowflakes were falling as I walked back to Settle Street after the concert. The following morning I was roused by one of the 'Mistees', as we dubbed them, to look out of the window.

I did. The garden was buried under six inches of snow. A quick panicky telephone call to Workington elicited the reply that so was the Derwent Park pitch. My broadcasting debut was off. That weekend was as miserable as the Wembley trip had been happy. I was utterly disconsolate and must have been wretched company at the Saturday dance at the Victoria Park Hotel where each week John and I would hope to find local damsels who would eventually become life-partners.

The gloom hung about only until Monday. Around 10.00am a call came to the *Evening Mail* newsroom from Pat Thorpe, Robert Hudson's secretary, commiserating with me on the Workington postponement and offering me another chance. The game was Leeds versus Oldham in early March in the third round of the Challenge Cup.

It was back to the drawing board, or more accurately to the landing mirror, for more voice exercises while absorbing photographic images of players. With virtually no television games in those days and no recorded snippets, all in the future, to peruse, it had to be newspaper pictures, or copies of official club programmes as memory aids.

On Saturday 3 March 1956, the delayed debut finally happened. During the previous fortnight, with the guarded pessimism that passes for other people's guarded optimism I had waited for another snowstorm or heavy rainfall to wipe out Headingley for the Leeds versus Oldham game. Or an earthquake, or a typhoon.

None occurred and on that Saturday morning, again with pounding heart, I set off for Leeds by train, because I was not then a car owner or driver. With me was my fiancée Sheila from Barrow, who would later become my wife and mother of my two daughters.

Little did Sheila know as we set off that she would be used that day as a ploy in ensuring that my first broadcast would be heard and analysed by at least one radio listener. Nor did an innocent and unsuspecting Headingley householder who had the misfortune to live near the stadium. I still blush and quail mentally at the memory. Excitement and anticipation must have momentarily turned my brain.

As we alighted from a bus which took us from the station to the ground I somehow persuaded Sheila to take part in my plan, which was to knock at the door of a house close to the ground and persuade the householder or resident to allow Sheila to listen to my first-ever broadcast on his or her radio.

Bizarre though it sounds the house was opened by a middle-aged, comely and very friendly lady who was at first startled and then amused as I outlined my scheme to secure a listening figure of at least two for my debut on air. I left a bemused Sheila with the helpful Yorkshire lady, and walked into Headingley. There I was met by Alan Clarke, a famous soccer commentator of the time and a North Region sports producer, and my co-commentator Harry Sunderland. Both welcomed me warmly, which helped calm my trembling nervous system.

An engineer had laid out two microphones and earphones on a bench in the Headingley press area, with a third set of equipment for Alan Clarke to maintain contact with the outside broadcast van just outside the ground. As I recall it was second half commentary only, which was ideal for me, because I could spend the first 40 minutes matching the faces and figures on the field with those in my pictures and cuttings I had so assiduously studied. In addition, I had seen both Leeds and Oldham in action when covering their matches against Barrow for the *Mail*, so I was not entirely unprepared for action.

Nevertheless, I remember the butterflies swarming around in my stomach as, after 20 minutes of the second half, Alan Clarke waved his hand in my direction. It was time for the handover. I remember Harry Sunderland's words to this day. In his Australian twang he said: "It's time now for me to hand over to a new young commentator making his radio debut today, I hope you will all give him a warm welcome". He handed the mike to me with the words "Good Luck, Keith".

Bless you, Harry. I can no longer say that to his face, alas, because he died in the 1970s, still living in England, and bemoaning the fact as I sat by his hospital bedside that total weekly attendances at rugby league grounds - at a mere 31,000 - were falling and the game, like he himself, was terminally ill. Thank heavens he was wrong, and how sad that he did not live to see the subsequent revival.

But back to my first commentary. Thanks to all the preparation I was able to launch into an early stride, and got through the final 20 minutes with some degree of animation. For the record Leeds beat Oldham, and both Alan Clarke and Harry Sunderland said nice things about my efforts as we went our separate ways after the match. I left Headingley relieved that I had emerged unscathed, and walked to the house where I had left Sheila. To my relief it appeared that after introductions the pair of ladies had got on famously over a pot of tea and had chatted virtually throughout my commentary. I thanked the helpful woman profusely and regret that she and I have never crossed paths since. However, I am sure she got much mileage out of the story. When we arrived back at Settle Street that Saturday night the Mistees were a-flutter with excitement. During the afternoon several telegrams had arrived and, like me, the matronly duo could hardly wait for them to be opened.

As I tore them open the compliments flowed from the pages: "Congratulations on a brilliant debut ... What a great commentary ...A star is born ... Well done, nobody would know it was your first time ..."

They were from auntie Janey and uncle Harold in Manchester; auntie Elsie and uncle Sam in Blackpool; auntie Bessie and uncle Clarrie in Earlestown; and last and certainly not least from Mum and Dad in Rainhill. Suspiciously, one had a 1.45 pm timing, more than an hour before kick-off. No matter, it was a great display of family support, and I was already in dreamland, and anxiously awaiting further reaction, most importantly from BBC North Region in Manchester.

Mercifully I did not have to wait long. Both Robert Hudson and Alan Clarke rang on Monday morning to say "well done", sounding as if they meant it, and asking if I would be free to do more games. After a quick and very helpful conversation with the *Mail* editor, I was able to reply in a still-dazed affirmative.

Tom Clark agreed to cover Barrow RLFC if needed, which was a nice gesture, and to my further astonishment and delight I was asked to do two upcoming commentaries. One was the Challenge Cup semi-final. The other was the 1956 Challenge Cup Final. The final! At Wembley! Me, a raw young 25-year-old novice commentator with only two live games under his belt would be at the holy of holies for what was then the crowning point of the rugby league season before it was usurped by the Australian-style Grand Final.

More than half a century later, I can still feel the strange mixture of emotions that gripped me when I received the formal phone call from outside broadcasts (OB) secretary Pat Thorpe inviting me to be part of the Wembley team. Excitement, intoxication, shock, bewilderment - all of these and more besides.

That early summer of 1956 was the time of my own personal salad days. I was happy with the day job at the *Mail*, had many firm friends, including John and Sheila, and had discovered a renewal of faith and church attendance at Abbey Road Methodist Church, at which John was organist and choirmaster.

The semi-final draw was also on my side. Barrow met St Helens in two pulsating games, a splendidly fought 0-0 draw, which was genuinely gripping because of magnificent defences and some nail-biting near misses, and an extra-time replay win, in another low scoring game, by Saints. There followed a wait of several weeks before the final, weeks of intense mugging up on St Helens, the team I had followed as a boy, and Halifax. Again, just I had done 12 months earlier I counted the days, but with even greater excitement and anticipation. The 1955 final had been my Wembley debut as a provincial newspaperman, the 1956 final would see me at the historic stadium as a national radio broadcaster at a time when the nation did not have saturation television coverage of rugby league, and there would be a big audience in the North.

Again I made the train journey out to Sidcup, had a pleasant evening with George and Sheila, boring the patient Sheila rigid with more RAF memories, and getting the early train to London. At this point the ritual changed, as it would do for nearly three decades. Instead of accompanying George, standing strap-hanging on the sardine-packed noisy tube trains to Wembley Park, I got a cab at Euston, which I could charge to the Beeb, to Broadcasting House, where I would join London outside broadcasting director Ken

Pragnell, Alan Clarke, Harry Sunderland and two OB engineers. We then went round the corner to a pleasant little pub, had lunch on the Beeb, and then out to Wembley in Ken Pragnell's spacious Humber car. Again I had to pinch myself to make sure this was really happening to the wire-mill fitter's son from Lancashire. But it was, and Ken Pragnell's car replaced the tube trip as we drove through the North London suburbs to Neasden and on to Wembley.

I felt a little pang of sadness as the car with its BBC pass went through all checkpoints to the official car park, thinking of George making the cheerful trek up Olympic Way without me, but consoled myself that I would see him outside after the game and renew Wembley weekend practice. Then it was time to calm down the twanging nerves, and take the lift and steps again to the huge and wide press box with its glass cubicle at the top where the radio broadcast for the North Region Home Service would take place. Another look around at the impressive vastness of the Wembley stands and the terraces that still existed before the arrival of all-seater stadia showed that they were rapidly filling up with a crowd that would number more than 80,000. The previous year I had come with pen, notebook and telephone: this year I would be sitting at a desk in an enclosed glass cabin holding a microphone and wearing headphones, talking not to one copy telephonist but to hundreds of thousands (I hoped) of listeners.

Before the broadcast began at 2.30pm we got a pep talk from Alan Clarke, who told me to treat the match as if it was an ordinary league game. As if I could. We would do previews and team news up to the 3.00pm kick-off, stop talking and fade up the mike's volume for *Abide With Me* and the National Anthem, then do full commentary. When we went on air I got a serious lesson in the superb professionalism that only comes through years of experience, though I would not recommend Alan Clarke's 1956 preparation to any of today's young would-be broadcasters. For Alan Clarke enjoyed a glass of gin and tonic, or two, before a game, something less frowned upon then than in today's super-professional broadcasting environment.

He also spoke from only a handful of roughly scribbled notes, yet once he had welcomed listeners to Wembley he gave a flawless performance. Setting the scene, previewing the game, cueing in myself and Harry for comments, painting word pictures of the stadium, crowds and atmosphere and pausing for the mass singing of *Abide with Me* and the National Anthem, Alan Clarke got it absolutely right. I knew then that I had a lot to learn. Clarkey was a great pro despite his somewhat unorthodox preparation, and the early deaths of both he and another commentating colleague and friend, Alan Dixon, a few years later were sad blows. Within a decade I was to lose the two Alans and Harry Sunderland, all great friends, helpers and colleagues.

The pre-match activities on the pitch and the crowd participation were all part of the magic of Wembley. One stirring fixture then was the marching and counter-marching in their colourful uniforms and tall bearskins of the bands of the Grenadier Guards, Coldstream Guards and the Brigade of Guards. They played rousing marches like *Colonel Bogey* and *On the Quarterdeck* and accompanied the enthusiastic community singing and the anthem. It is a source of personal regret to me that this splendid tradition at Cup Finals and Grand Finals has often been replaced by the uninspiring warbling of pop singers and pop groups, but times and tastes sadly change.

The game itself, while a huge professional thrill for me, was a disappointing anti-climax. I made sure that my share of the commentary did not show any Saints bias, but the pleasure of seeing St Helens win at Wembley at last was tempered by an unfortunate blow to Halifax.

The first half was hard-fought but unspectacular, and ended up 0-0. Then Halifax suffered a terrible mishap which swung the game irreversibly towards Saints. In the early stages Johnny Freeman, the speedy Halifax winger, suffered a painful leg injury. Under today's substitutes rule he would have been replaced. But in those days there were no substitutes, and Freeman had no choice but to carry on, hobbling on his one good leg.

St Helens, understandably, professionally and cruelly, took full advantage. The ball was moved repeatedly towards Freeman's wing, and Saints' winger Frank Carlton swept easily past him for a long-range try. Steve Llewellyn and Alan Prescott also went over for tries, and Austin Rhodes kicked two goals in a 13-2 win. Tyssul Griffiths landed a goal for Halifax which was scant consolation for their ill-luck.

It had gone well for Saints, badly for Halifax, and luckily for me. Circumstances had contrived to establish my credentials as a radio commentator after just three games. The daydream of the 14-year-old boy at Old Trafford cricket ground had been fully realised.

5. Television debut

Life continued on its pleasant, almost dreamlike, way in the next year. While I attempted to get home to Rainhill for occasional weekends, I was thoroughly contented with my Barrow lifestyle. Perhaps, even at 25, I had still not quite grown up, with the harsher realities of life still to come. My cup, if not overflowing, was full to the brim.

I was enjoying being a mini-celebrity in the shipyard town where an 'offcomer' from South Lancashire had been accepted, not merely into the ample bosoms of the Mistees, but into a host of local families.

Social life was a fulfilling break from journalism and broadcasting, but it was not that I needed one because I enjoyed following Barrow and doing the occasional radio commentary as an accepted member of the BBC team. However, to top things up, my relationship with Sheila was developing and, after being reintroduced to the Methodist Church at Abbey by John, I had decided to become a local preacher in the Carlisle circuit and was studying the Old and New Testaments and Christian doctrine. On this latter point I was constantly being wound up and leg-pulled by people asking how I reconciled the Christian ethic of turning the other cheek with reporting on big forwards knocking seven bells out of each other on the rugby field. I replied, I hope convincingly, that it was all part of the game and that everybody became matey and no grievances were held in the bar after the game.

On the leisure scene I had also branched out into amateur drama and light opera, producing plays with a good moral message for the Barrow Methodists and singing in the chorus of the town's Gilbert and Sullivan musical society, with an occasional step up to minor principal roles.

One of these caused a minor and perhaps laughable crisis of conscience. I was given the small singing role of the Foreman of the Jury in the short G & S curtain-raiser frolic *Trial by Jury* which was performed as a warm up for *HMS Pinafore*.

It is a typical G & S farce, and the foreman is a leering, lecherous Leslie Phillips type who offers consolation to the jilted bride and sings the line "If faint you're feeling, recline on me" with accompanying gestures. It took months for me to live down the accusation that my leering demeanour and gestures were remarkably realistic and unbecoming a Methodist local preacher.

The Wembley Challenge Cup Final of 1957 was to be the last hurrah of my brief but happy time as the *Mail's* rugby league writer. It was not destined to be a particularly happy occasion, because before a crowd of 76,000 Barrow lost 9-7 to Leeds after a late try-scoring chance was fluffed and, for the second successive final, a player suffered a personal career tragedy. My arrangements in the build-up to the final had changed for professional reasons. The *Mail* sports editor, Eric Hulley, decided it would be a good idea if I joined the team at their pre-match hotel and training venue from Wednesday to Saturday and filed daily reports.

It was an excellent idea - a four-day break at a luxury hotel alongside the Thames at Maidenhead culminating in the Cup Final. It was a mini-holiday in fact. I am not sure to this day whether Barrow's team and management thought it such a good idea, but they had not booked the whole hotel and my booking had been done quietly and unobtrusively as a certain Mr L.K. Macklin. Nobody spotted anything until I turned up at a table for one at dinner on Wednesday evening, and by then the deed was done. In the event I got on well with the official party, reported positive vibes from training sessions, and things went well until just before dinner on Friday when the Barrow squad was summoned to a meeting on the spacious and sunny lawn alongside the Thames to hear the announcement of the team to play Leeds on the morrow. I cannot now recall the club official who actually read out the team, but the names of the regular XIII who had played throughout the tournament were mechanically reeled off, moving smoothly from number 1 Joe Ball to number 9 Maurice Redhead. Next name up was sure to be Frank Barton, the veteran former Wigan forward and no stranger to Wembley finals. There was a loud and sustained gasp when the announcement came: "Number 10 …. Parker"

The selection committee had chosen Reg Parker, a good second-row or utility forward but not a regular at that time, to replace the seasoned veteran Frank Barton. By unhappy coincidence I was standing on the lawn with my notebook just alongside Frank. His face literally drained of colour; his lips opened as if to speak, closed again, then quivered open.

"Fair enough… fair enough," he almost gasped, walked off the lawn into the hotel, and while he stuck out a weekend of torture for team solidarity's sake, he retired from rugby league from that moment on.

A tainted weekend for Barrow ended with defeat the following day and although things had again gone quite well professionally, and Tom Clark had reported the match while I did the commentary, it was rather anti-climactic.

This honeymoon with life could not last for ever, and didn't. Sheila quit her job in the Barrow area, and got a post with, ironically, Pilkington's, the famous St Helens glass manufacturing company. John was getting dissatisfied with lack of promotion prospects in Barrow Library and libraries elsewhere, and was planning to emigrate to Australia and I was having difficulties balancing my *Mail* role with increasing rugby league commentating and reporting engagements with the Beeb. In addition I had a nasty experience with a tooth extraction which became septic, and life's realities began to bite. Eventually I resigned, with considerable regret, from the *Barrow Mail*, left the town which had made me welcome and happy, and got a reporting post back on a weekly, the *St Helens Reporter*. It was, on the surface, a slight backwards step, but it took me back to my home in Rainhill, nearer my betrothed and to one of the great rugby league strongholds.

In addition - and what was a very important point - the management of the Reporter Group, who ran a prosperous and well-written chain of local weeklies, gave me freedom to continue broadcasting without inhibition, provided I put in a certain number of hours each week.

This move, apart from being convenient, was yet another example of the mystifying workings of fate. For in 1958 there came another incident which projected my career onto a higher plane by a series of coincidences.

In the summer of 1958 Great Britain made one of the regular tours of Australia which had resumed after the Second World War. Rugby league had not yet reached the status that required a reporter on tour, so we followed it at a distance of 14,000 miles.

Great Britain lost the first test in Sydney on 14 June 25-8. To save the three-match series they had to win the second Test in Brisbane. In what was to go down in XIII-a-side lore as 'The Battle of Brisbane', the match produced acts of bravery and victory against the odds that produced more 'Rorke's Drift' headlines. These referred to the famous victory by a handful of British soldiers in the 1879 Zulu War, an event later commemorated in a 1914 British rugby league test victory in Australia, and now to be repeated in 1958.

In the early stages of the game the British front-row forward and captain, Alan Prescott, fell awkwardly and broke his arm. The Wigan stand-off David Bolton fractured his collar bone and several other tourists received heavy knocks. In those no-substitute days, the British party and their badly-stricken skipper, knew that the loss of another player would probably mean the loss of the game and of the series.

Remarkably, and astonishingly, because Prescott must have been in considerable pain from his broken arm, he declared after receiving an injection in the dressing room that he was going back onto the field. Despite efforts to dissuade him by the tour doctor and management including warnings that his arm might be permanently damaged, Prescott went back on to the field with pain-killing injections and a strapped-up dangling limb. Bolton, meanwhile, was definitely out of action with his collarbone injury.

Incredibly, Britain's 12 men led 10-2 at half-time, and then increased their lead to 20-7 as Prescott's bravery inspired the team. Australia scored two tries and gallant Britain seemed likely to fold when the youngest player on the field, later to become a rugby league legend, scored a brilliant individual try. Cheeky, irrepressible Alex Murphy, the St Helens scrum-half, dodged and corkscrewed his way through the Australian defence and Warrington full-back Eric Fraser, also suffering from a painful knock, kicked the goal. Australia came back to notch another try, but Great Britain won 25-18 and went on to clinch the series with a 40-17 win at Sydney, despite the fact that they were without Prescott and Bolton who were forced to fly home for treatment to their injuries.

Alan Prescott was to pay a heavy price for his bravery. After recuperation his playing career was cut short and he turned briefly to coaching. However, his ill-fortune in Brisbane was to prove extremely lucky in the long term for a young radio commentator following Great Britain's exploits at home.

Shortly after the injured skipper's return a member of the production staff of the BBC TV *News of the North* six o'clock bulletin read Prescott's story somewhere, and suggested it as an item. The problem then was that no one on the production staff knew anything about rugby league. Someone must have contacted the OB department and got the name of a freelance radio reporter/commentator who might help out, and as a result I got a phone call at home one early afternoon asking if I "could get this chap Prescott over to the Manchester studio for an interview in the six o'clock show". They said I would get a fee for doing the errand, but I needed no such bribe: to meet up with the hero Alan Prescott would be reward enough.

Luck was again with me. I got his home telephone number and address from the St Helens club, shot over in my newly acquired motor, and found a rather disconsolate skipper nursing a heavily splinted and bandaged arm. At first he was reluctant to leave the house for the journey to Manchester but, generous man that he was, agreed to do it as a favour to me. We sped over to BBC Piccadilly, and Prec, as most people in the game knew him, was ushered into the make-up room.

My job done, I prepared to leave, only to be stopped by the producer of the programme. He said that because nobody on the staff knew anything about rugby league, would I be kind enough to do the interview? It took a nano-second to reel back and say "Yes", and then I followed Prec into the make-up room.

It was audition time all over again. I was given two and a half minutes on air, tried to ignore the cameras, and just did a radio interview with the cameras eavesdropping.

Afterwards both the injured Great Britain skipper and I were thanked, and the producer said to me as we left the building: "We might call on you again when we have a sports story".

Yet again I had ascended to cloud nine, and it was with total sincerity that I thanked Prec profusely both on the journey and as I dropped him off at his home. Like my other mentors Alan Clarke, Alan Dixon and Harry Sunderland he had given my fledgling career a wonderful boost. Sadly, like the others, this brave and generous giant of a man has gone to the great stadium in the sky but, as with the others, I will always remember him with gratitude.

The Manchester producer was as good as his word, and television sports interviews came with increasing regularity, culminating in yet another massive dose of good fortune two years later in 1960.

Rugby league had by then entered the television era. The BBC was for the first time allowed access for live broadcasts, primarily for the Saturday flagship show *Grandstand*. Arguments and counter-arguments had raged as the sport's council members debated the issue. Proponents said television would raise the profile of the sport at national level and provide a source of income. Opponents said that presence of live cameras at games would affect attendances across the board. All the claims had some validity and after much council and media debate the BBC won the day, and Eddie Waring was on his way to becoming a nationally known voice and face.

I must here admit that my own feelings - and I tried to be honest about them both publicly and privately - were that live coverage would undoubtedly affect attendances. Certainly in the early years, this proved to be the case. But the decision had been made and, in a strange way, the decision helped me. While Eddie, with his broad Yorkshire vowels, fractured English and catchphrases became a television figure, both revered and reviled in equal quantities by the two schools of thought, the increased interest in rugby league by the media brought me, as a freelance specialising in the sport, plenty of work in television and radio bulletins, and in newspapers like the *Sunday Express* and the *Liverpool Daily Post*. There were also spin-offs because I was able to give fee-earning talks and after-dinner speeches.

Another area that opened up for me was writing a book. There is a saying that every person's life carries the seeds of at least one book, usually a novel, and in or around 1959 the bug came to the surface in my mind. The thought had come to me when browsing through library shelves to find that in the sections marked 'Sport', there were vast numbers of books on football, cricket, rugby union and minor sports, but little or nothing on rugby league. Certainly there was no detailed history of the game.

On one of those whims that seem to have punctuated my life, I wrote to one of the leading London publishing houses, Stanley Paul, who specialised in sports books, and to my surprise and delight received a letter from publisher Roddy Bloomfield accepting my suggestion and commissioning the book, which was first published in 1962 under the straightforward and prosaic title of *The History of Rugby League*. It was pleasantly received in both national and local newspapers, and was reprinted, and bought up to date twice, in 1974 and 1984. Roddy also commissioned a follow-up book, *The Rugby League Game*, a series of general essays, published in 1967, which also went moderately well. He also, on a totally contrasting plane, published in 1975 *The Sunday Quiz Book of World Religions*, which I co-wrote with Bill Weaver, and arose from our 1970s Yorkshire Television show.

If ever there was a labour of love, the *History* was it. In addition to the heady prospect of becoming an author there was the added pleasure of writing about the game I enjoyed. So for the better part of two years I spent any spare time between *Look North* and other television and radio commitments sitting in public libraries in Manchester, Leeds, Huddersfield, St Helens, Warrington and Widnes browsing through dusty old newspaper files and microfilm for articles, match reports and any snippets I could find about rugby league. I also received considerable help from figures within the game, local sports historians, and last, but not least, collectors of memorabilia who were all wonderfully co-operative. It was a great feeling when the book came out, and I still feel a pleasant glow when, after all these years, fans bring copies, well-thumbed and timeworn, to the press box for a signature.

My private life had moved on pleasantly. In 1959 Sheila and I were married at her place of worship, Beacon Hill Methodist Church in Barrow and, back in South Lancashire, we elected to live in a pleasant new bungalow in a quiet cul-de-sac alongside the golf course in another rugby league town, Widnes.

People ribbed us about the choice at the time, for the rugby league team were not nicknamed the Chemics for nothing. The town had grown and thrived during the late 19th and early 20th centuries around the chemical industry, brought in by German industrialists and firmly established by the giant Imperial Chemical Industries or ICI. These and other factories brought growth and prosperity to the town on the banks of the Mersey opposite Runcorn, but its chimneys sent out a variety of chemical aromas, ranging from the sickly sweet to rotten eggs, giving Widnes in those days the reputation of being a town with a stinky aura.

However, the advantages of Widnes were that good housing came at a reasonable price, and the town was on the main express railway line between Liverpool and Manchester, then my two main broadcasting and journalism outlets, which saved a lot of tedious driving. Eventually the M62 opened up the way to towns and grounds across the Pennines. Another huge asset was that it was in the centre of a rugby league area with the Chemics, Saints, Wigan, Warrington, Leigh, Swinton - then a top side - Salford and even struggling Liverpool City all within easy reach.

I must also place it on record that in the 22 years I lived in the town, I found Widnes folk wonderfully warm, friendly and honest, providing excellent neighbours and good friends, and I am always given the warmest of receptions whenever I return. In addition, smokeless zone legislation and the arrival of new, clean industries mean that the town's aroma is no longer repellent and is in fact indistinguishable from neighbouring boroughs.

A year after marriage and the move to the bungalow in Woodland Avenue, Widnes, the train journey to Manchester became five days a week as my career took another giant leap forward. The BBC decided to expand its regional coverage to fight back against the growing strength of ITV. In the north west this successful challenge had come from one of the bigger and livelier companies Granada, based in Manchester and a big audience-puller. So BBC bosses decided to replace the regional evening news bulletins with a nightly news magazine, at first titled *North at Six*, to cover a huge and well-populated trans-Pennine area, covering Lancashire, Yorkshire, Cheshire and parts of South Cumbria and North Wales.

Colin Welland, the well known television actor in the popular police series *Z-Cars*, prolific playwright and, like me born in Newton-le-Willows, was chosen as the big-name presenter. The lesser role of sports reporter was given to me.

North at Six went on air in 1960 with a fanfare of publicity, but failed to make the expected impact. This was primarily because Colin, although a huge name as a police dog-handler in *Z-Cars*, and a very successful scriptwriter and playwright, did not have the journalistic and presentation skills required of a television news magazine front man.

The search was on for a replacement presenter and, like everyone else on the programme, I threw names of other well known faces in the north and nationally into the ring.

Then, totally out of nowhere, at least as far as I was concerned, I arrived at my small sports desk on the Friday of the third week of

North at Six to be summoned immediately to the office of Jim Entwistle, the producer. With him, oddly it seemed, was Maurice Taylor, the chief programmes finance officer.

What happened next left me, in the crude modern vernacular phrase, completely gobsmacked. "We want you to take over from Colin," said Jim Entwistle, a quiet dedicated news editor who never wasted words. I must have looked uncomprehendingly at him, because Jim continued: "Colin isn't comfortable with the role, and wants to be released from his contract forthwith. We think you can do the job because you look and sound relaxed."

I didn't at that moment.

I genuinely found it hard to believe that, while my four years in broadcasting had given me confidence that I could make it a career, I had not dared daydream beyond being a television and radio reporter.

I had kept in touch with news and current affairs via the press and broadcasting media as part of a journalistic background, but I had never envisaged moving out of sport. Nor had my dreams of advancement ever stretched into the realms of news magazine presentation.

The following Monday brought the first night for the new anchorman of *North at Six*. I was conscious yet again that I was on trial before a wider audience, one that regarded me as someone from the small pond of sport getting a trial in the big lake of news, current affairs, films, theatre, art, literature et al. Human nature being what it is there would be those out there wanting me to fall flat on the seat of my pants, and I was very much aware that this was a possible outcome.

The programme editors and Jim Entwistle made the task easier by not giving me an interview in the studio on the first night, allowing me straight-forward autocue links into items while news reporters brought in film stories and did any extra studio work. As a result I got through without mishap, everybody made kind comments afterwards and as the weeks progressed I was eased into a role I would occupy for the next six years.

However, it was not all plain sailing. Quite a few viewers wrote in to ask tartly why a sports person had been chosen to front the North's flagship programme. One or two complained that my Lancashire accent, which I thought had been ironed out, kept coming through. Others said that occasionally my attempts at post-item ad-libbing were too flippant. After a few months, the barbs thinned out and when the post began to bring in fan letters, requests for autographs and invitations to open fetes and bazaars, it sank in almost unwittingly: I was becoming a minor local celebrity.

Debut on *Look North* in 1960. This photo was taken of the television screen by Keith's mother, using a Box Brownie camera.

It seems strange to think back to those comments and complaints about my traces of accent. Nowadays local accents seem not merely irrelevant but even a qualification for a regional reporting role. Nearly 50 years ago, while the Reithian and Oxbridge traditions still held sway, the first sign of a flat northern vowel would bring an instruction to sign up for elocution lessons.

Fortunately for my peace of mind, despite the demands of the linkman's job at what soon became *Look North*, my sporting contacts were not tainted. At weekends I still did rugby league reports and commentaries, and it became a six-day television week when the BBC's North Region introduced a Saturday night *Rugby League Extra* which lasted seven minutes on screen. It included contributions from Eddie Waring and another new young upstart named Stuart Hall, who would later take over from me on *Look North* when I moved across to ITV.

While my prime responsibility on *Look North* was to present the programme I occasionally got out of the studio, and these were not always pleasurable jaunts. In 1964 there was a terrible train crash at Cheadle Hulme station near Manchester, in which three people were killed and many injured. A train travelling on the Stafford line to Manchester took a curve near the station at what the official report described as "an excessive speed" and derailed.

For some reason on that particular morning I had caught an early train from Widnes. As I ambled into the production office Derek Maude, a fine editor who had learned the journalistic trade on Fleet Street newspapers, barked at me: "Get a crew and get yourself out to Cheadle Hulme railway station. There's been a bad accident." A camera crew was ready and we drove out to the station, where the inevitable crowds of sightseers had assembled. Police cars, fire engines and ambulances were flashing their lights and sounding off sirens. Above us we could see carriages leaning almost over the parapet at a crazy angle.

There was also a scrum of reporters jostling for interviews with any passenger, railway official or member of the emergency services they could find. I managed to obtain one or two interviews, which were picked up at the scene by a staff car sent out by Derek Maude, taken back to the studios, edited and transmitted on network bulletins throughout the day. Other reporters were sent to relieve me and the tragedy topped the news, including *Look North*, with updates on radio and television.

As an exercise in dramatic journalism Cheadle Hulme was a highlight but, as a human tragedy it left me shaken and depressed and reminded me that there is far more to life than sport.

Such is human nature, however, that the daily stint on television quickly erased the worst of the memories and it was back to the pleasurable ephemera of life. *Look North* was now established with a loyal, steady audience, and by 1964 Sheila and I had two daughters, Heather Jane and Tracy Elizabeth.

Professionally I was getting busier, having to take more time off from the nightly half-hour in Manchester to present a series of new shows. I was still the new kid on the block, a new face at network level and pleasingly and hectically in demand. There must have been an awful shortage of presenters in the 1960s.

6. Union adventures

Certainly I must have seemed a useful guinea pig for producers launching new programmes for in the 1960s I was invited to front up the first series of *Pot Black*, *Rugby Special* (the other code, that was quite a surprise), BBC North-originated *A Spoonful Of Sugar*, *Songs Of Praise* and an outdoor pursuits magazine called *Time Out*, which was produced by former Olympic athlete Chris Brasher. The snooker and rugby programmes and *Time Out* were all on the fledgling new channel BBC2 which was trying to find a niche in the television market and build up a following.

Pot Black was recorded at the BBC studios in Birmingham, with Philip Lewis as producer and 'whispering' Ted Lowe as the commentator. My job was simple enough, just topping and tailing the action and providing any necessary links.

Rugby Special, produced from club and international grounds by Alan Mouncer, was an edited outside broadcast, featuring early-evening programmes of recorded action, led by the international games at Cardiff Arms Park, Murrayfield, Lansdowne Road and, of course, Twickenham. Again it was a question of opening and closing with that magnificent broadcaster, Hawick schoolmaster Bill McLaren, providing his peerless, model rugby union commentaries. But it felt odd to be a rugby league commentator introducing rugby union. I saw myself a traitor, and I am sure that rugby union greats like Cliff Morgan, who later had a stint at presenting, regarded me as an upstart and an interloper, which, to be honest, I was. However, Bill McLaren made me feel at home, and one or two memorable incidents stand out.

One was quite bizarre, almost surreal, and I still have to pinch myself to ensure that it was not just a dream. I was due at Cardiff Arms Park on a Saturday to introduce and sign off the Wales versus Ireland international.

On the Thursday afternoon I had a car accident during a fierce gale in Lancashire, mistiming a turn and crashing into a lamp-post. My chest and teeth hit parts of the steering wheel and, when they took me out of the car and delivered me to a Blackburn hospital, I had badly bruised ribs and some gum damage, though all my teeth were still intact. Medical opinion was that I should stay in hospital for at least 48 hours, then have more tests.

That would have meant missing the Wales versus Ireland game at Cardiff. Against medical advice I signed myself out of hospital, and despite the aches from my injured ribs and stitched-up gums, took a taxi home and on Saturday, despite family and friends' misgivings, caught an early train from Runcorn to Cardiff. There was nothing brave about the action: I had become a workaholic and hated missing assignments.

The journey became a nightmare. As the train went through Abergavenny on its way to Cardiff for a lunchtime arrival it broke down. Eventually the guard came along to tell us that a replacement engine was on its way, but would take between two and three hours to arrive. In other words, I would miss the kick-off, and possibly the game, which I had to introduce and round-off for the evening highlights.

Unless... no doubt the powerful painkillers had partially scrambled the little grey cells, for I took a weird action.

Making sure no guard or policeman was around I jumped painfully from the stationary train, and hobbled as quickly as I could down the embankment like a Second World War prisoner escaping from Colditz. In the town below I saw what I wanted, a taxi rank, crawled into a passenger seat and asked the puzzled taxi driver to take me on what proved to be an expensive journey to Cardiff, explaining my predicament as we went along. In addition I asked him to put Radio Wales on the wireless. I needed to know the score.

It was a slow journey, the clock ticked round remorselessly, and when we finally reached the approaches to the Arms Park the referee blew the final whistle. The game had been played in teeming rain in awful conditions, and Ireland had pulled off a huge shock by winning 3-0.

I knew the final score. I could see the horrid weather and imagined the conditions. I had made it and if Alan Mouncer, who would be wondering where the heck I was, accepted my pleas to be allowed to top and tail the action, I would be on the show in three hours time.

There was one more huge obstacle for a man with sore ribs. I had to walk to the television gantry by going through the stadium concourse as 50,000 rugby fans were coming the other way. It was a painful, bumpy ride, but eventually a sopping wet, gasping and sore presenter climbed up the gantry to the astonishment of Alan Mouncer and crew, who looked as though they were Macbeth seeing Banquo's ghost. I breathlessly pleaded to be allowed to retain my 100 per cent attendance reputation by recording the match preview I had written on the train, and then ad-libbing a back reference about the shock to Wales, the awful conditions, the delight of mud-caked Ireland, and so on. And then I would say "See you next week".

Mouncer could hardly refuse under the circumstances. He told me to compose myself, take a few deep breaths, comb my hair, look at the camera, take a practice run, then do the intro and cue

Bill McLaren for the commentary. Then pause and do the summary and closing. These would then be edited into the highlights. The job finally done, I said my thanks and farewells, hobbled back down the ladder, made my way to Cardiff station, and got the last train back to Runcorn and Liverpool. Mad, barking mad. But I had made it, and viewers of the programme spotted nothing unusual in the transmission. Indeed, producer Alan Mouncer had literally the last laugh. On Monday he rang me to say: "Keith. Don't bother to come to matches any more. We'll put a camera in your garden. You watch the game on live telly, then do your links afterwards." Point taken.

Another memorable rugby union occasion was a midweek live television broadcast of the Varsity match, Oxford versus Cambridge at Twickenham. On this occasion I was unexpectedly asked to share the commentary with another virtual novice, but one with an athletics pedigree. He was never to make it as a commentator, but earned millions as novelist. His name was Jeffrey Archer.

If I flirted with danger on other programmes, one live outside broadcast during the 1960s proved a positive disaster, and ended what had been a reasonable run with the BBC2 leisure, adventure and outdoors programme *Time Out*, produced by Chris Brasher.

My appearances on the show tended to be studio-based so it was something of a surprise to be asked to do an outside broadcast from Northolt Airport near London. The occasion was one of the major record-breaking flights by aviator Sheila Scott, a 1960s Amy Johnson or Amelia Earhart. The precise city-to-city record she was attempting to break escapes me, but she was due to bring it to a climax by touching down at Northolt, where a BBC Outside Broadcast team would be awaiting by arrangement between BBC executives and Sheila Scott's advisers.

The OB was open-ended, to allow for any delay in the arrival of Scott. Chris Brasher had arranged for lots of film reports to be made to fill in the time, but the Scott plane was delayed and we ran out of film. Just when panic was about to set in an exultant roar went up from the assembled Northolt ground staff and all BBC personnel. The aircraft was there in the sky and would land in minutes. The OB production assistant thrust a bottle of champagne for her in my hand, the floor manager cued me to start talking and I opened up with the well-rehearsed lines about this great woman aviator coming into land after another record-breaking flight.

Only she wasn't coming in to land. Well, not at Northolt. To the consternation of the television crew, and my own gut-wrenching horror, Sheila Scott did not even lose height as she passed Northolt and flew off to an unknown - to us - destination.

It was one of the lowest points of my career, before or since. For in those less sophisticated and much less technically advanced days of outside broadcasts the only contact I had with the producer Brasher was by signals mouthed with gestures from the floor manager on site. Worst of all, there was no film left at base to cue in to cover our, and particularly, my embarrassment. I waffled for as long as I could about there having been some breakdown in communication with Sheila Scott or perhaps she had developed signs of engine trouble, or had accidentally overshot... but at last the studio took over leaving those of us at Northolt with eggs on faces and devastated with the anticlimax. As the frontman, most of the egg was on my face and despite the fact that her failure to land had created the chaos, that was the end of my brief spell with *Time Out*, though mercifully not with the BBC.

If it can be possible for a crass and repeated error to be a source of uproarious humour, then what must rank as the worst, yet perhaps funniest, gaffe of my career must qualify in that category. It happened in one of my Saturday commentaries on BBC North Region radio.

I was scheduled to do a second-half commentary on the Hull Kingston Rovers versus Leigh game on Humberside. On the day dense fog came down as I drove over the high Pennine trails, because the M62 motorway was not yet completed. Fortunately I had set off early and struggled over the top, through to the foggy environs of Kingston-upon-Hull, and over the bridge to a fog-shrouded Craven Park to arrive with an hour to go before kick-off. The spectators, 99 per cent of them from Hull, had been admitted, but to me the game looked certain to be postponed. From the broadcast point in the stands I could barely see a quarter of the pitch; with threequarters covered in dense fog.

However, the referee was able to see both sets of goalposts, and both touchlines from the centre spot and, according to the then rules, the match was on. When I turned to the producer of the day and asked plaintively: "How can I describe a match when I can barely see a quarter of the pitch?" his reply was: "Describe what you can see, and make the rest up. It's radio and no one can argue with you".

I devised a plan. When the ball was in the fogbound area I would know who had possession because of the noise coming from the home fans. When there was virtual silence, Leigh were in possession. When the noise reached a crescendo it was a score or heavy pressure from Rovers. Therefore, according to the noise levels, I would pick a name at random from the printed programme. Fortunately, the official scoreboard was on my side of the pitch, and when the only try of the second half went to Rovers in the fog I correctly guessed from the direction of the noise that it had been touched down by the left-winger. The only other score, a penalty to Leigh, happened on my side. During the second half spells in the fog, when the lack of noise indicated Leigh in possession, I would look at the Leigh names in the programme and choose one or two. In particular my eye seemed to catch every time on Ted Brophy, a South African second-row forward. He did little on the clear side of the fog, but in the swirling mists he had an absolute stormer, a heroic man-of-the-match display. At last the whistle blew, I had kept it going and, with the aid of the scoreboard, had got it right at the end.

On being kindly invited for a warming drink in the Rovers boardroom, I was approached by a Leigh director, who said in a splendid Lancashire accent: "Well done, Keith lad. We couldn't see t' match, so we listened to thee on t' wireless. You only made one mistake."

"What was that?"

"Brophy weren't playin'. He cried off sick just before t' match".

Oh dear, oh dear. How could my career survive this?

Mercifully, it did. People had a good laugh about it and to cap it all Ted Brophy wrote a letter to the Leigh secretary claiming his match fee because, contrary to reports, he had played in the game and had a recorded copy of a radio commentary to prove it.

My favourite of the shows I fronted, principally because it was created, staffed and marketed to the whole BBC network was *A Spoonful of Sugar*. The format, developed by a North Region programmes executive John Ecclestone and directed by Nick Hunter, has since been adapted and copied many times throughout the world, but four decades ago it was something of a trail-blazer. Barbara MacDonald and I presented a recorded OB which consisted of the pair of us visiting a hospital to give long-stay patients fantastic surprises in the shape of bedside appearances of a long-lost relative from thousands of miles away, or their favourite film, stage, television or radio star. Sometimes, if they were mobile, we took them on a holiday or tour abroad which they could never have afforded.

Of course, as with the *This Is Your Life* television format, complete secrecy was imposed on hospital staff, families and friends, and on the day of our visit the recipients of our surprises were fed some cock and bull story about the interviews being recorded for a series of documentaries on hospital life. We would worm out of interviewees the details of their family lives, interests and favourite personalities, and then, hey presto, in would walk the long-lost relative or friend, or a current star from entertainment or sport.

Millions of people appeared to love the show but one television critic, Milton Shulman, of the London *Evening Standard* wrote a savage review accusing *A Spoonful of Sugar* of being gooily sentimental and patronising to patients. BBC top executives in London had an immediate knee-jerk reaction to bad publicity and, after two successful series it was taken off, only to reappear in various 'new' guises in succeeding decades with such show-business luminaries as Cilla Black and Jimmy Savile in charge.

Life was by now teaching me the cardinal truth that sometimes you win, sometimes you lose, immortalised in Kipling's adage about triumph and disaster. I was busy, probably too busy for a man with a wife and two young daughters, and the downs had to be taken with the ups.

There were also difficult decisions to be made about priorities. Freelances do not like turning down assignments, and not always for mercenary reasons. Rejecting jobs, even with apologies about being already booked, could lead to someone else doing them, doing them well, and taking over on a permanent basis.

Amid all these hectic comings and goings something eventually had to give. My absences from the anchor role on *Look North* became more and more frequent and often lasted for more than one day. Jim Entwistle's considerable tolerance finally gave way, and after an amicable chat it was decided that while I would continue to report and present features, a new full-time presenter would start. Arthur Murphy, a well-known compere on Irish television magazines did a short spell, then Stuart Hall, much as I had done six years earlier, stepped up from presenting sport into the hot seat. He soon made it very much his own before moving to *It's a Knockout*, a huge network success. For me, my busy freelance work continued. I even deputised for Eddie Waring on three commentaries when he was in hospital for a minor operation.

What could be seen as a gap in my journalism portfolio, the Sunday papers, was briefly filled during my frenetic activity in the late 1960s and early 1970s by invitations to cover rugby league and football, and write the occasional column, for the *Sunday Express* and the *Sunday People*.

I have yet another of those guilt filled memories from my brief time with the Sundays. Names of the paper and football manager involved are omitted to shield me, the guilty party, from reprisals.

It was, and still is, normal practice after reporting a game to get a quote from a manager or player. I did this faithfully and I hope accurately until one occasion, and I still wince at the memory, when I went down to the dressing rooms rather belatedly to find that the team and manager of the defeated visiting team had boarded their coach quickly and left.

I returned to the rapidly emptying press box, and got a couple of off-the-cuff quotes from colleagues. They were not enough for the long quote I needed, but, using them as a base, along with my knowledge of the manager's personality and vocabulary, I sent a detailed quote, two thirds a sheer invention, to the newspaper.

The paper gave it considerable prominence the next morning, and for weeks I waited for an angry telephone call from the manager denying that he had spoken to me. Thankfully it did not happen. Perhaps he purred with delight at the eloquence he had displayed in the 'interview'. Perhaps he did not read the paper. I was lucky, and I have never committed that misdemeanour since.

In 1969, there came another seismic shift. I had maintained my rugby league connections by doing matches on radio but my stint on *Look North* had included football features and the odd report.

Independent Television was by now an established power in broadcasting, and Yorkshire Television was the new force on the east side of the Pennines. The independent networks throughout Britain were establishing their own strong news, sport and outside broadcast departments and association football – soccer - was a central audience-getting feature. Each independent region had its own local football match coverage slot, with matches recorded on Saturday and shown on Sunday afternoons.

In 1969 Yorkshire TV were, according to the internal grapevine, seeking a football commentator to replace Danny Blanchflower, a magnificent and legendary Irish player, but not a natural broadcaster. I applied for an audition, hoping that my specialisation in rugby league would not rule me out of contention.

Fortunately for me it did not. The head of sport at Yorkshire, former BBC *Grandstand* editor Lawrie Higgins, invited me over, along with several other auditionees, and we were each given spells at a closed-circuit recorded broadcast at a pre-season Sheffield Wednesday game.

Luck was again on my side, as it had been at Swinton in 1956. I got the job, and ironically enough I was told sometime later that one of the deciding factors was not so much my knowledge of football but my years of experience in sports television and radio.

After 13 years of specialisation in rugby league, including writing two books, I would now have to give priority to soccer, with the emphasis on Yorkshire clubs like Leeds United, the two Sheffield sides, Huddersfield Town, Middlesbrough and Hull City. Though I would keep in touch with rugby league, and still do occasional radio commentaries when I could get permission from YTV, for the next seven years my number one sport would be soccer, which I had watched as a boy and played at school. It was a huge wrench, but the challenge was too good to miss.

Keith and Sheila with their children Heather and Tracy in 1965.

On location with Border TV in lakeland.

7. Yorkshire Television

The years at Yorkshire Television were meant, at least in my mind, to be the time when the manic dashing from programme to programme, location filming to location filming, would be put behind me. While retaining my love of and occasional reporting on, rugby league, which was then in broadcasting terms very much the exclusive province of the BBC and Eddie Waring, I would concentrate on being a football commentator and reporter, attempting to do the job properly and to prove to sceptics that the XIII-a-side code was not the only sport on my personal planet.

Some hope. In reality the Yorkshire years saw me as manically and diversely active as at any time with the Beeb. I would cover Wembley rugby league finals for radio, boxing, snooker, show jumping, cricket, women's hockey, head tennis, and such bizarre sports as shove ha'penny and table football. Non-sporting outside broadcasts would send me to Robert Brothers Circus and church services and to the wonderfully colourful Spalding Flower Parade.

On a more global scale there would be network assignments to the 1972 Olympics and the 1974 World Cup, where I would come within a couple of inches of crashing a Hamburg Police motor launch into a bridge on Lake Alster.

The football scene was exciting and rewarding, though it tended to be centred on the exploits of just one team, Leeds United, to the oft-expressed annoyance of officials and supporters of other Yorkshire, Lincolnshire, Humberside and north Derbyshire viewers.

The problem was that, while other teams had sporadic bouts of success, such as Huddersfield Town achieving successive promotions, Leeds were perennial trophy chasers and the team everyone wanted to beat, for worthy and unworthy reasons. For Leeds under Don Revie were disliked and reviled everywhere outside their own city and fan base.

Between 1969 and 1975 Revie's United won the First Division title twice, the FA Cup once, and were beaten finalists in both the European Cup and the European Cup Winners Cup and in the FA Cup twice. They also won the former European Inter Cities' Fairs Cup once.

But they were not a popular side by any stretch of the imagination. In today's game Manchester United and Chelsea have become the clubs everyone wants to see knocked off their perches and Sir Alex Ferguson and José Mourinho would never top the poll in best-loved managers. However, reactions to perennial success at Old Trafford and Stamford Bridge have never been as grudging or as rancorous as those accorded Revie's Leeds on their travels, despite the fact that they were, and remain, one of the outstanding teams of the late 20th century.

However, Revie was a ruthless pursuer of success, and in that pursuit he produced a team that was equally ruthless and, to coin a euphemism, extremely uncompromising. They knew how to win, and had so many fine players that they could play it pretty or play it ugly depending on the opposition. They were both admired and feared, and they had great players throughout the team.

Players like the superb half-back line of Billy Bremner, Jack Charlton and Norman 'Bites yer legs' Hunter controlled midfield long before the semi-meaningless word 'midfielder' was confusingly coined. Gary Sprake and David Harvey were quality goalkeepers, Paul Reaney and Terry Cooper were tigerish tacklers at full-back and good at getting forward. The front line consisted of Peter Lorimer, the winger with the most powerful shot in football; goal scorers Allan Clarke and the willing workhorse Mick Jones; the cunning, skilful and lethally tackling Johnny Giles, and on the left wing the Scotsman Eddie Gray who had dribbling skills to rival the peerless Stanley Matthews. Gray scored the finest individual goal I have ever seen in a 2-0 Elland Road win against Burnley.

Leeds had excellent fringe players too, who fitted in seamlessly. Paul Madeley, Terry Yorath - father of Gabby Logan - Terry Hibbitt and Mick Bates were among a pool of players who could have walked into other first teams. They won consistently, were always in contention, and as a result were constantly on television.

Yet Leeds, for all their success, never won hearts outside their own parish. Credit, yes. Grudging admiration, yes. Accolades and trophies, yes. But they were unloved because of the widely perceived overexposure on the box, and the equally widely criticised combination of skills and hardness of their game.

The architect of their success, Don Revie, eventually had a spell as England manager, but he never received the warm general acceptance and even affection that was given to Leeds's contemporaries and challengers, Bill Shankly and his Liverpool team.

That negative public conception eventually spread into an occasional reaction to YTV and to me as commentator. For the most part the crews, producers Geoff Hall and Andy Gullen, and me were warmly received and well treated at other grounds, particularly in the lower divisions, but from time to time an undercurrent of resentment came to the surface. The more vocal fans would accuse YTV of being 'TV Leeds United', and therefore anti everyone else. Accusations of bias would inevitably arise. The city of Sheffield, whose denizens felt that the main ITV studios should have been based there, were almost comically abusive, for when they were not charging us with Leeds bias, they alleged collusion with their city rivals. At Hillsborough we were 'United-ites', at Bramall Lane we were 'Wednesday-ites'! It was a pity, because all of us working on the football programmes wanted every club in our area to do well and were thrilled and delighted to be there when it happened.

Sunday football coverage aside, the Yorkshire period was pleasantly varied and far more eventful than anticipated. There were boxing tournaments in Bradford, and a women's hockey tournament in Thirsk where, perched on a hastily assembled platform on the touchline on a bitterly cold midwinter day I was frozen rigid, and several times dropped the microphone from nerveless fingers. At the Robert Brothers' Circus in Leeds we did a live Boxing Day OB from Leeds during which, as a stunt, I was invited to take part in an act. This involved, as I recall, picking up a large hammer and slamming it down on the rigid stomach muscles of the Strong Man, who was billed as Ivan, the strongest man in Russia, brought over from Moscow at huge expense.

As I hesitated, not wishing to inflict a painful death on Ivan from Russia through severe internal damage, I was startled to receive from him the whispered injunction "Gerrit done, lad. Tha' cawn't hurt me wi that thing". Either Ivan was not from Russia, or he had studied English regional dialects at school.

At Leeds University we filled an afternoon with a football head-tennis tournament, which was won by two well-known Manchester City footballers Neil Young and Mike Doyle.

A source of much humour, on both sides of the camera, was the networked show *Indoor League*, which was hosted by Fred Trueman, with Sid Waddell, Dave Lanning, Neil Cleminson and me doing commentaries on pub games like darts, skittles, carpet bowls, shove ha'penny and table football. Fred hammed it up wonderfully in his best "Sithee in a tick" accent, but the commentators took the games seriously.

It was great fun except for one particular night at the Irish Centre, now a snooker centre near the YTV studios in Leeds. In the absence of Fred on a more pressing engagement, I deputised, linking the show and acting as master of ceremonies on the stage. All went well for an hour or so. Then, not to put too fine a point on it, all hell broke loose.

A fight broke out at a table. Others joined in, including the bouncers, as fights began all over the place, and the producer of *Indoor League* told me to "go out on stage and restore order".

What a joke. I could no more have restored order than I could have extinguished an eruption of Vesuvius by pouring in a glass of water. I decided that survival was the better part of valour when a half-full glass of beer whistled past my ear, soaking me and causing a rapid flight to the safety of the OB vans.

The summer months brought more variety with the splendidly busy OB department, including show jumping, starring that other larger-than-life Yorkshireman Harvey Smith, at the magnificent Great Yorkshire Show in Harrogate. There was more show jumping at the Lincolnshire Show in Lincoln, and at Scarborough.

Inevitably, this being the White Rose county, there was cricket. One afternoon in April, as pre-season training began, we went to the Indoor School at Headingley and there filmed Don Wilson, a cunning left-arm bowler, and Barrie Leadbeater, an opening bat and later a distinguished first-class umpire.

The producer, as producers are paid to do, had a bright idea. He would film Don Wilson running up, turning his arm over, and spinning one off the indoor wicket at Leadbeater.

Foolishly, I stood on the opposite side to Wilson, just feet away as he trundled up with that deceptively lazy action. Over came his arm, he tossed up a juicy half-volley, and Barrie Leadbeater hit a perfect skimming on drive, inches off the ground. It hit me right on the edge of the shin bone, and I went down howling with pain as my right leg turned every colour of the rainbow and blood dribbled into my socks.

The physio, I think it was Paddy Dalton, was quick off the mark. He squirted some freezing substance on the swollen, multi-coloured limb and as he stepped back I looked up and from my prone position saw, looming over me, the large frame of Yorkshire and England captain and legend Brian Close.

What a moment to cherish. Here was I, injured in a cricketing incident, and the great Brian Close was about to offer comfort and solace. His face close to mine, Closey whispered; "Now you know what we have to ------- put up with all the time". Cheers Brian.

Perhaps, the most career-crowning days of the period were those as part of the London-based ITV team at the 1972 Munich Olympics and the commentary team at the 1974 Football World Cup in Germany.

While the London end of the operation kept me indoors at London Weekend Television for three weeks, away from the front line in Munich, it was a great experience just to be asked to take part.

The 1972 Games were, of course, disrupted by the ghastly incident of the kidnap and slaughter of 11 members of the Israeli team by Black September terrorists, and the subsequent killing of five terrorists by Munich police in a botched rescue attempt. However, after a one-day suspension and a memorial service the Games and television coverage went on.

In London, it was very much backroom work, receiving incoming recorded commentaries from the Olympic venues and editing them into broadcast packages. Occasionally the incoming action would be of minor events like rowing heats and shot-putting qualification. They would have no commentary, and those of us on duty in the London studios on the south bank of the Thames would have our brief moments of glory on the screened highlights by cutting a short item and writing and recording a commentary. We might even get a name credit on air.

The 1974 World Cup was compensation for the fact that I had missed out in 1970 primarily because I was a new kid on the ITV block. I was one of the five commentators in Germany headed by the late Brian Moore. The others were Hugh Johns, Gerald Sinstadt and Gerry Harrison, and it was a privilege to be part of the team. Inevitably the top games went to the senior men, Moore and Johns, but it was a thrill and an experience just to be there, and the tour of Germany provided several moments to treasure.

The two most memorable ones both came in Hamburg, that lively city on two lakes, the Great Alster and the Little Alster, where in the space of just one evening one could enjoy a sail on a lake, an opera performance, and a tour of the infamous red-light district, depending on tastes and interests. Geoff Hall, my producer, and I eschewed, of course, the last of these options, and were eventually glad to escape with our lives on the Great Alster sail. It was not on a pleasure boat, but on a Lake Police launch as guests of the chief officer, plus the crew of three or four officers who got more than they bargained for when, in a brief but foolish moment they invited me to try my hand at steering the speedboat.

I must have rather exaggerated my experience of such a skill, which consisted entirely of piloting gentle paddle-boats at Fairhaven Lake near Blackpool or in a Scarborough Park. It all went reasonably well on the placid waters of the Great Alster as I controlled the accelerator pedal rather timidly. But then the chief officer said that "I could go a little quicker if I wanted to". I put my foot down much too enthusiastically, and the speedboat nearly leapt out of the water and careered across the lake, mercifully missing other craft with panic-stricken occupants.

Suddenly a bridge loomed in front of us and I was heading straight for its left-side stone support. As I closed my eyes and prepared to meet my maker, the chief officer grabbed the wheel and we missed the bridge by inches. Afterwards the atmosphere was distinctly frigid and it is unlikely that any English tourist or journalist has been granted such a privilege again by the Hamburg police.

The other memorable Hamburg incident was at the studios of Norddeutsher Rundfunk - North German Radio. As visiting broadcasters, producer Geoff Hall and I had been invited to have lunch and a tour of the studios by our German opposite numbers, a visit which pointed up our perceived insularity as a nation. It can be a source of puzzlement to people of other nationalities that we do not readily converse in any language other than English. While it is gratifying and comfortable to know that our native tongue is the world's most popular second language, it must occasionally grate that foreign-language teaching has never been a priority in our educational systems, and is even less so nowadays.

Certainly, on that 1974 afternoon in Hamburg, Geoff and I took it for granted that our hosts would speak fluent English, and so it proved. We were entertained to a splendid lunch in an excellently appointed staff canteen, and then taken on a tour of the radio and television studios.

Throughout the conversation we were staggered at the fluency of the German producer and commentator, who seemed able to speak not merely in standard English sentences, but also in clichés and football vernacular.

Eventually came a passage of conversation which, though I forget the subject, remains imprinted on my memory to this day. The conversation in English had been pretty fluent, with few pauses, and we had all chipped in with our contributions to the four-sided natter. Suddenly, with a perfectly natural turn in the subject, our two German hosts discussed the football point at issue with each other. As Geoff and I took on the role of listeners they chatted for about five minutes.

In English, as naturally as if it was their native tongue. Whether it was sheer politeness to guests, or a natural fluency in what to them was a foreign language, the two Germans never paused, we never felt excluded, and I still marvel at it to this day. I can only recall one other similar occasion, although the opposite happened. It happened at Cardiff Arms Park during a *Rugby Special* at an international rugby union recording. However, on that occasion producer Dewi Griffiths and commentator Onllwyn (Onkers) Brace, two smashing chaps and proud Welshmen, conducted a conversation entirely in Welsh, pausing only occasionally to smile or nod in my direction.

But back to Germany. It was a fascinating tour and a memorable experience which took me to games, interviews and social visits in Cologne, Düsseldorf, Hanover, Gelsenkirchen and Stuttgart. Not quite a paid holiday, but close enough to it to cause occasional bouts of puritanical guilt.

It was to be the only football World Cup I would cover, for in less than two years my stint as YTV's commentator, with its attendant range of other assignments, would end, and rugby league, which had never for a moment been far away, would again take over as number one sport in the diary.

Throughout my hectic and mostly happy YTV stint I had reported on rugby league Challenge Cup Finals and the occasional club game for radio when they did not clash with television assignments, and this very retention of interest would prove a small element in the eventual parting of the ways in 1976.

But before leaving my Yorkshire days I must find space to mention one more programme.

While sport, and particularly football, provided the bedrock of the hectically crowded YTV years, one programme stands out in memory for a bizarre mixture of reasons. It was not a standard mainstream show. It was born of a whim, a brainwave; it was bitterly opposed by some elements of the Independent Broadcasting Authority, it was scheduled in the obligatory Sunday religious hour, named by cynics and sceptics 'The God Slot', and it was barely 25 minutes in length.

Against all the odds it reached audiences of between 10 and 12 million, but was then killed off, a victim of a lengthy ITV technicians' strike.

The idea of *The Sunday Quiz* came unbidden to mind during an evening of mental doodling. It was quite simple in concept, and very basic. Rather than focusing on serious academic analysis, an act of worship, or a documentary based on religious orthodoxies, primarily Christian, the quiz would ask questions of Judaism, Hindu and Islamic teachings, Buddhism and other faiths, and would include visual artefacts and dramatic enactments. At a time when interest in comparative religion was growing both in schools and in literature, the format seemed an ideal subject for the television religious hour, and the quiz format would give it added pace and competitive appeal.

A YTV producer, Tony Scull, took up the idea and with researcher David Wilson gave it shape and a variety of ingredients to lift it out of the mere question-and-answer convention. Then came the tough bit, getting the idea past the hardest obstacle, the religious programme decision makers in London. Understandably, there were voices raised against what could be seen as a flippant, entertainment-led quiz disguised as a serious religious programme. A compromise was reached whereby *Sunday Quiz* would be given a short trial run, fully networked, to see how it worked, and I would act as question master.

The format varied between single contestants and teams of two and included the two sections which lifted the show above the normal quick-fire question-and-answer routine. The first section included dramatic monologues by famous actors impersonating historic religious figures. These included Marius Goring as John Wesley, George Baker as St Augustine and William Simons as Martin Luther.

The second, and a real scene-stealer, was the collection of historic religious artefacts brought on by Bill Weaver, now the Reverend Canon Bill Weaver, who was then a lecturer in the theology department of Leeds University. Bill unearthed such objects as an Egyptian funerary boat which dated from 2000 BC, ancient statues of Buddha, Shiva and Hanuman and a Sikh dagger.

To our pleasant surprise, and ultimately astonishment, the programme caught on. No doubt this was partly due to the fact that in the early 1970s there was no powerful mass opposition from new terrestrial, cable and digital channels, and the BBC would also be showing religion-based programming.

The *Sunday Quiz*, quick-moving under Tony Scull's direction, with informed questions on a variety of topics and faiths from Bill Weaver, and not least Bill's weird and wonderful collection of artefacts, received remarkable official viewing figures. I have a small contemporary cutting from *The Sunday People's* television gossip column in which, to the author's obvious surprise, it was revealed that the programme had a regular audience averaging 10 million and at one stage hitting 12 million.

It ran for six series including two for schoolchildren, and one series was recorded at the Tyne Tees TV studio at Newcastle. The *Sunday Quiz* came to an end in 1976, much to my regret, for it was great fun, informative about faiths, and a break from sporting matters.

However, during the recording of the Tyne Tees series of the quiz I had one of the most frightening, potentially embarrassing, yet in retrospect, funniest experiences of my career.

It happened at one of the plusher hotels in Newcastle, where I was staying overnight on generous company expenses, with an early start in studio in the morning. In an act of sheer self-indulgence I decided to have an early night, take a leisurely bath, order a room service meal, watch some telly, then have a good night's sleep. Sheer Babylonian excess.

I ordered a cheese and ham sandwich, with crisps, salad, and a pot of tea and gave the room number. The order seemed to take longer than anticipated, so I undressed and started running the bath while I waited. When the knock came on the door I looked in vain for a dressing gown and, not wishing to appear at the door in the nude, shouted to the waiter to place the tray outside the door for me to pick up. When the footsteps had disappeared down the corridor I opened the door slowly, looked to left and right to ensure no one was in sight, then nipped out quickly to lift the tray. As I did so I heard a horrible sound. The door, on a spring mechanism, had clunked shut behind me. I was on a second-floor corridor of a posh hotel in Newcastle as uncovered and helpless as a new-born baby.

Don't panic I thought. There has to be one of those in-house white telephones somewhere on the corridor. Sure enough, there was one, some 30 yards to my right, at the top of a flight of stairs. I could ring reception, explain my predicament and hope that a tactful porter would come to rescue me with a service key. But then there came more disturbing noises. The sound of human voices. A party of fellow guests was coming up the stairs and would reach the top at roughly the same time I got to the house phone.

Again, as at Hull KR versus Leigh, I felt that my career was about to end in shame and ignominy. I could see the headlines in the Newcastle papers, and probably further afield:

"TV man runs naked along hotel landing … shame of Sunday quiz presenter".

The divinity that shapes our ends came to my rescue again. About 10 yards to my right on the wall was a red fire extinguisher, tastefully-covered with a red plush curtain. I whipped inside and behind the curtain, alongside the extinguisher and stood stock still, hardly daring to breathe. The babble of voices neared the extinguisher, went past and, as they disappeared slowly to the left there was a short pause in the chatter, then giggles as an incredulous female voice said: "I'm sure I saw a pair of man's feet behind that curtain".

Horror of horrors, I was nicked. The game was up. The curtain did indeed end inches from the carpet, and my feet must have been clearly visible. Mercifully, everybody roared with laughter, made rude remarks about the lady's eyesight and carried on. I waited a couple of minutes, crept out from behind, carried out Plan A with the house phone, and was rescued by a porter who discreetly avoided looking in my direction as he opened the door with his master key and let me in. I did not sleep too well that night and it took me a long time before I saw the humorous potential of the tale, and incorporated it in many after-dinner speeches.

But to return to the end of the seven busy years at Leeds, which was partly precipitated by perceptions of a clash of loyalties between sports, which would not have been a problem with today's multi-purpose commentators.

There were other pressures in the football front. One came in a semi-jocular remark delivered in all apparent innocence by Lawrie McMenemy, manager of Southampton when they shocked Manchester United in the FA Cup Final in 1976. In the popular weekly programme *Yorksport*, hosted by Fred Dinenage, also a presenter of the network *How* programme. Dinenage referred to me as "our football expert" during an interview. I have always cringed at this use of the word 'expert', since only those who have played or managed at the highest level of sport deserve the accolade. Reporters can be highly knowledgeable, and accurate and responsible in their judgements, but only practitioners within a sport can be real experts.

Be that as it may, when Fred used the word 'expert', and quoted my comment, a beaming McMenemy, with whom incidentally I got on famously, jocularly replied "Oh, he's a rugby league man really". Jocular or not, I winced. Another straw in the wind was that an outstanding young commentator, Martin Tyler, was emerging in the sports department of London Weekend TV and was understandably being pushed hard by John Bromley in London and other senior network executives.

Add to these pressures the fact that again quite justifiably, the feeling had grown among the top brass at YTV that I was doing too much and was in the industry's parlance, 'over-exposed', leading to a deleterious effect on some performances. The ground was obviously shifting. Amid the uncertainty a lifeline emerged which, amazingly, solved the problems with minimal damage and maximum possible satisfaction all round.

Border Television, based in Carlisle, is one of the smaller television stations but a thriving concern attracting top-10 majority audiences in Cumbria, southern Scotland, parts of Northumberland and the Isle of Man. They were looking for a new main presenter for their six o'clock flagship news magazine *Lookaround*. I applied for the job and was offered it by the Border head of programmes Derek Batey, himself a well-known network broadcaster with the *Mr and Mrs* show.

Yorkshire released me from my contract as football commentator, while offering continued freelance work in other areas. Martin Tyler took over at the football microphone, rapidly established himself, and ultimately became Sky TV's number-one commentator and one of the most outstanding, dedicated and consistent practitioners in the art of football commentary. And although I did not know it at the time, the path was then cleared for my eventual return to rugby league at the highest level on both regional television and network radio.

8. And on to Border

If there is some substance of truth in the phrase a 'seven-year itch', then my career seemed to be following that sort of pattern. At *Look North* and then at YTV this had been certainly the case, and any hopes that Border TV would break the mould of my career did not prove to be well-founded. Again the truth of another adage, that variety is the spice of life, was to foreshorten what was otherwise an extremely happy two and a half years, in one of Britain's and the world's loveliest environments.

The time at the *Barrow Mail* had included trips up into Cumbria and into that part of north Lancashire which was later absorbed into south Cumbria, so I was happily attuned to mountains and fells, rivers and streams, agrarian communities and wide stretches of peaceful countryside. These factors and the consequently slower and more relaxed lifestyle made life at Border TV a rest cure after the relentless, albeit exciting, flurry of cross-Pennine and national network schedules.

The offices and studios, small and compact and creating a family atmosphere based around a spotlessly clean and comfortable canteen, were the perfect cure for any semblance of bruised ego left over from the fiercely competitive and demanding national networks. The transmission area is vast, but the centres of population, outside of the cathedral city of Carlisle, are small. It really is a geographical patchwork quilt, stretching north over the border near Gretna through the towns of the central Borders of Scotland and up and over to Stranraer, and east to Berwick and Northumberland. On the Cumbrian west coast are the industrial towns of Whitehaven and Workington, south are the agricultural market towns of Penrith and busy Kendal. So many ways of life; so many different accents.

The editors and producers of *Lookaround* performed - and presumably still do in the six o'clock slot - minor miracles in covering so many diverse and disparate parishes. Any single nightly programme might see me introducing a court story from Carlisle, an industrial dispute from Workington, or Hawick's textile industry, an agricultural feature from Penrith or a gentle arts feature from Kendal. Sports items would include a preview on what was bizarrely referred to as a Borders football derby match between Berwick and Stranraer, two clubs on opposite sides of the country! There was rugby league in Whitehaven, Workington and Carlisle, rugby union in Hawick, Galashiels, Jedforest, Selkirk and Langholm. Because of this television fusion of the two rugby codes Border can justifiably claim to have created a television 'first'. For I was eventually asked to co-host a monthly half-hour programme *The Union And The League*, in which both codes were featured side by side, without demarcation. More often than not a pre-programme canteen meal would see my rugby league interviewee chatting amiably and animatedly with John Smail, a Borders man and *Lookaround's* XV-a-side reporter, who co-introduced the programme with me, along with a Scottish international figure like Jim Telfer. Or perhaps we would feature John Jeffrey, the union player who became notorious for allegedly playing football with the Calcutta Cup after an international game. John always played down the incident though he never quite denied it.

Filming was often sheer joy on *Lookaround*. There was no way I could be allowed to idle around in the studio while others did the road work of film stories. I had to do my share with the camera crews before coming back in time for rehearsal and the six o'clock show.

Not that it was a problem. Quite the reverse, particularly in spring and summer, for hardly a day went by without a trip to Windermere, Derwentwater, Coniston or Bassenthwaite to mix with holiday makers while ostensibly working. There was clay pigeon shooting at the Annan Game Fair, just over the Scottish Border, and a day spent at John Jeffrey's Borders farm on a mission to preview a forthcoming Scotland game at Murrayfield. There would be a day at the races at Kelso or Carlisle; a trip on the Ravenglass to Eskdale railway through the hills and dales of West Cumbria, Cumberland and Westmorland style wrestling at Grasmere Sports. You could hardly call it work, and in the golden glow of memory the sun always shone.

And, of course, there was rugby league at Whitehaven and Workington and, for all too brief a time, at Carlisle. Then, as now, Cumbrian rugby league faced a constant struggle to survive. Both clubs had known good days following their admission to the Rugby Football League. Workington won the Challenge Cup in 1952, led by their own legendary full-back Gus Risman, and with mighty forwards in Australian Johnny Mudge and canny loose-forward Billy Ivison. They beat Featherstone Rovers 18-10 in the 1952 Challenge Cup Final, Mudge scoring a magnificent long-range try to turn the game for the Cumbrians.

Town were to reach two more finals in those early golden post-war years, only to lose to Barrow in 1957, and to Wigan in 1958 in a match which produced a cliff-hanger finish, and one of the great match-saving tackles of all time, only matched by John Pendlebury's tackle on Mark Elia in the St Helens versus Halifax final of 1987. Favourites Wigan were leading 13-9 and by three tries to one with only minutes to go when Town's speedy Great

Britain winger Ike Southward broke clear and sped towards the corner.

The Workington fans in the 66,000 Wembley crowd were on tiptoe as they roared on their wing greyhound for the try which, if Southward could tack on the goal, would almost certainly give them an unexpected victory. But Norman Cherrington, the big Wigan second-row forward had other ideas. He galloped across field and as Southward got to within a yard of the line and lifted the ball ready for the touchdown, Cherrington launched himself like a ground-to-air missile and knocked him over the touchline as the ball flew from his grasp.

Town had other successes and reached finals in other trophy competitions in the 1960s, and they could still field a useful side in the 1970s but their great days were over at the latter end of the decade, and gates were well below their immediate post-war peak.

Whitehaven had also made a pretty good impact after their admission to the League but they had no major trophies to their name, the nearest they got to Wembley being in 1957, when they were heartbreakingly beaten by Leeds in the semi-final by a late drop-goal from the Loiners' scrum-half Jeff Stevenson. However, Haven made their own peculiar contribution to today's fast-moving game in the shape of their second-row pair, Dick Huddart and Geoff Robinson, whose ability to hold on to the ball like glue and grind out up to 60 and 70 yards, play-the-ball by play-the-ball was one of the reasons why, in 1958, the rule change was introduced forcing the acting half-back at the tackle to pass or concede a scrum.

The two clubs welcomed the publicity given by Border TV, and were always co-operative, well aware that publicity outside the boundaries of Cumbria was virtually impossible to come by.

This perceived remoteness created an additional problem which still exists in some degree today. Even when funds were available to bring in fresh blood from the Lancashire and Yorkshire heartlands of rugby league, players would at first seem attracted by a possible move, only to pull out because of the huge mileage involved in making the trips to West Cumbria. Consequently Town, Whitehaven and later the short-lived Carlisle club had to rely on home-grown talent to build their sides and here, at least, they were fortunate. For then, as now, Cumbria had a strong and thriving amateur game providing a steady stream of youngsters to the senior clubs.

Well aware of this, Border TV's cameras would regularly make the trip to amateur clubs who frequently reached the earlier rounds of the Challenge Cup, like Kells and Wath Brow Hornets.

Nor was football forgotten. In addition to regular previews and bursts of film action, cameras would cover the handily placed Carlisle United at Brunton Park just down the road. But the other side of the travel coin would be the route marches, or rather safaris, to the far north-west and the Ireland ferry port of Stranraer or east to Berwick.

Lookaround and its associated programmes must have made a reasonable fist of the job of covering this massive geographical spread, for the six o'clock programme, virtually from its inception, was always in the audience research top three programmes, and frequently number one, for the region's transmission area. Jokers and cynics used to say that this was because sheep and cattle were included in the figures but it was always a boost to get the weekly charts.

Sadly, my Border idyll was to last no more than two and a half years. I could comfortably have settled into a sort of double life in which after a day's television I spent three nights a week paying no more than £5 for a night at the Hare and Hounds Inn, in the tiny hamlet of Talkin, up a winding hill from the market town of Brampton, east of Carlisle. There I was treated like a member of the family by Les and Joan Stewart and their faithful ally, cleaner and waitress Mary and would often go to sleep at night, if I retired early to read a book, to the cries of the darts team when someone hit a double top or bull.

However, I was also a member of a real family, around 100 miles south down the M6 in Widnes. My daughters were growing up and in their teens, with the seriously mentally and physically disabled Tracy requiring constant care from her mother, sister Heather and the staff of a special school. Throughout my stay at Border I had driven home on Wednesday nights to spend a couple of hours with my family and an hour before school on Thursday morning before scorching up the M6 back to Carlisle.

A further problem domestically was the fact that the continuing professional log-jam meant that I would usually be covering either a rugby league game or football match - and very occasionally both - at the weekend which further reduced quality family time. While, as ever, I was happy to be working, it was becoming, rightly and understandably, a source of guilt that I saw too little of my family.

Something had to give, and in the late summer of 1978 I made a startling, knee-jerk career change.

Once again the situations vacant section of *World's Press News* provided the impetus. I was looking for a radio, television or journalistic post anywhere around the M62 area that would enable me to work from home in Widnes. In addition I hoped my future employers would show the same generosity in releasing me for weekend and occasional midweek sporting commitments as Border and earlier YTV had done. For weeks I scoured the columns in vain, until at last a panel appeared advertising a post in Warrington, the place where my career had started in 1951. There was just one small snag. Well, it could have been a sizeable snag. The advertisement declared that Warrington New Town Development Corporation was looking for a chief public relations officer. The salary was £8,000 a year, a sum worth three or four times more in today's inflated currency and, of course, I would be spending much less on petrol.

A possible drawback was that publicity was not an area I had practised or studied, at least not professionally. But my mind was made up and I posted an application to Warrington New Town's managing director David Binns.

No doubt there were many applications from experienced publicity men but, to my surprise, I received a letter asking me to come to the New Town offices in Buttermarket Street, Warrington, for an interview. The interview did not last too long and David Binns, a man of guardsman-like straightness and authority, welcomed me aboard.

I politely enquired why he had made the decision, in view of my lack of PR experience. He said that I should have no problem writing literate press releases, which would be provided by the departmental officers to be given a journalistic gloss by me. Other assets were that I could front public meetings and coach the rest of the staff in how to do interviews about the New Town's services and plans. Finally, which he seemed to regard as an ace card, my regular television and radio appearances over the years had made my face and voice reasonably well-known in the Warrington area.

Thus began a new career step and, to my gratitude and relief, it would be allowed to go hand in hand with the existing one. I could live at home, spend real time with the family, and juggle the PR job with broadcasting assignments. Again I had struck lucky, but it left me with the painful task of saying farewell to the lovely Borders country and folk although in the event it turned out to be more of an *au revoir* than a goodbye.

When I explained my decision to move south the Border management team readily accepted the situation. Indeed they made it a satisfactory one for both parties by offering me freelance work which would enable me to continue to make regular trips up and down the M6 working on their rugby union half-hour, Cumberland county cricket at Netherfield, Barrow and Millom, rugby league and even occasional return stints in the presenter's chair on *Look Around*. There were to be many more trips from Warrington to Cumbria and the Border towns.

However, amid a decade of pleasant professional jaunts there was one assignment which was one of the two saddest and most depressing days of my life. It was the aftermath of a tragedy of worldwide implications, one of the most evil manifestations of international terrorism: the 1988 Lockerbie disaster.

I must say immediately that I played no part whatever in the actual coverage of the horrific event on 21 December, when the terrorist bomb exploded as the plane was passing over the small Scottish town killing everyone on board - 269 passengers and the crew. Wreckage from the plane dropped like bombs on Lockerbie, killing 11 people in Sherwood Crescent and leaving a massive crater amid the carnage. Like everyone else I followed the 24-hour coverage of the disaster by ITV, spearheaded by Border, the BBC and the international networks.

Towards the end of the week I got a surprise call from the Border news desk. Their staff had been working round the clock covering the disaster brilliantly, and were exhausted. The initial 24-hours a day coverage had been scaled down, and since it was Christmas time they wanted to know if I would mind manning the desk on Boxing Day. Since the major networks would be filling the holiday schedules, there would just be mid-morning headlines, plus a five-minute round-up of news and sport around teatime.

After spending Christmas Eve and Christmas Day with family and friends, I drove up to Border and found a message from the news editor Andy Leitch, suggesting that I should go up to Lockerbie after writing the morning headlines and do a piece with the people of a town who would spend Boxing Day grieving for their dead and injured while the rest of the country celebrated.

It was a heart-rending experience. No one in the town was smiling, there were few, if any, pathetically ironic celebrations and people stood, in silent vigil or numbed grief around the crater where once stood the houses of Sherwood Crescent. That day will stay with me forever. I returned to the studio, wrote and recorded the piece almost mechanically and drove home with a leaden heart.

It is a proven fact that all major tragedies, personal or public, eventually fade in their impact, life reverts to normal, and the time comes, all too soon perhaps, when the result of a sporting encounter assumes ridiculously exaggerated importance, or a minor setback assumes the weight of a major tragedy. Time heals, human nature reasserts itself, life goes on, but sometimes I remember Lockerbie and hope that I learnt something from all the horror.

But again I digress. I must return to 1978, my new role in Warrington, my first Australasian rugby league tour, becoming rugby league correspondent for *The Times* and for BBC Radio 2 and sadly, but not unrelated, the end of my marriage.

9. Warrington New Town

When David Binns, general manager of Warrington New Town Development Corporation, gave me the job of what came to be known, rather pompously, as head of public relations, one of the reasons was my experience of the media. Unfortunately that very fact boomeranged unexpectedly, and not in the New Town's favour.

I tried conscientiously to fulfil my responsibilities, chairing meetings and publicity panels, and writing and editing public relations releases on the New Town's state-of-the-art factory estates, a variety of housing and community schemes, leisure facilities and roads.

At least, I worked on these things when I was at the desk at New Town headquarters in Warrington. But within a month or so of my arrival, more developments in broadcasting led to ever more frequent absences from PR. The excellent and conscientious staff covered my absences well, though under some strain, and my double professional life can hardly have endeared me to my colleagues.

One instance of this resulted in another remarkable and thoroughly undeserved slice of luck. In 1978 I was asked by Don Mosey, then head of outside broadcasts of the BBC North Region, to become senior rugby league correspondent and reporter on a fee-paying freelance basis. Because of the verbal gentleman's agreement brokered with the New Town I was able to accept this and, at first, it caused no problems, since the PR role was Monday to Friday with rugby league previews and games on Saturday.

The significance of the new role became quickly apparent, however. There was an Australian tour to Britain in 1978 which featured three test matches in October and November. Then, the following year, there would be an immediate back-to-back series with a tour of Australia and New Zealand. The 1978 Kangaroos were to maintain their immunity from test series defeat in Britain since 1959, winning the first at Wigan but losing the second at Bradford, where outstanding performances by the Castleford centre John Joyner, Brian Lockwood, the Hull KR forward, and Stuart Wright, the Widnes winger who scored two tries, gave the home side a thrilling win.

It all depended on the third test at Leeds on 18 November, and the result had unfortunate repercussions for the Great Britain coach, Peter Fox, and for my professional relationship with him.

Peter was an outstanding coach who had led Bradford Northern and earlier Featherstone to trophy triumphs, often with limited material, and had been justifiably lauded by the media. However, some of his selections, particularly of older players, for the test series had received criticism, and even though the second test had been won, many scribes dubbed the side, and particularly the pack, 'Dad's Army', comparing them unflatteringly with their young Australian counterparts. When the Australians won the third test and the series 23-6 at Headingley the criticisms seemed justified, and the post-match media reports were not kind to the coach and his selection.

Alas, and by sheer force of circumstances, the first man to report the bad news on the final whistle was the Radio 2 man, who added the line, quoting current speculation in saying: "This might mean that Peter Fox will not get the coach's job for the Australian tour". When ultimately the selectors, who would be sitting in the stand when my words went on air and did not hear it, made that very decision and appointed Eric Ashton, Peter laid much of the blame on my observation, and it soured our relationship for years.

Ironically, while the dedicated and bitterly disappointed coach did not make the tour, I did. I had not held out much hope of getting on the trip, because I was not a full-time correspondent and I did have a full-time post, in theory, at Warrington. To my astonishment and then delight, when I tentatively jokingly put the point to Don Mosey he consulted network bosses and got the go-ahead, subject to certain provisos. These were that while the Beeb would pay travel and hotel bills, I would not be treated as a staff correspondent, and would have to subsist on freelance fees for previews, match reports and interviews.

It was too good an offer to resist. I would make no profit on the tour, but all the travel and accommodation details would be covered and I would have the pleasure and experience of having, let's be quite honest, a paid holiday watching Great Britain's rugby league tour. But it would mean two months away from promoting Warrington New Town. A considerable part of that would be deducted from a generous holiday entitlement, but it was still a lengthy absence. David Binns, a true gentleman of honour, swallowed hard but accepted the situation. However, the patience and loyalty of the PR staff must have been stretched to their limits, particularly when I returned to duty two months later to be greeted by another staggering piece of unwarranted good fortune, bringing a massive pay increase. More of that later.

It was to be for me the summit of every rugby league journalist's ambition: the chance to watch test matches between the two leading powers in the game while enjoying Australia's exotic South Seas scenery and fabled lavish hospitality, even if it meant leave of absence from Warrington duties, and more sombrely, yet another spell away from the family. At the end of May it was with something akin to schoolboy excitement that I boarded the plane at Manchester Airport with the playing squad and media corps in our smart Great Britain blazers and trousers. If I had foreseen some of the discomforts and hazards that were ahead on the 36-hour flight I might have been much less euphoric, although there was one slightly farcical incident which relieved tension and tiredness.

The route took in several stops. It went via the Syrian capital of Damascus - which in the darkness was just a sea of lights when we arrived - Bahrain, Kuala Lumpur, Singapore, Sydney and Brisbane, ending at the small coastal Queensland town of Mackay on the Great Barrier Reef.

Three memories stand out from the trip. One was distinctly unpleasant, one was a complete eye-opener for one unversed in the wider aspects of global travel, and one was extremely funny, which showed how camaraderie soon builds up among sporting tourists.

The thoroughly disagreeable factor began to happen roughly halfway through the long flight. Despite being a party that included sportsmen representing their country abroad, we were travelling economy class. The spaces between the seats and behind the person in front were tight, with the result that for long periods we were sitting immobile, unable to stretch our legs. Once or twice we could struggle out of our seats to go for a leg-stretching stroll in the aisles or answer a call of nature, but they were rare moments and because my seat was a window one, I felt trapped.

Eventually my legs began to feel heavy and sore, and when after 20 hours or so I investigated I found they were swollen to nearly twice their size. The rest of the journey was not comfortable, and on arrival at Mackay my first stop was bed with my feet up on top of a pile of boxes and bedding. The swelling mercifully went down within 24 hours.

Before the discomfort became really irksome there came another eye-opening experience for those of us whose experience of flying had remained within Europe's boundaries. When we touched down at Singapore the pilot told us over the intercom that we had a re-fuelling break of several hours, and recommended a tour of The Great Shopping City at the airport. This may not be its real name, but it is one that fits this spectacular shopping concourse, brilliantly lit, and containing luxuriously appointed and colourful malls and emporia either belonging to, or modelled on, Tiffany's, Harrods, Selfridges or Bloomingdales. It was stunning. If a compulsive shopaholic were to imagine heaven, it would look like Singapore airport.

The moment of light relief, amounting almost to slapstick, passed the time amusingly for an hour or so, which was very welcome for the aeroplane insomniacs like myself, who can never snatch more than a couple of hours sleep on aeroplanes.

The central figure was a scrum-half, Gary Stephens, from Castleford. It became obvious very early on that Gary was a compulsive chatterbox. He never stopped, at least in the early stages of the flight when, under normal circumstances at home, we would all be in our beds asleep.

Yap, yap, yap. At first it was funny, and media men joined in the laughter determined to be part of the British entourage.

Yap, yap, yap. Stephens went on, and some of his fellow players became irritated, particularly those who had managed to nod off. There were shouts of 'Shurrup you little _____" and one or two cuffs behind the ear from forwards anxious to silence this noisy imp of a half-back. But nothing could shut him up, until suddenly a burly frame got up from a seat just a couple of rows behind Stephens. It was the giant figure of Welshman Jim Mills, the Widnes front-row forward, a renowned on-field enforcer who had a season-ticket booking with the Rugby League's disciplinary committee, and left a trail of prostrate opponents behind him as a memorial to his robustly turbulent career. Mills advanced upon the more diminutive form of the still prattling Stephens, then produced something from behind his back. Two things in fact, a gag and a piece of cord.

Castleford's finest number seven realised the futility of resistance, and within minutes he was securely fastened to his seat and subsided into mumbling incoherence behind the gag. Where Big Jim got the cord and gag from I never discovered, but they did the trick, Stephens was reduced to virtual silence, and we all got some sleep.

However, after the long flight, cramped seats and fitful dozes, it was a dishevelled-looking gaggle of rugby league tourists and journalists that finally stumbled down the steps from the connecting internal flight in Mackay, North Queensland.

Jet lag had us all in its grip, though some recovered more quickly than others. Veteran journalist Jack McNamara of the *Manchester Evening News*, took longer than most. When a group of scribes finally emerged from their hotel bedrooms to go for our meal, Jack remained as chirpy as ever for a while, but then sank into a deep sleep. This resulted eventually in his slumping forward, in very slow motion as we watched in fascination, until he buried his nose in a dish of ice cream and remained there, presumably breathing through his mouth, till the end of the meal. He then awoke, looked around a bit sheepishly, wiped the ice cream from the end of his proboscis, and resumed the conversation as if nothing had happened.

After a night's sleep, we managed a full Australian day, and got our body clocks in sequence by walking round the small town in the scorching sun, gazing in wonder out to sea at the coral outlines of the Great Barrier reef.

While other press men in the party had done the Australasian tour before and were therefore old hands at the game, it was all marvellously new to me. The sun's rays bathed the Pacific Ocean in varying shades of blue and gold as far as the horizon beyond the reef. The blazing sun in a cloudless sky was hotter than anything I had experienced in England, despite the fact that this was what they called winter in Australia. Britain was more than 14,000 miles away, and seemed it.

The first press conference, for the match at Mackay against North Queensland, brought another strange excitement, one that seems naive and schoolboyish in retrospect, like the day I gazed up at the Old Trafford press box at the age of 14.

It was held in the tour manager's room at the hotel, very simply furnished like ours. Harry Womersley of Leeds, was the man in charge with Dick Gemmell, a former player with Hull, as assistant manager. A team was selected for the game with North Queensland the following day at a local ground, and then we dispersed to our rooms to file our previews. It was then that I got the tingle of excitement. I had filed telephone reports before, but in England and Europe, and it did not sink in at first that, while I was talking into a hotel bedroom telephone on an Australian evening my report was, because of the 10-hour time differential, being listened to at early breakfast time in England many thousands of miles away across the globe.

However, the euphoria soon evaporated the following day when I was summoned to a hastily convened gathering of the British daily newspaper men covering the tour.

Their grim-looking faces indicated that the meeting was not going to be a friendly one, despite the fact that two of the daily lads were former colleagues. Alan Thomas of the *Express* was the same man who had felt the wrath of Harry Bath of Warrington. The *Mail's* Brian Batty had covered Barrow Football Club when I was at the *Evening Mail.*

The spokesman was Arthur Brooks, of the *Mirror*, later to die at an unfairly early age. The case against me was that my live report on Great Britain's team selection had gone out on BBC radio news bulletins from the crack of dawn onwards, whereas their own pieces, filed late at night in Australia, would be too late to print and include in the first editions and, in some cases, the later ones. This consequence of the differing times had not occurred to me, but I saw their point. Solving the problem proved hard, since there will always be an inevitable time lag between an instant telephone call on radio and even the speediest print and distribution process. However, a combination of strategically timed press conferences and agreed delays on my part created a moderately successful compromise, albeit an uneasy one.

There were good times, mostly social, on the 1979 tour, but it was not by any stretch of the imagination a successful one on the field. The warmth of the welcomes was unstinting as the party moved around the vast, beautiful, often wild country with its glorious seascapes and mountain ranges, its plains, bush and forests, and the huge expanses of land between what were called 'neighbouring' towns.

At luncheons and dinners held in the tourists' honour the tables would groan under mountains of steaks, a huge variety of fish and exotic southern hemisphere fruits and vegetables. Handshakes and slaps on the back were genuine, and one quickly learned an essential lesson for Poms visiting Australia. If an Australian detects any real or imaginary aloofness, or any indication that the perceived impression of his country is that of a line of convicts shuffling along in clanking chains, then an icy politeness will ensue. But accept the warm, unaffected and natural ebullience and national pride that are the hallmarks of Australians of all ancestries, and an Australian can be your friend for life, even if he enjoys nothing more than seeing England beaten in any and every sporting encounter.

They also have a robust sense of humour and like to be experts at pomposity-pricking. Early on in the tour, at Mackay perhaps or maybe Rockhampton, the whole touring party, including journalists, attended a dinner of local businessmen and worthies. At the end of a sumptuous, and, for some, a well-liquefied meal, the assembled gathering of locals raised their glasses to the tour manager Harry Womersley and sang lustily:

"Hooray for Harry
He's sure got class
Hooray for Harry
He's a horse's ass"

Nobody laughed louder than Harry. He had to.

There was time for just one more moment of light relief before the tour began to fall part, with some unconvincing up-country performances ending in a 3-0 test whitewash.

It happened at Maryborough, a small Queensland town where incidentally, a shop keeper described a temperature of around 70 degrees as 'cold... but then it is winter".

The 'joke' was perpetrated on David Barends, the Bradford Northern winger, though I doubt whether Barends saw the funny side of it. We were housed in comfortable ground-floor chalets, and the nights were sufficiently balmy to allow windows to be left open. Early one morning David was awakened by a rustling sound near the window. The next second a long, writhing green snake came through the window and quivered on the bed. The Bradford winger let out an almighty scream, leapt out of bed and ran, almost gibbering with fright, out into the courtyard and through the tennis courts to safety. When he finally calmed down it transpired that the snake was a lifelike plastic toy supple enough to wind and unwind when airborne. No one owned up to the prank, but huge suspicion fell on Steve Nash, the Salford scrum-half and a renowned joker. He, of course, unconvincingly denied it.

The lighter moments became fewer and fewer, particularly after the first test at Brisbane on 16 June. Great Britain were never in the game, which was so one-sided that the hapless tourists were unable to score a single point, not even a penalty or drop-goal. They were hammered 35-0 before a gleeful but below-par Lang Park crowd of 23,000, itself a disappointment.

More rather meaningless state or district games followed, with occasional short-lived bouts of euphoria when a victory was recorded. However, when the tests came around the results were inevitable and morale was not improved by the loss of several players through injury, including Jim Mills, for whom the return home was not entirely unwelcome.

For, surprisingly for such a short-fused giant of a man, Big Jim had an unexpected soft centre. In a one-to-one chat with me early in the tour he revealed that he was suffering dreadfully from homesickness. So were we all, to a degree, but Jim's version of the malaise was tragi-comic. He confessed that at times he would ring his home in Widnes even if he knew nobody was in. He said that the simple sound of his telephone ringing in the hallway conjured up a picture which gave him comfort.

My own occasional bouts of homesickness, which arrived after the excitement of seeing Australia for the first time, were considerably eased when we flew into New South Wales. There I was reunited with John Taylor, who had shared my Settle Street digs with the Mistees in Barrow in the 1950s before job disillusionment took him to a new life. He had become the chief librarian of the large town - virtually a Sydney suburb - of Parramatta. He had married Bev, and had four children, three boys and a girl.

I was able to leave the comfortable headquarters of the Rushcutters Bay Hotel in Sydney to spend several nights with the

Taylors. Their house was in North Epping, a comfortable train journey from Sydney, and we enjoyed Bev's splendid meals, the odd glass of wine, family chatter, and the inevitable Barrow memories. On my days off from writing and recording tour pieces we spent the time exploring the wonderfully recreated Old Sydney model township, the many natural seaside resorts, and walks through the neighbouring bush. It went a long way towards easing the frustrations of the disappointingly poor British form. Not that John and his brood cared about that: John had become an Aussie, through and through with an accent that was half-Oz and half-Yorkshire, and Bev and the children could not resist crowing at the success of their national team over the Poms. Their house was just a stone's throw from the North Epping Oval sports centre, of whose facilities the family made full use, and it was obvious that my old chum John, ex-choirmaster and local preacher in the Barrow Methodist Circuit, had made the right decision when he emigrated. He had carved out a fulfilling new life, was still playing cricket, and he and Bev were, or eventually became, members of the Sydney Cathedral Choir.

Happily, the relationship has survived the years. I was to make three further trips down under and John, following retirement, has been over to England several times, having been granted leave of absence from his now extended family as recently as summer 2007.

It's clear my memories of that first tour have little to do with the rugby, for we had nothing to crow or be exultant about. The second and third tests in Sydney were lost 24-16, a better effort but unavailing, and 28-2, again with moderate crowds of 26,000 and 17,000, a far cry from the 70,000 at Sydney in June 1962 and 43,000 at Brisbane in June 1972.

Nevertheless, my first tour had been a wonderful and eye-opening geographical and social experience, and had re-united me with John. Professionally, despite the contretemps over my live broadcasts scooping the newspaper reports because of time zones, the broadcasts had been well received. Inevitably I did not sleep well in the 28-hour flight back, but there was a warm welcome awaiting me at home, and a very, very unexpected and totally unearned pleasant surprise at the headquarters of Warrington New Town.

10. Red Rose Radio

After a couple of days spent mostly in bed recovering from reverse journey jet-lag, I resumed duties at the New Town headquarters two months after setting off on the Australian journey. The touring party had gone on to New Zealand, where they salvaged some respect by winning the series 2-1 but I could not take any more time off, and anyway Radio 2 did not regard the Kiwis as sufficiently attractive to a rugby league audience to warrant a special correspondent out there.

When I walked through the door that Monday morning there was an atmosphere in the PR suite of offices which, though not tense or unpleasant, was rather charged. The staff had done splendidly in my absence, the New Town's industrial and housing estates had continued to prosper, and my presence at the helm had not been missed in the slightest degree, which made the opening gambit of senior colleague Christine Boughey, all the more staggering.

"Have you heard the good news? While you were away your salary went up by 75 per cent."

It was true. A body called the Whitley Council, in this case making a judgement on bringing New Town senior officers' remuneration in line with Civil Service national rates, had awarded this thumping rise while I was sunning myself on Australian beaches. Life can be very unfair at times. The Warrington PR staff, including the secretary Ethel, were conscientious and skilled operatives yet I, after a couple of months swanning about watching rugby league down under, had got a massive rise. It was again a time of mixed emotions. I knew that I had done nothing to warrant such good fortune, but was human enough to enjoy the thought of having what economists call 'more disposable income'.

For a while I resolved to put my nose to the proverbial grindstone, write more than my share of press releases, host public meetings and generally earn my huge allocation of corn. For a while it worked, and I settled into a routine of extolling the genuine virtues of the New Town's expansion as it created state-of-the-art factories, homes and leisure centres. In the evenings I would clock out on flexitime, and go home to be with the family, and share some of the responsibilities of bringing up two daughters, one, Heather, about to start Leeds University, the other, Tracy, showing increasingly worrying symptoms of the severe neurological complaint that would eventually take away all speech and movement and end her life prematurely. For a while I shared at first hand the problems with which Sheila and Heather had coped over the years when broadcasting had seen me rushing off to all points of the compass, with many enforced overnight stays.

But the new routine was not to last long. Within weeks of my return from Australia, freelance radio and television demands began to mushroom again. There were television reports and commentaries for Yorkshire and Border, and more Radio 2 rugby league work. There had also been another major freelance development which in itself could easily have provided full-time work. It sprang from an idea which came to me when idly perusing a copy of that august journal, mover of governments and royals, and bible of the nation's intelligentsia, academics and opinion makers, The Thunderer itself, *The Times*. The most lofty and patrician of newspapers had undergone remarkable and unforeseen changes. The historic front page of advertisements had suffered a revolutionary makeover and had become a front page of headline news, stories and pictures, in line with 20th century newspaper practice. Its literary style, while still serious, had become more relaxed. And, most significant of all, the sports pages were beginning to take rugby league seriously instead of reducing it to tiny paragraphs in 'minor sport' round-ups.

That niche-finding instinct which had, for better or worse, never been far from the surface prodded me again. Just as I had buttonholed Robert Hudson in the 1950s I wrote to the sports editor of *The Times*, Norman Fox, enclosing a short CV, and suggesting that the modernisation and expansion of the sports pages should include wider coverage of rugby league, which I would be only too happy to provide.

Thus began a happy and rewarding decade and more as *The Times'* first officially recognised rugby league correspondent, albeit as a freelance, which expanded to include cricket in the summer and occasional football matches.

The log-jam of varied assignments was building up again, although *The Times* unwittingly eased the pressure by having an early evening printing deadline, which meant that I did not have to cover evening matches. Still, with the New Town day job, Radio 2 rugby league doubling up conveniently with *The Times*, and the other more occasional items in the freelance portfolio, my diary was getting crowded, and soon it would be over-full once more forcing separations both personal and private.

There are two other special rugby league memories from that time. In September 1980, Fulham RLFC was launched by Harold Genders and Ernie Clay. It was the first professional club to be based in the capital since the 1930s. This venture outside the game's traditional boundaries gave me another 'first' and a totally

Fulham versus Wigan 14 September 1980 – the inaugural rugby league
match at Craven Cottage. Fulham's Reg Bowden looks to pass.
(Photo: Ken Coton)

unexpected one, an appearance on the BBC's *Match of the Day*
programme, talking about rugby league.

The football programme, then as now a weekend institution,
covered the team's opening game on Sunday 14 September, a 24-5
win over illustrious Wigan. A crowd of nearly 10,000, including
many Fulham football fans, came to Craven Cottage to help launch
the great ground-breaking experiment.

The RFL's David Howes had asked me to set the scene over the
PA by doing an illustrative commentary on a specially-arranged
warm up match to give the locals some idea of the laws and
scoring methods of this alien game. The many Wigan fans present
greeted my efforts with good humoured laughter and derision.
After the match Tony Gubba did an interview with me which was
featured on *Match of the Day*.

The game itself resulted in the Fulham team, led by player-
coach Reg Bowden, playing out of their skins for a famous victory.
The atmosphere was a frenetic mixture of carnival and pantomime,
with the Fulham supporters cheering even the knock-ons and
forward passes. Afterwards the Fulham players did a lap of honour
for their delighted fans. It was a truly memorable day.

During this period, the town where I lived celebrated the most
successful era in the history of Widnes RLFC. The 1975 Challenge
Cup saw the beginning of the emergence of the Chemics as a
major force in the game. They had notched up occasional triumphs
in the past, including two Wembley Challenge Cup wins, but long-
term dominance eluded them until that 14-5 win over Warrington.

Between 1975 and 1984 Widnes appeared in seven of the 10 Wembley Challenge Cup finals, winning four and losing three. They were also the team to beat in the league and other cups. This was a wonderfully consistent and competitive Widnes team, with most of the players being home-grown. A glance at the teamsheets over the years shows only rare evidence of imported stars from Australia, New Zealand and the South Seas, although Kevin Tamati and Kurt Sorensen did inject some Kiwi fire in later years.

Outstanding names from that period included Doug Laughton, Stuart Wright, Jim Mills, Mick Adams, Eric Hughes, Dennis O'Neill, Reg Bowden, Ray Dutton, Malcolm Aspey, Mick Burke and Eddie Cunningham. Two great players who won honours with Widnes, Andy Gregory and Joe Lydon, went onto even greater things with Wigan. Symptomatic of the hometown loyalties which bound the side together were two sets of brothers, David and Paul Hulme, and Mike and Steve O'Neill.

The years of Widnes success gave me particular pleasure, putting impartiality to one side, because I lived there for those 22 years. I am not a native of the town, but was, and still am, treated like an adopted son on my frequent match-reporting visits. And to me they will always be the Chemics, despite today's vogue for Australian-type nicknames.

****

In the late 1970s and early 1980s, with BBC local radio well established, the government had begun to open up the market to commercial radio franchises. I had done some BBC local station work with presenters such as Ray Stubbs, Eddie Hemmings, Ray French and the late Gerry Burrows at Radio Merseyside, and had enjoyed the relaxed and cheerful camaraderie. Therefore, when an invitation came out of the blue in late 1981 to join a Lancashire radio consortium in a battle with four others for a commercial station covering a large chunk of the west of the county, I quickly accepted. At that stage it did not involve breaking any other ties, because the preparation of a submission and prospectus largely involved drumming up support and financial backing by the directors, headed by chairman Owen Oyston, and programme executives, managing director-elect David Maker and head of news Julian Allitt, the latter two both journalists of considerable experience in local radio and newspapers respectively.

My role, in the event of Red Rose Radio getting the franchise, would be the not unimportant one of programme controller, and in the year or so of campaigning I would appear at, and occasionally speak at, evening public meetings. Great support was also given by star name company directors including Victoria Wood, Clive Lloyd,

Bill Beaumont and the late Russell Harty, whose presence lent considerable weight to the application. It was not an easy campaign to win for the four other consortia had the big names too, and we were jokingly referred to by the other groups as Red Nose Radio. There was a final mass interview in London from an Independent Radio Authority panel, chaired by Lady Mary Warnock, a profound intellectual who gave me a fearful grilling on programme content, and then we waited for the outcome.

For several weeks we were all on tenterhooks, knowing that the decision would be a close-run thing. However, when I returned from lunch one afternoon there was a telegram from Owen Oyston, the flamboyant self-made multi-millionaire estate agent, chairman of our consortium. It said: "No longer Red Nose Radio... Red Rose Radio is officially now in existence".

It was another twist in the tale. After less than three years at Warrington New Town Development Corporation, and at sundry television and radio stations, plus *Times* newspapers, yet another change of direction was in the pipeline. When I handed in my notice to David Binns he was as courteous and polite as ever, and understandably made no attempt to dissuade me. After all, he could now appoint someone who would devote all his or her time to the job, rather than a will-o'-the-wisp who was constantly disappearing on broadcasting assignments elsewhere. There were few tears shed in the office, because the staff had carried the PR burden so many times in my absences.

The brand new Red Rose Radio station was due to open in early October 1982, and Owen Oyston, David Maker, Julian Allitt, sales director Peter Salt, chief engineer Dave Cockram and secretary Roxana spent around three months in temporary office accommodation on Fishergate, Preston, interviewing and hiring staff for the big opening. As programme controller-elect I had to listen to more than 200 tapes from would-be presenters and disc jockeys to allocate around a dozen hopefuls seeking a new career or a new start in radio. Julian Allitt, Peter Salt and Dave Cockram were also choosing their people, but the programmes in-tray groaned daily under the weight of stardom seekers' tapes.

Would-be broadcasters came from a variety of sources. Clerks, postmen, mature students, tax inspectors, there was even a chef, plus of course, journalists and hospital radio presenters.

It helped that many of the applicants had neither the experience nor the voice to make the grade and, sadly for them, the standard printed rejection slip was sent out. I hated doing this, for I know what pain and disappointment it would cause the recipient: I had been in that position myself a generation before, but had been one of the lucky ones.

Eventually the better talents were winkled out of the mass, although even then there was the feeling that some of the near-misses deserved better and in different circumstances might have made the cut. Indeed, it became one of life's ironies that in succeeding years, presenters who had received rejection slips entered the radio profession elsewhere and achieved success. One of them, Dave Shearer, eventually joined the staff under a subsequent management team, and went on to gain an executive post at Radio Piccadilly in Manchester. He never fails to chivvy and chide me about it when we meet, and rightly so.

The big day dawned early in October 1982, in the studios built inside the thick, soundproof stone walls of the derelict St Paul's Church in Preston. In those opening months the station had a licence to broadcast only between 6.00am and 10.00pm to an area covering East Lancashire as far as Nelson and Colne, Preston and Central Lancashire, North Lancashire to Lancaster and Kendal, Blackpool and the Fylde Coast down to Southport and Formby, and parts of south Lancashire including Wigan. It was a large and challenging area.

The opening was a moving, exciting and nervous experience. Although it was 6.00am on a cold October morning, every single member of the Red Rose staff, numbering more than 40, was present in the reception area.

There was also a photographer, David Mycock, who had captured on camera every stage of the 150-year-old church's conversion from the beginning.

Breakfast show presenter Dave Lincoln was ready to go with the mix of music, chat and hourly news bulletins, but the first voice would be the deep, almost stentorian tones of the chairman of Red Rose Radio, Owen Oyston, a tall, flamboyant character with an impressive beard and whiskers.

Owen was another classic case of the working-class lad - this time from the industrial villages of Tyneside - who had made good. He had built a small empire of estate agencies bearing his name after moving to the north-west, and had won a showbiz type of notoriety with a series of television commercials including personal pratfalls in one of which he fell backwards into a swimming pool.

It all went smoothly. Owen warmly welcomed Lancashire's listeners to their brand new station in his patrician voice, and then handed over to producer/news reader Mike Green. Mike, later to become head of media news studies at what is now the University of Central Lancashire, read the mixture of local and national news faultlessly, and then Dave Lincoln's cheerful and relaxed voice got the programmes on their way.

Thankfully, Red Rose Radio was an instant hit, and the presenters that David Maker and I had whittled down from more than 200 hopefuls soon slotted comfortably into their positions. Except perhaps, the one allocated to the head of programmes: me. In addition to handling and monitoring the progress and impact of the presenters I had agreed to present *Midday with Macklin* between noon and 2.00pm with the luxury of having Mike Green as producer. In those early days of commercial radio Red Rose was not the totally pop-music oriented venture that it, and most commercial stations, have become by economic necessity today. Ours was an eclectic mix of the current popular musical favourites, plus big band, jazz and soul, and, remarkable though it may seem today, magazine programmes with interviews, and a flagship one-hour news magazine *Red Rose Reports* which was to win a national award in its first year.

Midday with Macklin was a magazine programme, consisting of star interviews interspersed with tunes from the current Top 20. It was well meant, but it had one fatal flaw, apart from the fact that I was presenting it.

The programme was to be built around lively sub-Parkinsonian chats with showbiz personalities who would be appearing at Blackpool's theatres and at Preston's Charter Theatre. We could also rely on our Red Rose directors Victoria Wood, Russell Harty, Bill Beaumont and Clive Lloyd to weigh in. However, on a five-days-a-week show we very rapidly ran out of star guests. Les Dawson, who lived in Blackpool, got the ball rolling superbly and comically on the first day, and the others followed in a stellar procession. But after a few weeks the supply had dried up, the programme became more and more music, and less and less chat, and David Maker and I decided that I would be better off at my desk, or arranging sports interviews, rather than trying, leadenly, to introduce pop records.

Fortunately the mix of Red Rose programmes seemed to go down well with Lancashire audiences, and after one year both audience share and advertising revenue were healthy.

However, all too familiar problems had arisen in my private life. Sheila and I had separated prior to divorce. No third parties, other than my jobs, were involved. Sheila went on to take a BSc degree at a university college in Liverpool, Heather was at Leeds University, and Tracy was in full-time residential care.

On the jobs front the log-jam had built up again, bringing the usual logistical dilemmas. Again the opportunities, and one from Granada TV in particular, had been too challenging to refuse.

The surprise call was from Paul Doherty, head of sport of Granada TV in Manchester. After nearly three decades of a BBC monopoly on televised rugby league, ITV had negotiated a foothold in the coverage - quite a substantial foothold in fact. Agreement had been reached with the Rugby Football League for Granada, Yorkshire and Border to broadcast selected games, primarily on Friday evenings, and Doherty, aware that I was no longer with Radio 2, wanted me as commentator. Again there was the thrill of being asked, but as ever there was the awkward problem to face of asking permission, this time from the Red Rose Radio managing director David Maker. David was reluctant at first to release his programme controller so early in the station's life, but agreed on the proviso that if ever there was a clash of loyalties, Red Rose would win the day.

The merry-go-round was whirling faster. I now had *RL Action* to add to daytime coverage for *The Times*, and the odd summons from Border. Nevertheless for three seasons I managed to juggle the balls reasonably successfully before *RL Action* ended, to be revived briefly with a new title *Scrumdown*, a new production company, YTV, and Yorkshire's own commentator John Helm.

RL Action provided two moments to remember. At Knowsley Road, St Helens, a successful kick at goal produced this bit of commentary for the archives.

"The kick's on its way... straight through the middle of the posts ...and straight through the window of the directors' room, showering the directors with glass."

On another occasion we were at Headingley for a Leeds home game and were all set up to go, with the two teams warming up on the pitch, when there came an unexpected hiccup.

A Leeds official came out on to the pitch and spoke animatedly to the referee, and then to the coach and skipper of the Leeds team. A state of some confusion developed and, somewhat reluctantly, the teams left the field as a message came up to the commentary box that the match might be postponed.

This was very puzzling, since there was nothing wrong with the weather or the pitch, and no potential crowd problem. Geoff Hall, who again was the OB director, hurried off to the dressing rooms, and some 20 minutes later came back with the news that the match was indeed postponed, for a bizarre reason. In those days of the early 1980s rugby league club players were not allowed in television matches to wear sponsors' names on the front of their shirts which were larger than a certain size by an agreement between the Rugby Football League and the ITV authorities. Leeds did not have a spare set of jerseys without the advertisers' insignia, so reluctantly the match had to be postponed. There was nothing else for it. We had to pack up, dismantle the cables and camera equipment and go home. The disgruntled spectators also filed out, although they were given vouchers entitling them to free admission once the match was played.

The television games provided some lively and enjoyable matches and, like *Scrumdown* later, briefly challenged the supremacy of the BBC in rugby league. With the advent of Sky and its admittedly first class coverage of Super League, together with the Beeb's continued coverage of the Challenge Cup, ITV pulled out of regular screening. But it was fun while it lasted.

Talking of fun, there were the Rugby League Roadshows to keep me occupied in the evenings throughout the 1980s, particularly in the aftermath of the ending of my marriage, when despite the warm hospitality of close friends who treated me as an extra member of the family, there were inevitable bouts of loneliness.

The Roadshows, sponsored generously by the *Sunday Mirror*, were staged to raise money for players' benefit years. They were expertly and enthusiastically organised by David Howes, then the RFL's public relations and press officer, and were held in social clubs, public halls, hotel function rooms and at clubs boasting their own suites. They invariably raised a thumping four-figure sum for players whose broken noses, scars and occasional black eyes from a weekend game bore ample testimony to the toughness in combat that had richly earned their reward. For unlike the 21st century's pampered and overpaid football superstars and their obscene salaries, these men were comparatively ill-paid, particularly among the lower levels of the game. David Howes did the spadework and on-site organisation, columnist John Huxley provided *Sunday Mirror* inputs, former player Mick Morgan told ripely funny jokes which lost nothing in comparison with Bernard Manning and Roy 'Chubby' Brown, and there were model girls to mix with the audience and sell raffle tickets. My role was to compere the show and interview the recipients and many players who turned up to support them. It was a good, wisecracking team, the rugby league fans were good-humoured, noisy and supportive, and inevitably there were unscripted moments to savour.

At one venue, either Batley or Dewsbury, there was an incident which came straight out of northern pub humour and jocularity. It was life mirroring the comic's art.

At a packed house in the social club, David Howes had run through the Roadshow sequence, whose centrepiece would be a Mick Morgan auction of sports memorabilia, and I went on stage to start proceedings with a rundown on the beneficiary's history and virtues.

After a while I became conscious of the fact that the small but insistent figure of a man was standing just below me under the stage footlights. He was tapping on my shoes urgently to grab my attention. From his apparent agitation it was obvious that he had something important to tell me that was more urgent than my script.

"Mr Macklin... Mr Macklin..." he intoned, stopping me in mid-sentence. It most definitely was some sort of emergency.

I bent down and put the microphone to his lips.

"Mr Macklin. Will you inform everybody that the warm pies have come at the bar counter?" It got the biggest laugh of the evening.

At another Roadshow I found myself stuck on stage with a sticky and potentially professionally damaging dilemma. The routine was that David Howes would line up the interviewees off-stage, and when their time came usher them up to me, whispering the name into my ear just in case I did not instantly recognise them.

On this occasion, contrary to normal practice, he brought two players up together. The names were familiar from newspaper reports, but I had never seen them play. As David stepped down I realised with horror that I would not recognise either of them and was in with a 50/50 chance of making a public and professional fool of myself by guessing wrong and asking the right opening question to the wrong player.

It constantly amazes me how quickly the human mind can think in a crisis. One of the two players had a surname which was difficult to spell and pronounce. Without looking up from the microphone, and turning as if to involve the audience, I asked: "John, how do you pronounce your surname correctly?" When I followed the direction of the reply I had my first interviewee tagged - Phew.

11. Tragedy at Abbeystead

Somehow or other the various pieces of the broadcasting jigsaw kept falling into place, but only just, and it eventually became obvious that David Maker was beginning to feel uncomfortable about my absences, even though Red Rose continued its successful entry into the radio market. However in May 1984, still early in the life of the station, there came an appalling public disaster during which Red Rose Radio came of age, albeit in the most tragic of circumstances.

The event in its sadness and suffering was like Lockerbie again, on a smaller scale, but still ghastly in its toll of human life. Only this time the involvement of the radio station was immediate and not retrospective.

Wednesday 23 May 1984 had been a normal type of evening. My good friends, Alan and Rickie Jones of Rainhill, two of many friends whose hospitality eased the pain of divorce, had invited me for dinner. After a pleasant repast we settled down to watch the 10 o'clock news on ITN.

At first the newsreader's voice did not penetrate the post-dinner warm haze. Then a map appeared on the screen. It was a section of Lancashire in a rural area on the River Wyre, west of Preston and Lancaster and heading towards Blackpool and Fleetwood. At its centre was a village, St Michael's, towards which an arrow was pointing, and close to the village another arrow pointing to Abbeystead water pumping station.

The newsreader's voice was chilling. A massive explosion had taken place underground in a valve house at the water pumping station and a sheet of flame had enveloped a tunnel in which a touring party of sightseers was watching a demonstration. The number of casualties was unknown; ambulances were ferrying them to Lancaster Royal Infirmary and other hospitals.

Thanking my lucky stars that I had not imbibed too liberally I shot out to the car and drove to the studio in Preston, where the then news editor Mike Henfield and reporters Chris Rider and Juliet Burns, who had been playing tennis and were still in their tennis outfits, were already in action putting out the latest news.

There were huge decisions to be made. In those still-early days of Red Rose Radio the broadcasting hours were restricted by the Independent Broadcasting Authority (IBA). We would have to close down at midnight, coming back on air at 6.00am, and that would be a clear dereliction of duty and a dreadful anticlimax.

As programme controller the decision was mine to make. After a quick conversation with Mike Henfield and engineer Dave Cockram it was made, and later fully endorsed by MD David Maker and the IBA. We would stay on air throughout the night and continuously until the horrific tragedy of Abbeystead had run its course.

Juliet went out to the Abbeystead pumping station where the fatal methane gas explosion had happened. Sally Moon would stay at the presenter's desk, Mike and Chris would direct the operation at base and I would drive out to St Michael's, the village at the epicentre of the tragedy.

However, there was a major logistical problem for Juliet and me. Mobile telephones were then only in the experimental stage and local radio budgets did not run to outside broadcast vans. We would have to use public telephones for live external reports. This would prove difficult, and almost impossible under the circumstances. Even if a public phone was available, we would need a mountain of coins to feed it because there was no switchboard on duty back at Red Rose to field and hold reverse charge calls. It would also make for a physically uncomfortable night in kiosks.

In the event I was lucky. I called at the village post office in St Michael's and, late at night though it was, found that no one in the stricken village would be going to bed that awful night as people waited for news of the casualties from Abbeystead. When I asked the favour of being allowed to use a telephone to make my initial call, the family running the post office took me to a private room, gave me a telephone, a table and a chair and said they were mine as long as I needed them. It was a magnificent gesture and it enabled Red Rose to ring me and run continuous reports as news filtered back from all sources.

We quickly learned how the tragedy had unfolded during the afternoon and early evening.

Towards teatime on the warm sunny afternoon of 23 May a group of 44 people from St Michael's and surrounding villages and hamlets had set off by coach to Abbeystead. They were attending a Water Board presentation to allay anxieties about possible flooding of the lower Wyre Valley. Official reports state that part of the presentation would see water pumped over the weir regulating the flow of water into the River Wyre. Shortly after pumping began there was an "intense flash" followed by a huge explosion as a mixture of methane gas and air ignited. The burning flash shot through a tunnel and hit a valve house where the villagers were gathered. Of the 44 in the valve house, 16 of those were killed, none escaped without injury, and many injuries were serious and disfiguring.

Throughout the night two-way reports, unconfirmed at first and later confirmed, filtered through from Red Rose studio and, in St

Michael's, there were interviews with shocked and weary villagers as they returned from seeking news of relatives. Our telephone reports went out live, were recorded, and sent out as bulletins by Mike and Chris to radio and television stations not merely in England but throughout Europe and the world. I had one awful moment when I seriously doubted my own judgement in releasing a story. The first identification of a fatality, a boy in his early teens, unofficial but from the mouths of distraught family and relatives, went out before official police or hospital identification had been cleared. However, when official notice came out, it proved only too sadly correct.

Daylight came, and all day Thursday came and went as reporters and camera crews from far and wide came to Abbeystead and St Michael's. Red Rose kept going with updates and follow-ups as members of staff joined or relieved those who had been up all night.

Then Thursday night came and went as the clearing up of the Abbeystead site came to a conclusion and the final official harrowing list of casualties was released. Mike Henfield and I had somehow managed to stay awake through sheer adrenalin flow, and at 8.30am on Friday I went back to the studio where Mike and the news staff had prepared a half-hour bulletin condensing the elements of their tragedy together with interviews. We provided live voice links in the studio, and wrapped up at 9 o'clock.

I looked at my watch: 9.00am Friday 25 May. Without realising it, the two of us, supported by a magnificent team effort by station staff, had stayed awake and on-air for the better part of 34 hours without a break.

It was time to get some sleep.

Like Lockerbie, Abbeystead will stay in the memory for the saddest of reasons. But, as the comforting cliché puts it - not always convincingly for those who have suffered - life goes on.

After two years as programme controller during which time Red Rose Radio, by its own momentum and the hard work of others, had established itself as Lancashire's number one station, both David Maker and I were ready for a change. I needed to get back to regular broadcasting and particularly commentary, leaving the deskwork and staff responsibilities to someone more temperamentally suited to it. Mike Henfield deservedly took over, leaving me free to take up a contract as sports editor and commentator. With fewer office and management responsibilities, I could also work for *The Times* and report for Border TV with a much clearer conscience.

In addition, Granada TV came up with another broadcasting venture, crown green bowls, a traditional northern sport at both professional and amateur levels with official betting licences. In the 1980s and for decades if not centuries before, this variant of flat green and French boules had been played in northern counties, particularly in Lancashire, on special bowling greens at the rear of pubs and clubs. Sadly, although crown green survives, many pubs have abandoned their greens to expand their drinking areas, launch fitness clubs, or provide overnight accommodation. However, Blackpool is still a magnet for the professional crown green bowler with its prestigious Waterloo and Talbot handicaps.

In the early and mid-1980s Granada TV picked up on this interest, and *RL Action* producer Paul Doherty asked me to be one of the commentators at the launch of a series of televised tournaments at St Helens, Warrington and Ellesmere Port, with Bryan Brett as co-commentator and Elton Welsby as presenter.

I was not unfamiliar with the 21-up sport, having been born and raised in the south Lancashire hotbed. I had even tried my hand with friends in early manhood at the Ship at Rainhill and the local cable works social club greens at Prescot. I knew about thumb and finger bias on the 'woods', as the bowls are called, and about the tortuous complexities of some of the rougher greens which slope up to the 'crown' in the centre and down the other side. A couple of inches misjudgement at the delivery, or wrong choice of weighted bias, and a wood can end up among the spectators! The tournaments made for pleasant days out in the summer, though again it meant time away from Red Rose as I rushed to the events, and eventually a former ITV soccer colleague Hugh Johns took over from me.

I seemed fated, partly through choice, partly through circumstances, to play the role of juggler, moving from sport to sport, from radio to television, and from broadcast company to broadcast company. Life had become, particularly since divorce, a seven-day week merry-go-round. Some might even describe it as a treadmill with Monday to Friday radio sports bulletins and occasional forays into news. Then there were Saturday afternoon radio commentaries at one of the Red Rose station's regional grounds, Blackburn Rovers - whose matches I covered regularly - Blackpool, Burnley, Preston North End, Wigan Athletic and Wigan rugby league club, then a perennially mighty power in the XIII-a-side code.

Occasionally I was again poised perilously between two stools. On one such occasion I had an important Blackburn game at pre-Premier League Ewood Park and a big rugby league game for *The Times* at Headingley, Leeds on the same day. The game at Headingley kicked off early, and I managed to get the bulk of the first half watched before rushing to my car and, shamefully, burning up the M62 while watching the mirror for police cars, to get to Ewood to do second-half commentary while monitoring the rugby on radio. A colleague had held the fort at Blackburn with score flashes. Since the report in *The Times* would be a subsidiary addition to the Sunday games (one of which I would cover in full) I managed to cover both matches adequately, but my physical and nervous systems took quite a hammering.

Less nerve-wracking were the occasional summer days at cricket. *The Times* used me occasionally at county matches at Old Trafford, Headingley, Southport, Harrogate and Scarborough, and Border sent me to knockout cup giant-killing tilts by Cumberland, against senior counties. One sunny day at Netherfield's lovely little ground below the castle at Kendal they ran Lancashire very close.

The trips to Old Trafford, which also included official Red Rose Radio ones, meant that, after a lapse of nearly four decades the little boy's 1945 dream had literally come true. Forgive another divergence, but there was something special about these cricketing days, something which, alas, seems to have been lost with the emergence, to popular acclaim and large crowds, of the 'pyjama game'. One-day cricket, and particularly 20-20, has replaced the measured, steady rhythm and occasional bursts of final-day excitement of the traditional stylised county game. It has replaced those matches with flailing bats, shots that must make cricketing purists cover their eyes with horror, even from the best and most stylish of batsmen, and crowds of rumbustuous booze-fuelled spectators who wouldn't recognise a late cut from a thick edge, or a cow shot from a leg glance, because all that matters is that the ball scurries to the boundary while fielders throw their arms up in the air with disbelief and the batsmen scurry through for runs like hunted foxes.

Admittedly these variations of the game pull in the crowds and the sponsorship without which most counties would eventually go to the wall, and they can be said to have revived cricket as a national sport. This is particularly so among today's younger spectators, weaned on millisecond sound bites and video flashes. It is a long way from the more leisurely pace of the county game, which can be a relaxing four-day escape, with hamper and flask, from an increasingly turbulent world. It saddens me that outstanding former professional players and particularly Lancashire and England captain Michael Atherton, of whom a little more anon, play down the importance of county cricket, despite the fact that he is one of the most talented batsmen to learn his trade with a county side.

It is also the opinion of this particular layman and cricket-watcher, and one offered with due respect to those infinitely more qualified to comment, that county cricket produced some of our greatest-ever players, and Test-winning sides long before the one-day game was dreamed of. The lately departed Fred Trueman and Brian Statham, and battling greats like Len Hutton, Peter May, Ted Dexter, Ken Barrington and, yes, even the obdurate and unyielding crease-occupier Geoffrey Boycott did not hone their skills slicing on drives over the wicket-keeper's head or turning the bat round to 'nurdle' it through a huge one-day fielding gap. And if today's cricketers suffer alleged burnout - how Fiery Fred would have snorted and harrumphed about that - then put it down to all-the-year-round one-day cricket all over the world, not to the whipping boy, the traditional county game.

Just one more choleric blast before resumption of normal service, including a gentle tale about Michael Atherton. Whatever use central contracts may be, financially or otherwise to players, they do no favours at all to counties. As a lifelong avid Lancastrian, I object to the fact that Andrew Flintoff, the most exciting hitter of a ball since the likes of Ted Dexter, Colin Milburn and Ian Botham, and an equally devastating fast bowler on his day, has played little part in the county's championship campaigns in 2005, 2006 and 2007. It is not just personal bias which makes me assert, with proper recognition of the achievements of Chris Adams and Sussex, that Lancashire might have nicked the county championship had the cavalier Freddie, with due acknowledgement of his injury problems been a little more available.

Yorkshire were luckier, they achieved county success a few seasons ago despite the fact that Darren Gough played in just a handful of county games. I recall that Headingley worthies, on and off the field, had fairly strong opinions about that.

Having sounded off like Fred Trueman at his truculent best, back to the main thread, and a distinctly pleasant and quirky personal memory of Michael Atherton.

The meeting occurred when Lancashire were playing a home county game at one of the 'out grounds' away from Old Trafford, places such as Blackpool, Liverpool and Southport, and which proved a treat for local cricket lovers who usually turned out in force for these special events. A blip in memory prevents me identifying which particular ground it was, but I think it was the compact pretty ground at Lytham on the Fylde coast.

On Red Rose Radio duty I went to Lytham, and during the lunch interval one day I saw a youthful, twenty-ish Michael Atherton, then emerging as a highly promising young batsman tipped for future greatness, chatting to some friends outside the pavilion. I approached, microphone in hand, and with due deference to a potential interviewee asked if I could speak to him. "Certainly Mr

Macklin, where would you like to do it sir?" came the staggering reply.

Staggering because never before or since have I received such a doubly polite reply from a professional sportsman, young or old. Most replies are helpful and friendly, thank heavens, but never so self-effacing and well-mannered - *Mr* Macklin, and *sir*. I could hardly believe my ears, and to this day I like to think the source was the patrician influence of Manchester Grammar School and sound middle-class values rather than the too-obvious greying hair and spreading tummy of a middle-aged broadcaster.

The interview was a cracking one, too, with the young man showing the lucidity that nowadays illuminates his television cricket commentaries. However, after my earlier comments I might not get such a polite reception next time.

The early and mid-1980s while comfortably busy, were much less frenetic than earlier decades and I was able to devote much more time to local sport. Indeed, while Sundays were the preserve of *Times* rugby league round-ups and midweek days brought the occasional television trips to the Great Yorkshire Show and Border cricket games, a closer relationship developed with the five Lancashire football clubs, and particularly Blackburn Rovers.

At that time Rovers were a mid-table side in the old Second Division, now the Championship, with a tired old stadium and average gates of 8,000. The amazing renaissance created by the Jack Walker millions was still a few years away, and following Rovers everywhere was something of a roller-coaster experience. But it was fun, with defeats and victories alternating, and a growing sense of belonging to the town and its team, and being engaged in earnest conversation by neighbours, the barber, and the proprietors of local shops.

I was even forgiven, once the damage had been paid for, by the owner of the local paper shop, Tim McNamee, when my car caused considerable damage to his shop window.

I was not in the car at the time. Nobody was. I had parked in a side road opposite the shop with the car facing it. The gradient slopes downwards from the side road to the shop, and I had pulled up on the way to an Ewood Park match to collect my evening paper. As I collected it and chatted at the counter the senior lady assistant, who still works there, said to me in a very matter-of-fact voice: "Is this your car approaching the window?"

I looked up. Yes, it was, approaching at a very gentle pace and it crashed through the glass, mercifully coming to rest on impact.

I had forgotten to put on the hand brake. I gulped and walked out to survey the damage. Within minutes a siren-blaring police car arrived, the crew having been tipped off by a phone call that a ram raid had taken place at the newsagent's shop and the gang had not yet made their getaway.

A couple of Bobbies got out and I was asked if I was the owner of the car. Out came the notebook and I half expected a pair of handcuffs to follow. Just when it seemed that I would be spending the night not at the game, but in the local slammer, mercifully Tim and his staff member jumped in to corroborate my tale, and when I offered to pay for a replacement window the constables decided not to arrest me on a charge of dangerous or careless driving, because I was not in the car at the time. It was a lucky escape, but quite an expensive one when the bill for the huge, reinforced window came. The hand brake has never since been left off when I park the car.

This was one of the few unpleasant experiences I had had since moving to Blackburn, and one of the many pleasant ones was the event which put Blackburn Rovers back on the football map, albeit briefly, in 1987. I was already involved with the side through regular reporting of matches. As I have said, the Blackburn Rovers team, club and ground in the 1980s were far removed from the Premiership club of today, with its modern Jack Walker-inspired stadium and ability to compete at the highest level of British football and in European competitions.

Rovers' attendances at the time-worn Ewood Park ground rarely exceeded 10,000, and normally averaged 8,000. The manager was Scot Don Mackay who had just replaced Bobby Saxton, and in his first season he steered Blackburn out of relegation trouble to the final of the prosaically-named Full Members' Cup, a trophy played for by clubs in the lower reaches of Division One, plus the bulk of Second Division clubs.

Rovers had last won a trophy of any real substance in 1928, when they beat Huddersfield Town 3-1 in the FA Cup Final at Wembley and the town's football fans were hungry for any kind of success to break the half century of up-and-down mediocrity.

Rovers had last reached a Wembley final, the FA Cup, in 1960, only to lose in unhappy circumstances, 3-0 against Wolves. In those unenlightened days no substitutes were allowed, and when Blackburn full-back Dave Whelan, now the multimillionaire founder of JJB Sports and owner of Wigan Athletic and Wigan Warriors (at the time of writing), broke his leg, Rovers were down to 10 men and paid the price.

Thus, when the Mackay-inspired mini-revival came in 1987, and the Full Members' Cup Final was reached, the Blackburn public turned out in remarkable numbers to enjoy a trip to London and Wembley for the game against Charlton Athletic. The match was played on Sunday 28 March, and the attendance was 43,789.

This is a small crowd by Wembley's standards. However, the Blackburn contingent numbered more than 30,000 - just under a fifth of the town's population.

Followers of more exalted clubs like Manchester United, Chelsea, Arsenal and Liverpool tend to sniff and give patronising smiles at what are unfairly dubbed Mickey Mouse tournaments like the short-lived Full Members Cup. Even the Football League Cup, under a succession of sponsorships, has struggled to attract interest and crowds in its early stages.

Yet those who patronise the minor tournaments, in both football and rugby league, are unaware of the immense civic pride that is generated and revived by a successful trophy run. Fans and families who have ignored their local team for decades are galvanised into flag-waving and coach-booking action once a final is reached.

This is what happened to Blackburn in 1987. Charlton supporters were outnumbered and out-shouted, and ultimately silenced when in the 85th minute Colin Hendry, later Scotland's captain and centre half, but then playing in a makeshift centre forward role, shot home Ian Miller's cross to give Rovers their first Wembley victory since 1928.

For me, up in the press box for local radio, it was as great a thrill as Barrow's Challenge Cup win in 1955 and St Helens' win in 1956. One of the good things about working for a local paper, or television or radio station, is that there are no impartiality restraints on the commentator. Joy was unconfined, and there was even a moment of comedy to top it off when the Blackburn skipper and centre half Glenn Keeley was handed the trophy and, after his faultless display in the game, promptly dropped it with a resounding clang. There followed the heroes' welcome when the team returned home and were given the traditional civic reception at the Town Hall. It was a grand day out only eclipsed eight years later when a reborn Rovers won the greatest domestic prize of all, the Premiership. And as the Welsh comedian Max Boyce used to declare: "I was there!"... both times.

Jack McNamara asleep at dinner on the first night of the 1979 British Lions
tour, in Mackay, Queensland. At the table with Keith and Jack are
Ernie Christensen (Australian journalist), Dick Gemmell (GB assistant
manager), Harry Womersley (GB tour manager) and Alan Clarkson
(Australian journalist)

Keith with the Great Britain squad at the Brisbane Expo exhibition in 1988.

12. Adventures with Screensport

March 1987 brought a night of joyous celebration in the town centre of Blackburn: 16 months later the night of 9 July 1988 brought similar massive celebrations 14,000 miles away in Sydney but on a much larger scale. It was an evening when, for a few euphoric hours every Britisher, on tour or resident expatriate, painted Australia's capital city red, white and blue.

Not since 5 November 1978 - 10 years previously - had Great Britain won a rugby league Test match against Australia. Fifteen tests had been played against the understandably cocky, swaggering wearers of the green and gold, and all 15 had been lost, home and away. Britain had not won a series since 1970, and in all honesty, had not looked remotely liked doing so. Nor did they win the 1988 series, and it looked like another Kangaroo whitewash until that amazing match at the Sydney Stadium at the end of an otherwise disappointing, in the playing sense, tour. A fuller account will come later.

Meantime, having missed out on the 1984 Australasian tour, I had been lucky enough to join the 1988 party to the Antipodes. In 1979 it had been generously sanctioned by Warrington New Town Development Corporation. In 1988 the generosity, again in the form of leave of absence, came from Red Rose Radio, who allowed me to go as *The Times* correspondent only on the justifiable condition that I filed regular reports to the radio station in which I would emphasise the contributions of the large Wigan contingent which went on the tour. For Wigan, always a force in the XIII-a-side game, were about to embark on an amazing run of eight Challenge Cup wins in a row, and outstanding talents were emerging.

It was a great feeling, after a nine-year gap, to have another chance to tour the vast spectacularly beautiful, wild and faraway island, a European civilisation in South East Asia, while watching and reporting on rugby league football.

On the tour, another off-the-pitch diversion, and a series of comical highlights, was provided by one of the Queensland up-country preliminary games.

The match was staged at Gympie, an old gold-mining town nearly 100 miles north of Brisbane where gold was first discovered in 1867 by a poverty stricken lone prospector James Nash. He struck lucky in a dry creek with his panning dish and sparked off the Red Creek Rush: Queensland's Yukon. Nash and his dog walked all the way to Brisbane with his find. He sold it in the state capital for the then massive sum of £200; he registered his claim, became a millionaire and sparked the rush which brought prosperity, and scenes redolent of the Wild West, to the town which mushroomed and became Gympie, named after 'gimpi-gimpi', the Aboriginal word for a local stinging tree. The gold seam ran out in 1925, though it is commemorated in Gympie's Gold mining museum.

It was to this town, and to its rather primitive ground, that the touring party repaired for a warm-up game. I remember little about the game itself, but events before and after still bring responses varying from a chuckle to a guffaw. The crowd was understandably small, and the local club officials suggested that everybody should pay to get in - including players, officials, press and travelling fans - to help club funds.

Not everyone agreed with this enforced generosity, particularly because the turnstile was actually a wooden gate policed by a gateman who was unfortunately blind in one eye. Those who objected to the charge quietly skulked past his blind side, leaving the more honest, or timid, members of the touring party to pay up.

This unwillingness to part with cash, or maybe it would be described as good stewardship of personal finances, was replicated in one quarter, after the game.

Not everyone had travelled up on the official coach. David Howes had given three journalists a lift in his car. The quartet faced the 100 miles or so journey back to the hotel and, understandably, Howesy was anxious to get back as quickly as possible.

He put his foot on the accelerator, occasionally hitting around 90mph on the needle, and suffered the misfortune of catching the attention of a Queensland police motor patrolman.

Caught red handed, Howesy discharged his criminal responsibility with an on-the-spot payment of the $80 fine. On the return to the hotel it was suggested that to ease the financial burden on the tour's co-manager, the three journalists should each contribute 20 dollars. Two readily agreed, but one declined, informing Howesy that "It's your own fault – you shouldn't have been driving so fast!"

There was to be one more repercussion of the trip to Gympie. It came several weeks later, some time after my account of the game had appeared in *The Times*. Somewhat unfairly, because I had only seen the rugby ground and its approaches in the evening light, I had tongue-in-cheek described Gympie as "a one-horse town", in an allusion to its gold-mining past.

A senior officer, the mayor or town clerk, of Gympie, had got hold of a copy of the newspaper and had written to the sports editor complaining about my comment.

Quite justifiably exception had been taken, because my glib comment had, literally and metaphorically, merely skirted the town, which had developed into a thriving centre of agriculture, forestry and timber with its major tourist attraction a gold and mining museum. Though I never saw a copy of the letter myself, and assume *The Times* staff replied to it with the necessary apology, it made its point. As Peter Wilson of the *Star* jokingly put it: there were obviously two horses in Gympie.

Once more I was reunited with John Taylor and his family for pleasant social outings, and also with another close friend who had emigrated. Norman Smith, also of Rainhill, watched many St Helens games with me during our teens. He had left school at 14, worked as a railway clerk at Prescot, done two years' national service in the medical corps, taken 'O' levels and 'A' levels during his service days and after demob, and to shorten an educational odyssey, had ended up as Professor Norman Smith, head of social work at Queensland University in Brisbane. We had many splendid meals together, including one on a superbly-appointed and floodlit houseboat on the Brisbane River which flows through my favourite Australian city. This visit also coincided with Expo 88, the splendid exhibition and worldwide cavalcade of shows, exhibitions and stands which was hosted by the Queensland capital.

On the playing side the tour was not particularly successful until the third and final test. There was the odd good performance and result in some of the warm-up matches, but the first two tests, at Sydney and Brisbane, were lost 17-6 and 34-14 and, when the third test at Sydney arrived the series was a 'dead rubber'. But there was still pride to play for, and that pride had been severely mauled throughout the tour by the scathing analysis and sometimes mockery of the Australian press. As every touring side down under knows, including rugby union and cricket, Australian journalists love to taunt and dig the dirt about the Poms. Off the field the hospitality of the public and hotel staffs is marvellous and the banter friendly and jocular. On the field, and in the media, the boot goes in from the moment of arrival. By the time the final test was due to be played on 9 July an imaginary headline might read "Do the Poms need to bother to turn up?"

The rugby fans in Sydney obviously felt much the same way. Attendances throughout the tour had not been brilliant, although there were 24,000 at Sydney and 27,000 at Brisbane for the first two tests.

The attendance was just under 16,000 for the anticipated anticlimax, but those Australians who came to the stadium were in for a stunning shock, and the travelling party of British fans, who had remained cheerfully loyal throughout the tour, were about to be given a magnificent surprise reward for their loyalty.

One of the factors which had dogged the tour had been the number of injuries and replacements to the playing personnel. Six players had to fly home injured, including two star men in Shaun Edwards and Garry Schofield. This meant that the tour managers Les Bettinson and David Howes, and particularly the coach Malcolm Reilly, had a huge selection headache in addition to the prospect of a Test whitewash. No wonder the Australian press had a field day, with one journalist tipping a 50-point margin for Wally Lewis and the rampant Kangaroos.

The script had thus been written beforehand but the Great Britain squad had not learned their parts properly. Early in the game, before the complacent Kangaroos had settled, a swift passing move sent winger Henderson Gill over on the right.

Like a boxer caught by an early sucker punch Australia were shaken and dazed, and were not allowed to recover by an increasingly confident Great Britain side playing the best rugby of this, or several previous tours. Form was turned on its head as the Lions, growing in stature and self-belief with every move, ran in five tries with two from Gill, and one each from Phil Ford, Martin Offiah and Mike Gregory, with three goals by Paul Loughlin.

The much-maligned tourists went on to win the match 26-12, and everything about the game brought joy to success-starved British hearts. Everyone at the match that sunny, in every sense, July day in Sydney has particular memories imprinted on the mind.

Two things stand out for me. The first was the sight of Mike Gregory, later to be sadly stricken by a neurological illness, striding through the Australian defence like a stag, head held high, legs pumping as he galloped 75 yards to the line. And, literally closer to home, the parts played in an all-round team performance by the two Widnes brothers David and Paul Hulme: David had been a regular at half-back, but Paul had been flown out as injury cover, and the sight of the two of them in harness brought delight not just to one family but to the whole population of Widnes.

After the game came an incident in the rapturous Great Britain dressing room which saw further sweet revenge for the coach Malcolm Reilly. Well-wishers, mostly British, called with their congratulations, but the mood changed abruptly when an impromptu press conference occurred. A well-known, outspoken Australian newspaperman, who had pilloried, mocked and in general vilified the tourists throughout the tour, made two cardinal errors. One was attending the conference. Two was offering rather guarded and qualified congratulations to Reilly. It was the proverbial red rag to the bull. Reilly, the former Castleford international who had played rugby league in Australia and built up a fearsome reputation similar to that created by Adrian Morley in recent years, yanked him off his feet by his coat collar. Reilly would have summarily executed him there and then on one of the dressing room pegs had David Howes not counseled the coach that throttling a prominent Australian press man would spoil the headlines in the following day's newspapers and detract from a great win.

The evening on the town which followed was one to remember. It was as if Great Britain, rather than losing yet another series, had actually won it. The team, officials and press party were guests of the tour sponsors Whitbread at an end-of-tour dinner at a hotel on the harbour. It was a very lively occasion rather than the expected wake, and the celebrations continued at the team's hotel, the Manly Pacific, until the early hours.

The red, white and blue fans, at last given something to celebrate made a night of it in Sydney's cosmopolitan variety of hostelries, cafes and entertainment venues, while the local populace looked on with good-humoured indulgence, as indeed they could afford to. It was quite a night.

Although we did not know it at the time, the totally out-of-the-blue win was to be a catalyst for a genuine revival of international rugby league in Britain over the next two decades, with the gap between the southern and northern hemispheres becoming narrower but, frustratingly, not quite closing. However, in 1988 it was enough that the Lions had not been whitewashed, and we had witnessed a stirring win, which not even an anticlimactic 12-10 World Cup defeat to New Zealand in Christchurch the following week could spoil.

The long flight home after the tour was made more endurable by the Gympie stories and the Sydney victory, and after the usual couple of days getting jet-lag out of the system, it was back to domestic business, primarily with Red Rose Radio and *The Times*. However, there was to be little time to unwind and relax or to settle down to an ordered routine. In 1990 there would be another tour followed by the two more sadly short-lived, television opportunities. Together they created yet another extremely hectic log-jam of diary engagements.

During the late 1980s there was a short-lived attempt to gain a foothold for rugby league in the United States. An energetic American entrepreneur, who also happened to be an Anglophile rugby league enthusiast, Mike Mayer, was the driving force behind the venture. His aim, backed by the RFL in funding and publicity, was to persuade consortia of wealthy businessmen in the States to set up XIII-a-side franchises in major American cities, akin to those in baseball and American Football.

To galvanise interest in the States, Mayer, with the co-operation of the RFL and two leading clubs, Wigan and Warrington, arranged for an exhibition match between the two teams to be played at the baseball stadium in the beer-brewing city of Milwaukee, Wisconsin in June 1989. My minor involvement was to act as support commentator and explain the laws and techniques of rugby league to a local television station's own sports commentator.

Both clubs supported the venture financially, Wigan contributing £100,000 and Warrington £50,000, and two full-strength squads, captained by Ellery Hanley and Mike Gregory, took the field with the rugby league markings on the baseball pitch.

A crowd of 17,773 turned up, and the match was a fairly low-key affair, hardly surprising under the circumstances. Wigan won 12-5, and despite the advance publicity and our efforts in the commentary box, Mike Mayer's bold and ambitious venture failed to get off the ground, and no United States Rugby League emerged at this time from the seeds scattered at Milwaukee's baseball stadium. Gridiron football and baseball were too deeply entrenched.

The 1990s were to be a strangely topsy-turvy decade. All began well, as two television offers came right out of the blue. One should have gone elsewhere, dropping into my lap through the thoughtfulness of YTV and former Radio Leeds commentator John Helm. John had been offered work in a London studio dubbing commentaries on French rugby league games for a satellite television company Screensport.

For various contractual reasons John was unable to accept the work, and he kindly and thoughtfully passed on my name to the producer Colin Mitchell. The Screensport offices and studios were in Carnaby Street, still a chic fashion centre, and after a trip to London and a chat with Colin another television avenue opened. Satellite and cable were then in their infancy and audiences were small, but steadily growing. The commentaries would also follow a different pattern. They would not be live, or even recorded on-site. The matches would be filmed in France, with on-site crowd effects, and the film would be flown to London. They would then be tidily edited by Colin or a colleague, and the commentary would be dubbed in a Screensport sound booth.

Herewith, a shameful admission: The commentator would pretend to be live at Perpignan, St Esteve or Albi, and viewers would not be discouraged from thinking that I was sitting in a commentary box in the baking sun of southern France, while in fact I was working from notes in a small sound booth in a London studio.

There was to be an excellent bonus. The irrepressible, incorrigible Alex Murphy was to be the expert co-commentator and summariser. Over the years I had known 'Murph' as a player, coach, manager and outspoken pundit, and indeed as a friend whom I had interviewed in Bates Crescent, Thatto Heath, St Helens, at the start of his remarkable and explosive career.

It was to be an all-too-brief partnership, for the whole Screensport operation was wound up shortly after the end of a couple of seasons of French rugby league despite the high quality of the production values throughout the multinational and multi-sport coverage. Fortunately, many, if not all, the production staff found work with other companies, particularly Sky, as satellite and cable television burgeoned.

French rugby league on Screensport was huge fun while it lasted, thanks mainly to Alex, who proved about as easy to discipline as a commentator as he had been as a player.

He threw himself into the job with typical unbridled enthusiasm. His pronunciation of the French players' names was execrable, showing clearly that whatever subjects he had excelled in at school, one was not the language of de Gaulle and Chevalier. There were times when Colin, outside in the production area of the studio, was falling about with laughter, while I found it difficult to keep a straight face, and straight commentating voice.

Murph also enjoyed the harmless, I hope, deception that we were actually at the matches in France. On one occasion, when a game was flown back from St Esteve, he welcomed viewers with the cheerful comment that the sun was so hot that he had shed his jacket and tie and was drinking pints of iced water to keep cool. On another occasion he praised the quality of the red wine at lunch.

Another prize Murphyism was when he turned up at a St Helens match within hours of the screening of another game. When spectators asked him how he had managed to get back so quickly he said, no doubt with a twinkle in his eye, that we had taken a private plane back from France.

There was, however, one huge disappointment. While games were normally filmed and flown back there was an occasion in the early 1990s when the company adventurously decided to cover a game live, and an international match to boot; France versus Great Britain at Perpignan.

Everything began well with a short, comfortable flight to the historic town not far from the Spanish border. Then we took a delightful Saturday evening walk through the ancient streets and markets to a small bistro for a leisurely meal with the journalistic corps. This was enlivened by crassly unsuccessful attempts, no doubt tongue in cheek, by some colleagues, to chat up the waitresses in pidgin French. It was wonderfully good humoured. So far, so very, very good.

Sunday was a perfect southern France day - hot sunshine, but with a gently tempering breeze. We took up our commentary positions and the French engineer tested the lines and declared them to be in full working order. A line test to the London studio confirmed this, and we settled back in our seats for preview and kick-off.

Then the idyll ended, and Screensport's venture into live rugby league hit the rocks. When I was cued in for the preview I started to talk, but was aware of a hollow emptiness in my earphones. The French engineer looked worried and waved to me to stop talking.

The pictures were getting through to London, but the sound wasn't. At the moment I felt very sorry for two people. Myself and Ron Hill, the former goal-kicking centre with Salford who had, sensibly as it turned out, been roped into the team as a studio summariser and standby 'off-tube' commentator in London.

For the duration of the game Ron would have to do a live commentary alone, without the benefit of a summariser and without having had time to familiarise himself with the teams other than by the early test pictures. There is a world of difference between the comfort zone of describing edited pictures when the outcome is known, and live action. How Ron did it I do not know but he more than earned his fee that afternoon, while for us in France there was only anticlimax, a sense of professional loss, and an official evening dinner which held no real pleasure, despite the amiable company and the positive fact that Great Britain had won the match 8-4. As every reporter and commentator knows the first question anyone asks on returning home is: "What happened to you on Sunday?", and the explanation reignites the pain.

There was one other painful experience with Screensport. This time the ending was happier, but the build-up was difficult, and in many ways quite harrowing. As often happened, there was a tight margin of error between Saturday and Sunday engagements. On this particular weekend I was due to cover a Wigan Athletic home fixture for Red Rose, it was off then to London by car to put the voiceover commentary on a French game for Screensport on Sunday morning. Things went according to plan and I gave the last report from Wigan to the Preston studio at just after five o'clock. When I looked up from my notes, thick and heavy snowflakes were beginning to fall but at that point there seemed no need to worry. Nevertheless, I hurried to the car, to find the thick flakes gathering on the roof and windscreen. As I drove out of Wigan's old Springfield Park ground the snow got heavier and when I reached the M6 south it was inches deep and the windscreen wipers were struggling to keep up.

106

The car radio brought no solace. The forecast was bad: continuing heavy snow throughout the evening and, crucially, particularly in the midlands and south. By the time the traffic had crawled to Crewe the motorway was down to one lane and the radio was warning of possible total closure further south. I pulled into a service station and rang Colin Mitchell, who was fortunately at the London studios. When I told him the situation he was sympathetic but professional. There was no replacement commentator available at such short notice. If I could not make the morning session, the French rugby league broadcast would have to be cancelled.

There was no escape. The effort had to be made, though the decision was easier to make than to put into practice. The snow was piling up and the only lane open was beginning to harden with packed snow. Cars were beginning to stall and skid.

It was decision time again. The motorway was hopeless and would soon close. The only faint chance was an old car driver's ploy: get off the M6, and follow closely a massive lorry with huge wheels which would plough through the packed snow, and hope that it was on its way to London or its outer suburbs. After patient waiting I got behind a big lorry and trailer whose driver was signalling to pull off the motorway. By the grace of God (no blasphemy, believe me) he was heading south. The next four hours were torturous, crawling at 10mph keeping within thin, frozen tracks of flattened snow, and praying that the lorry would not stop or turn off the old A6 trunk road. He didn't, bless him, and in the early hours of the morning what seemed at the time a minor miracle occurred. The night skies became clearer instead of grey, the thick snow thinned out, then stopped, and about 30 miles from London the roads suddenly became swishy and passable. I waved a thumbs up to the lorry driver who had saved my and Screensport's bacon, and finally slumped into the overnight hotel bedroom around 4.00am.

After a few hours' sleep it was the short journey to Screensport, and a relieved and grateful producer took me to the studio. Never before had I been so grateful to see the pile of voluminous times, notes, and try and goal-scoring names, particularly because this time there were no idiosyncratic Murphy summaries to lean on.

There were to be few more French games to describe before the closure came. There was just time to describe an incident in one game that was so funny it was featured on the BBC programme *A Question of Sport* in the 'What Happened Next?' slot.

I cannot remember the French venue of the game, nor the teams, but that hardly matters, because the comic episode is what makes the match memorable. Well into the second half a spectator ran on to the pitch, approached the referee and threw something, possibly dust, into his face. He then decamped quickly back to the safety-in-numbers sanctuary of the pitch side spectators. Or so he thought.

The enraged referee set off after him, leapt over the fence and chased the miscreant halfway round the terracing before confronting him and flattening him with a right hook that Joe Calzaghe would have been proud of. He then dusted his hands, vaulted the fencing and ran back on to the pitch to loud applause from the spectators and players of both sides He whistled up, ruled a scrum where play had been stopped and gave advantage to the side which had been in possession.

It could only happen in France. And how we enjoyed it in our cubby-hole in London.

The team from the Rugby League Roadshow. From the top: Keith, David Howes, Mick Morgan, Neil Holding and John Huxley, with Elaine Burr from Hull, who was a Roadshow hostess for a couple of years.

Rugby League Man of Steel presentations

Top: Listening to Doug Laughton (Widnes & Great Britain).

Middle: Keith talking to the famous referee Billy Thompson.

Bottom: Sharing a joke with John Woods (Leigh & Great Britain).

Rugby League Roadshow interviews

Talking to Keith Mumby (Bradford Northern & Great Britain)

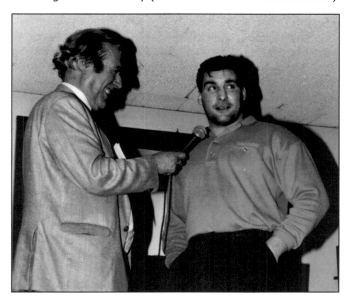

Listening to Trevor Skerrett
(Wakefield Trinity, Hull & Great Britain)

The 1980 Challenge Cup Final

Keith interviews Hull FC's Vince Farrar, while Hull KR's Roger Millward waits his turn to answer questions, before the 1980 Challenge Cup Final between the two Hull teams at Wembley. Hull KR won 10-5. Millward played at stand-off for Rovers, and scored a drop goal. Farrar came on as a substitute for Hull.

13. New Zealand and Australia

If the Screensport time had been short but eventful, British Aerospace Sportscast was even shorter, and only slightly less eventful. The invitation, again a surprise, came from a BAe press officer at the start of the 1990s, and it added two more sports to my commentary portfolio. One, professional boxing, I had dabbled in at Bradford hotel promotions during the YTV years in the 1970s.

The other, rather more exotic, was Thai Kick Boxing, and the occasion was the world championships of the sport. They were held at the huge sports complex in Edmonton, London, and beamed out live on Thailand TV, with me doing a commentary on a sport about which I knew nothing. Come to think of it, some rugby league and football fans might say "no change there, then".

However, the main sport to be covered was rugby league, and Sportscast would itself be exploring new and intriguing territory, for the telecasts, live from second and third division grounds, would be solely targeted at customers in hotels, pubs and social clubs, who could watch the games over a Sunday lunchtime pint. The licensees would pay a rental fee for a large set and aerial, and the hope and expectation was that customers would pack the function rooms and lounges for the novelty of seeing a game in warmth and comfort.

Inevitably, and for the umpteenth time, the clash of timings would cause logistical problems. I was still doing match reports and round-ups for *The Times* on Sundays, and I could see that there would be breakneck dashes ahead from a Batley versus York BAe telecast to a top division game at Wigan, St Helens or Hull.

Still, it was yet another challenge. The director of the matches, and head of the newly formed television arm of British Aerospace, was Huw Joseph, a Welshman with considerable experience on BBC outside broadcasts. He had put together an equally experienced team of cameramen and technicians.

Alas, the bold experiment was destined to last only 18 months before BAe decided it was losing too much money and attracting too few customers. Yet, as ever, there were moments to remember.

It was another time of frenetic activity, particular at weekends, when a Saturday game for Red Rose Radio would be followed on the Sunday by a mad dash for a lunchtime kick-off at Leigh, Halifax, Chorley, Dewsbury, Barrow, Keighley, Hunslet or any one of 22 clubs, to be followed by an even madder dash to the top game of the day, or the nearest First Division Championship match.

Two commentaries also meant two lots of homework. One aspect of an already limited private life did suffer, to my regret.

Because of the hours and the geographical variations in the Sunday fixtures, I had to suspend my pulpit appointments with the Methodist Church, though wherever possible I kept up irregular attendance at services and the situation eased when, within three years jobs in my portfolio began to fall like ninepins.

Several matches stand out from that all-too-brief 18 months. One fixture gave us an excuse to go to the seaside for a very short-lived experiment with a team called Scarborough Pirates, and we covered another gallant experimental failure in the midlands with Nottingham City. A match between Dewsbury and London Crusaders, who had begun life as Fulham, saw me thrown out of a dressing-room for the first time since Roy Francis ejected me politely but firmly from the Leeds Wembley dressing room before the 1968 Cup Final when I inopportunely interrupted his team talk.

The team coaches that day were Maurice Bamford, a vastly experienced manager and coach whose long CV included taking charge of Great Britain in 1986, and an Australian Ross Strudwick, who had built up a good reputation in his own country before trying his luck in England.

Looking for last-minute team news and background information for the Sportscast commentary I went to the London Crusaders dressing room first and gleaned a few useful statistics from Strudwick. I then crossed to the Dewsbury dressing room and at first was quite pleasantly received by Maurice, with whom, before and since, I have always had the friendliest of relationships.

I got as far as saying, as a preliminary to exchanging team news: "I've just had a word with Ross Strudwick and..." when Maurice grabbed me by the arm, not too fiercely, but firmly, led me to the door, and before the slightly embarrassed gaze of the Dewsbury players, ushered me out. I do not know whether history between Bamford and Strudwick was behind this, or whether it was a revival of some past Anglo-Australian needle, but it took a long time for the sense of surprise at this spontaneous snub to wear off. Mercifully it did, and Maurice and I have had many good natters since, the latest at a Batley game a couple of seasons ago. Maurice was plying his new trade, joining the press corps as a reporter and columnist, and obviously enjoying it.

The real highlight of the brief Sportscast era, primarily because of the bizarre nature of the task, was the live coverage of the World Thai Kick Boxing Championships at Edmonton Sports Complex in north London.

Obviously, I tried conscientiously to do some homework, only to be bewildered by the differences between Muy Thai, Thai Kick Boxing and a Japanese version introduced around 1950. Some versions allowed use of what was called 'The science of eight limbs' in which, gruesomely, knees and elbows and shins could be used to belabour a hapless opponent into submission. The less barbaric version appeared to be on view at Edmonton, but even then I struggled with concepts like the 'roundhouse kick' which seemed to involve rotating speedily on the toes of both feet and attempting in mid-flight to metaphorically slice one's opponent in half, or, with a higher trajectory, behead him.

However, help was at hand. Huw Joseph had helpfully arranged to have an expert summariser, a former kick boxer, and I did what every sensible commentator would do. I said as little as possible and let the expert do the talking. This meant merely announcing the number of the round, identifying the boxers, using normal boxing clichés like "an attack", "in defence", and "so-and-so appears to be building up a good lead", allowing the expert to fill in the gaps with due authority.

We got through the evening reasonably well, thanks mainly to our genuinely expert summariser. Afterwards the promoters expressed their satisfaction, Huw said he liked the way I had brought the expert in frequently and particularly at contentious points, though I suspect part of his tongue was in his cheek. It appeared, from later reaction, that the live telecast had gone down well in Thailand. No mention was made of the number of television sets in Bangkok where the sound was presumably turned down because of the English commentary.

The BAe experience was great fun while it lasted, and it was a gut-wrenching disappointment when the company cut their losses early in 1992 midway through the second of a three-year contract with the Rugby Football League. A happy team broke up, and when I last heard from Huw Joseph, whose full Welsh name was Huw Joseph Jones, he had moved to Toronto to work in broadcasting there.

Something very similar was to happen just over 10 years later, but at a higher and even more disappointing level. And just around the corner were other shocks to the professional and nervous system, as 1992 would develop into what could be termed - with acknowledgements to Her Majesty Queen Elizabeth II - my own *annus horribilis*.

However, in the first two years of the 1990s life was still good and still busy, despite the ultimate loss of Screensport and Sportscast. Red Rose Radio filled most of the week and regular studio work and filming for Border, plus daily pieces and weekend match reporting for *The Times*, ensured both steady employment, with seven days a week the unquestioned norm.

Most important of all, the 1990 rugby league international tour to Papua New Guinea and New Zealand arrived in the summer, and I would be sent again by *The Times*.

The 1990 tour broke away from the traditional mould by not including the usual major element, Australia. Instead, the Kangaroos would be coming to Britain in the autumn in a mini-tour lasting a month which would include three test matches.

Two warm-up tests were to be played in Papua New Guinea before the Lions went to New Zealand for three tests, the last of which would be one of the fixtures in the long drawn-out World Cup series, whose games were played sporadically throughout a four year period.

I would not be going to the Papua New Guinea games, which was no great hardship, because those who had braved previous trips spoke of the intense heat and often primitive conditions. This meant that, for once in a while, I could take normal holiday entitlement to make what was a mere three-week trip.

My first visit to New Zealand brought a reunion with my cousin Jean and her mother, my widowed auntie Bessie, late of Newton-le-Willows, who had emigrated many years before.

It also brought a trip to a racecourse which nearly resulted in myself and several journalistic colleagues being trampled to death by horses in the middle of a steeplechase event. Of that, more anon.

New Zealand itself was something of a surprise. Once the plane had touched down on the islands across the Tasman Sea from Australia I felt as if I had been transported in a time machine back to Britain in the 1950s.

While there is the danger of stereotyping, there do seem to be distinct differences in the feel of the two major South Pacific nations. Where Australia is extrovert, ebullient and particularly aggressive in sporting contests, New Zealand is relaxed, reserved and laid back, though certainly in rugby league, their sportsmen know how to battle. Where Australian cities, and particularly Sydney, buzz with restless energy, vivid life and multiethnic activity, the New Zealand lifestyle is much more placid and undemonstrative. Of course, there are variations from these stereotypes, but Auckland, Christchurch and Wellington have a conservative, non-restless atmosphere that reminded me of childhood and teenage years in England before the societal changes during the 1960s. Like Australia, the land of the Kiwi and the long white cloud has vast areas of open country, and these are largely populated by sheep, a fact which reinforces the sense of quietude. The weather, too, is temperate and often rainy, one more link with Britain.

The tourists arrived after two outings in Papua New Guinea; the first game was lost 20-18 at Goroka, the second won 40-8 in a World Cup game at Port Moresby. The first New Zealand test was played in the typically quiet, almost sleepy, town of Palmerston North before a small crowd of 8,073 in this rugby union All Blacks-dominated country. The Lions squeezed through 11-10, with the extra point coming from a Garry Schofield drop-goal. The second test brought another narrow win, 16-14 in Auckland, with the crowd barely touching 8,000.

The series was won, but the one match that really mattered, a World Cup qualifier at Christchurch, was crucially lost 21-18 before a somewhat pathetic attendance of 3,133. The frustration of all that was eased by the fact that my cousin Jean attended the game, with her two sons. They continually barracked for the Kiwis throughout the game, and were noisily overjoyed at the result, but we had an excellent meal together later.

Christchurch is my favourite New Zealand city, clean, compact, and with a river flowing right through the centre. You can walk into and out of the city centre along its banks and Jean had chosen well the place to start a new life. She worked in the advertising department of the local evening paper and a conducted tour took me back down memory lane to my early days at Liverpool, Warrington and Barrow.

While at Christchurch I took an up-country train to a small town called Ashburton to see auntie Bessie, who with her late husband Clarrie had sent me a pre-timed congratulatory telegram after my broadcasting debut in 1956. When my younger brother Brian and I were children we used to go to their trim and tidy house in Earlestown, Newton-le-Willows for Sunday dinner and she was our favourite auntie. Dark-haired, vivacious and pretty, she was always cheerful and jokey, and remained so until she passed away in her early nineties, still the life and soul of the party in her neat little flat in an Earlestown retirement home.

Forgive the indulgence if I tell one story that sums up Bessie Marriott. In her eighties, while still living alone in Ashburton, she had attracted amorous attentions from a wealthy businessman who, cousin Jean told me, was a millionaire. As the relationship developed the businessman offered to take her on a round-the-world cruise. Bessie, of course, accepted happily, but then cancelled abruptly when her would-be consort revealed that, without consulting her, he had booked a luxury double suite and bedroom. "I wasn't having any of that hanky-panky at my time of life," she declared. The relationship ended there and then.

Time now to return to the real highlight, or possibly lowlight, of the 1990 trip, the close brush with death by a group of rugby league journalists at an afternoon race meeting.

It happened at a between-the-tests midweek game in a place named Rotorua, which permanently stinks to high heaven of rotten eggs. This is because Rotorua is famous, certainly in New Zealand, for its hot sulphurous springs.

The temperature in the springs can rise to extremes and caution is required according to the publicity blurb. I bravely took a paddle in one ditch marked with a high-temperature sign half-expecting to have the skin removed from my legs. Fortunately they just felt rather warm, so either the temperature gauge was faulty or I must have the hide of a rhinoceros.

Anyway, the Lions were playing the New Zealand Maoris in a warm-up game, and the town's chief citizen had invited manager Maurice Lindsay, coach Malcolm Reilly, the players and the British press to be his guests at the afternoon Rotorua races.

For some reason or another, a group of pressmen, Ray French, Martin Richards, Alan Thomas, Paul Fitzpatrick, Peter Wilson and me, were late setting off for the racecourse and our taxi got us there well after the two o'clock start. To make matters worse, we were dropped off at a point directly opposite the pavilion where the reception party was being held, and it was a long walk round. After a hurried emergency consultation a decision was made. Because a straight line is the shortest distance between two points we would take a short cut, across the racetrack. Off we went, burrowing through a hedge, and setting off in the general direction of the pavilion.

We broke into a gentle trot. Suddenly, from our left we heard an ominous thudding and rumbling. To our horror we realised that a race was in progress and the horses were thundering towards us. We were about 20 yards from a fence. Our trot changed to a panic-stricken, frightened-rabbit scurry and we dived headlong behind and underneath the fence, seconds before the horses and riders arrived. We cowered there as the hooves passed overhead, and waited nervously until the rump of the last horse had disappeared into the distance.

To say that we were shaken up is the father and mother of an understatement, but even so we shared in the laughter which rang round the course when the public address announcer said "Would the party of journalists please get off the track?" We needed no second invitation.

The time in New Zealand sped by and I left with many pleasant memories, Rotorua racetrack excepted, of a gentle civilised country lacking perhaps the big city and wild-terrain excitements of

Australia, but a stable place in which to live, with its similarity to the bygone England I had known when growing up. One aspect of the country had been particularly impressive. The indigenous Maori population and descendants of the early settlers have blended seamlessly in most areas of life.

In the event, the parting from cousin Jean and auntie Bessie would not be long, for another New Zealand tour was on the near horizon, scheduled for 1992. And in the meantime the Kangaroos would be in England for what emerged as a most thrilling, cliff-hanging yet ultimately anticlimactic series as Britain's bold and unexpected revival in the Sydney test of 1988 continued its momentum.

On 27 October 1990, just three and a half months after the return from New Zealand, the Rugby Football League experimented by playing an Australian tour test match at Wembley for only the third time. On the previous occasions in 1963 and 1973 the matches had not been successful. Only 13,946 saw Australia win 28-2 in 1963 and even fewer, 9,874, attended to see England win 21-12 in 1973, both in series which were won by the Kangaroos. However, the great, unexpected win at Sydney, some well-orchestrated pre-match publicity, and the perceived quality of the tourists, resulted in a magnificent crowd of 54,569. The reward, certainly for the vast majority of the crowd, was a rousing game, and a 19-12 victory for the Lions which set up the remainder of the series perfectly. Great Britain rose splendidly to the occasion, and benefited from a 17-7 penalty count from French referee Alain Sableyrolles.

Unfortunately, by a weird combination of circumstance, the game and its postscript would result in my becoming public enemy number one to the Great Britain man-of-the-match, skipper Ellery Hanley.

Hanley's tremendous work rate and leadership had been a deciding factor in the win, along with the contribution of Hull winger Paul Eastwood who scored two tries and kicked three goals in the rapturously received victory. Hanley's Wigan team-mate Martin Offiah also scored a try and Leeds's Garry Schofield chipped in typically with a drop goal. But it was a magnificent team effort which beat the defiant Australians with, it must be admitted, some vital rub of the green in the shape of crucial penalties from referee Sableyrolles.

After the match the enthusiastic reports were filed and Hanley's performance took centre stage, not least in *The Times*. Some northern pressmen including me, stayed overnight in London. Sadly the halcyon days of Sidcup with George and Sheila were over following Sheila's tragically early death from cancer.

119

On Sunday I had arranged to cover a London Crusaders home game as part of *The Times*'s round-up underneath the test report. I duly watched the game, and telephoned my report, only to receive a message that the sports editor Tom Clarke wanted a word. Tom, to my astonishment and no little concern, had decided to run a big feature on Hanley alongside the match report. Would I kindly write between 500 and 600 words and telephone the piece in within the next few hours?

There was no way I could talk my way out of it, without losing professional face. I could not admit that, being 300 miles from home, I had no reference books to hand, and had no means of getting in touch with the man himself in the time allowed. I had to write a major article of several hundred words purely from memory.

To this day I do not know quite how I managed it. Fortunately, my memory for some salient facts and figures was still good, and over the years I had seen Ellery mature from the gauche, gawky lad from a disadvantaged background in the rougher quarters of Bradford to an outstanding rugby league professional and captain. I scribbled at a furious pace, and managed the deadline. The following day to my relief and pleasure the piece was given great prominence in *The Times* sports feature pages.

Succumbing to the deadly sin of pride I was particularly pleased with the banner headline 'The Black Prince of Wembley'. It was a phrase I had conjured up from the piece, and it looked rather splendid in large, bold type. But my pride and pleasure were short-lived.

A week or so later I covered a Wigan game and had heard rumblings and rumours on the grapevine that Ellery was gunning for me - not a comfortable thought.

Sure enough, after the interviews on the game I was walking downstairs when I saw Ellery alongside Wigan and Great Britain forward colleague Denis Betts, coming towards me. Denis walked past, somewhat hurriedly I thought, but Ellery stood in front of me.

He spoke. "Macklin," he said, "you are the worst commentator in the history of rugby league", suitably emphasising his point with emphatic adjectives and adverbs. It was a sentiment no doubt echoed in the minds of innumerable players and fans.

It was also a moment of truth. On my reply hinged the rest of the evening. I would either spend it enjoying a quiet dinner at home, or in the intensive care ward of the local infirmary on a saline drip. Timorously, remembering the proverb 'A soft answer turneth away wrath' I asked him what the problem was. It transpired that Ellery was annoyed at being made the subject of an article in a national newspaper by a journalist who had not afforded him the simple courtesy of meeting him, or at least telephoning him to get quotes and get the facts. The facts, happily, were reasonably correct, but despite the adulatory tone of the piece, my perceived discourtesy had not gone down well.

I tried in vain to point out the facts that I had cobbled the piece together on a deserted rugby ground in Greater London in just over an hour, but the Great Britain captain would not be placated and went on his way, having made his point forcibly.

The situation did, fortunately, have a happy ending, though some years of polite stand-offs intervened. Peace was declared after Ellery had ended his immensely successful playing career and was coaching St Helens to Grand Final victory over Bradford in 1999.

The match was Leeds versus St Helens on a pleasant evening at Headingley and it was a cracking game eventually won by Saints. I was covering it for GMR radio, and it was with considerable misgiving that I realised an after-match interview would be required by the studio producer and the following morning's news bulletins. When I made my way to the club's interview room I waited my turn, and then grasped the nettle. I asked Ellery if he would come to the grandstand and do a live interview. Without hesitation, and with the utmost good humour, he walked the 50 or 60 yards to the OB point, did an excellent and articulate interview, shook hands and went back to join his players. Perhaps he had forgotten the Wembley article aftermath. Perhaps it was time to let sleeping dogs lie. Or perhaps time had healed the rift. Whatever the reason, it was a huge relief. Ellery went on to make an impact in rugby union coaching and I rather regret that I have not seen him since that night in the Headingley grandstand, even if he still thinks of me as the worst-ever rugby league commentator.

To return to the wider picture of the 1990 visit of the Kangaroos: The Lions' win in the Wembley game had gripped the British imagination and optimists were beginning to suggest that, for the first time since 1970, Britain could win a series. We might even do it in the second test at Manchester United's Old Trafford ground on 10 November.

Expectancy and excitement were at proverbial fever pitch when the day dawned. Great Britain's preparations had proceeded confidently, and news from the Australian camp was that the wearers of the green and gold were genuinely worried.

A crowd of 46,615 came to Old Trafford for a game which lived up to its billing in sheer tension and drama if not in spectacular play. Australia held a narrow lead until the final quarter, when Great Britain substitute Paul Loughlin intercepted an Aussie pass, and ran over to make the score 10-8 amid thunderous noise. It looked like game, set and, at long last, series as the Lions pinned the Kangaroos on their own line with just 20 seconds left. Suddenly the Australian scrum half Ricky Stuart feinted to pass and, as a chink of space opened up in the British line of tacklers, Stuart dummied his way through. There was still the full length of the field to go and the British team raced desperately after him. At halfway Stuart unloaded the ball to Mal Meninga and he left bodies trailing in his wake to romp over. The goal was kicked and Australia squared the series with a 14-10 scoreline. It was a cruel, devastating blow. So near, yet still so far away. Now instead of clinching the series, the Lions had to go to Elland Road on 24 November with the series tied.

Once more the build-up and the anticipation were great, and 32,500 turned up at the Leeds United ground for the showdown. Alas, it was to end in anticlimax, as Australia having had two huge frights, took charge of the game to win comfortably 14-0. Again the dream was over, and again it was back to the drawing board. It was no comfort to know that Great Britain had been 20 seconds and one missed tackle away from a magnificent series win.

14. On tour again

In the early 1990s there were powerful subterranean rumblings in both rugby league and football which would soon explode, changing the games and their structures dramatically. In football the Premier League would arrive and, in 1996, after several abortive attempts to make two and three divisions work, Super League would be born. Both would be backed, and some would say manipulated, by massive injections of television money as fixtures were uprooted and spread around the weekend.

Momentous changes were just around the corner at the end of 1990, but for the time being traditional structures remained, and in the XIII-a-side code there would be another South Seas tour in 1992. It would prove to be the last of its kind. Indeed, the tour of 1988 had been truly the last of the long traditional tours of eight to 10 weeks, with 1990 and 1992 being truncated versions.

It was still a phenomenally busy time, so much so that a fellow sports journalist was moved to make the wryly amusing comment that "If Macklin retired tomorrow there would be seven jobs going at the Employment Exchange". The barb was not entirely accurate because Red Rose Radio, which would be split into two stations, Rock FM and Red Rose Gold, was still the 'day job'. But regular rugby league, and occasionally football and cricket pieces for *The Times* were augmented by visits to Border, Yorkshire and Granada television stations, and Screensport and Sportscast had their brief meteoric rises and falls. This glut of work could not last, and was not destined to do so.

There was still time for one last tour down under and a Kangaroos final full tour in Britain in 1994. Both were eagerly anticipated after Britain's renaissance and Australia's narrow shave in 1990.

Negotiating the 1992 trip with the radio station was a little easier, and less conscience-pricking than it had been on previous occasions. I had handed over the role of sports editor to Nigel Reed, who joined from Sheffield's Radio Hallam with an excellent track record. This released me to be a full-time commentator and reporter again, and Nigel was only too happy for me to combine regular reports from Australia for Red Rose in tandem with *The Times* pieces.

There was also a legitimate reason for giving extensive coverage. Wigan rugby league club was one of the core teams in the station's north-west area and, on the 1992 tour, they provided a staggering total of 13 players, a complete starting team, to the total squad complement of 32. The Wigan backs were Shaun

Edwards, Andy Gregory, Steve Hampson, Joe Lydon and Martin Offiah, and a complete pack of forwards was provided by Phil Clarke, Neil Cowie, Martin Dermott, Ian Lucas, Billy McGinty, Andy Platt and Kelvin Skerrett. Furthermore, winger David Myers was later summoned to the tour as an injury replacement. A further important Wigan connection was tour manager Maurice Lindsay, who was working with coach Malcolm Reilly in another attempt to end the invincibility of the wearers of the green and gold jerseys.

The right of Wigan to have such a huge representation could not be disputed. Their dominance of the domestic season in Britain was so complete that, had they been an industrial company, they would have been reported to the Monopolies and Mergers Commission.

Reporting on Wigan for commercial radio between 1988 and 1995 was an absolute doddle, though tinged with guilt at such obvious lack of competition. They were virtually unbeatable at their historic old Central Park ground, and at most away grounds. They were certainly unbeatable at Wembley in Challenge Cup Finals, rattling up a record eight consecutive victories. Wigan's appearances at Wembley were so predictable that they became monotonous to all except Wigan fans, who, as fast as one final ended, booked their tickets and coach parties for the next. In addition during that period they won three league Premierships and six consecutive Division One Championships. In 1992 the brilliance of their free-scoring backline was emphasised by their sinuous, speedy and elusive left wing Martin Offiah. On 10 May 1992, in a Premiership semi-final 74-6 crushing of Leeds, Offiah proved unstoppable, running in a record 10 tries. Most of them were bewildering, mazy individual runs that Brian Bevan, Billy Boston and Tom van Vollenhoven would have been proud to score. Scrum-half Shaun Edwards also rattled up 10 tries in a less important and less demanding fixture against Swinton in September of the same year. Both were among that huge contingent of Wigan players on the 1992 tour, and they and the rest of the 32-strong playing party were understandably full of confidence after the desperate closeness of the 1990 series in Britain.

One disappointing aspect of the forthcoming tour, as seen in the truncated 1990 trip to Papua New Guinea, and New Zealand, was its reduced length and number of sub-test fixtures. The old-fashioned eight and 10-week tour was being phased out and would only too soon, and sadly for traditionalists, be consigned to history.

However, Super League was still four years away and the Tri-Nations tournament even further towards the horizon, and one more happy working holiday in the South Pacific was there to be enjoyed. The press party included most of the usual suspects, but it also contained one man who had certainly earned the official right to the creature comforts, the long coach journeys and short flights, and the highs and lows of reporting on events on the playing field.

On the 1979 tour Dave Hadfield and the late Peter Ward, then freelances, had really roughed it to follow the Lions. Peter up to his sad and unexpected early death, was primarily a radio freelance. Dave worked for journals in Britain and Australia using the amusing pseudonym 'Old Dart'. The pair had followed the tour by booking the cheapest economy flights on minor airlines, by bus and train journeys and no doubt thumbing the odd lift. It was tough travelling but they never missed a match.

By 1992 Dave was very much part of the journalistic establishment as the rugby league correspondent of *The Independent* and reporter for Sky TV. We all got on well together and friendships made on the tours have stood the test of time with the tall stories and reminiscences getting a little taller with every retelling. There were more to come in 1992.

Pleasant reunions were enjoyed with John Taylor, Norman Smith and families in Australia, and with Jean and her sons in Christchurch but, the tour proved no more successful on the field of play. The Lions kept interest alive by winning the second test in Melbourne, thus squaring the series 1-1, but again they flattered to deceive as the Kangaroos wrapped up the third test and the series.

Perhaps the writing had appeared on the wall in the single warm-up game against Papua New Guinea on 31 May. I had again been allowed to give the baking heat and other discomforts a miss, and the few hardy trail-blazing journalists saw the tourists scrape out a 20-14 win with two tries from Martin Offiah and one each from Paul Eastwood and Phil Clarke, with Paul Loughlin kicking two goals.

The first test at Sydney was played 12 days later on 12 June, and Australia won comfortably 22-6 against a Lions side which included seven Wigan players, five of them in the pack. Castleford's Lee Crooks was the only non-Wiganer up front, and three of the four substitutes, Edwards, Lydon and Lucas, were from the Central Park club. Joe Lydon scored Britain's only try.

The second test at Melbourne's Princes Park was therefore critical if the series was to be kept alive and it was played at an experimental venue in the state where Australia's own invention, Aussie Rules football, was king. Huge crowds watch this strange, certainly to British people, variation on rugby, in which teams are 18-a-side, the ball is punched from hand to hand (throwing being illegal) there is no offside, possession is obtained by tackling or 'bumping' and there are four sets of posts at each end. Six points are scored by kicking the ball through the middle two posts, one point for the outer two.

It may sound weird, but do not knock it. Vast crowds watch it in Victoria and there are outpost clubs in England, Ireland and Japan.

Rugby league, whose strongholds were and still are New South Wales and Queensland, was in 1992 very much a stranger in town on the map of Australian sport, and the decision to take a test there was a chance-taking pioneering venture, very much a fingers-crossed exercise.

It was a cold and wet night but there were two pleasant surprises, indeed shocks, in store for the Lions, their enthusiastic travelling fans, British expatriates among the crowd and the press corps. The crowd of 30,257 was much larger and healthier than had been anticipated and the result, a 33-10 win for the tourists, was almost beyond belief. It was, and remains, the joint highest margin of victory by Great Britain over Australia, equalling the 40-17 triumph at Sydney in 1958.

We watched, at first disbelieving and then in raptures, as the Lions, playing excellent free-flowing rugby, ran in five tries through Clarke, Newlove, Offiah, Schofield and Steadman, augmented by six goals from Eastwood and a typical opportunist drop-goal by Schofield. Wigan provided eight players this time, including their complete pack of Skerrett, Dermott, Platt, Betts, McGinty and Clarke. Edwards and Offiah made up the eight, a record club representation for Great Britain which Wigan were to achieve a total of four times in all.

The series was squared and still open and up in the press box we had something to write about, plus plenty of cheerful tales to tell on radio, with accompanying interviews. The win crowned a splendidly sociable couple of days in Melbourne, where the night before I had been royally entertained to a family meal at the home of John and Bev Taylor's eldest son Andrew, who had built up a thriving motor accessories business in the capital city of Victoria.

The Lions bandwagon had gathered new momentum after the Melbourne victory, and the atmosphere was cheerful and optimistic as the touring party and various entourages went to Brisbane for the third and deciding test on 3 July.

Several days in Brisbane provided an additional tonic. We were comfortably, even luxuriously, housed in a riverside hotel with spacious gardens which led down to a landing stage for boats into the city. There were more social meetings with Norman, including a walk around the green and spacious campus of the University of Queensland, not far from the commodious house in Indooropilly of Professor Norman J Smith, formerly of Rainhill and the booking office of Prescot railway station.

It was in Brisbane that another comic episode occurred which severely damaged my reputation, if ever I had one, as a reliable guide to the gastronomic delights of Queensland's capital and its environs.

On a visit to Norman I had been regaled with glowing accounts of a tasty novelty foodstuff at eating houses named Sizzlers. The outlets, which were apparently building up a roaring trade, sold a wide variety of hot or cold fillings. The trail-blazing novelty was that these fillings were encased in hollowed cleaned out, spiced and cooked potato jackets, or what might be called in English vernacular, spud cases. These once-despised surplus-to-requirements pieces of waste, destined for the bin, were recycled into a hot delicacy, served under a banner which offered "as much as you can eat for one price", and every conceivable minced meat, fish, vegetable, crustacean and even exotic fruit filling was available.

The price was right too. Only a small fistful of $10 each, about £3.50, for as many filled spud peelings as a healthy appetite could manage, with unlimited trips to and from the counters. My enthusiastic sponsorship of Sizzlers, and the prospect of somewhere different to eat at a bargain price, won over enough of the press party to form a quorum, although a few misgivings were voiced when my colleagues were informed that the eating house was not in the city centre, accessible by boat, but out in the suburbs. However, upon my assurance based on my visits out to Indooroopilly that it was only a taxi ride away, doubts were allayed, and off we set.

My assurances about the cheapness and cornucopia of the filled potato jackets proved accurate enough. Alas, my estimate of the distance from the hotel out into the Brisbane suburbs was wildly inaccurate. When our bemused taxi driver finally arrived at Sizzlers after several false turns, the total on the clock indicated $30 a head, plus proportion of tip. To this would be added $10 a head for the meal, plus drinks.

Because we were coming to the end of the tour most of the party's finances ranged from 'reserve tank' to 'skint', so much so that between us we could not muster the $120 for the return journey by taxi, and would have had to walk or thumb lifts back to base had not help arrived in the shape of a van driver from Brisbane who had popped in for a bite, and who let us pile into the back, like cattle in a truck, for the journey home. Many unkind jokes, if they were jokes, were said about me and my suggestion on the bouncy, uncomfortable ride back, including the rather fanciful jibe that it would have been cheaper to have hired a plane to London for dinner at the Café Royal.

Nor did it enhance my Egon Ronay reputation or popularity to hear the gleeful comments of those who had stayed in Brisbane, and had found a smashing, cheap little cafe just down the road from the hotel.

Despite such minor hiccoughs the time at Brisbane passed pleasantly, particularly because the mood of the players, coach Mal Reilly and manager Maurice Lindsay was upbeat after the morale-raising win in Melbourne.

However, the Australians were once again in no mood to suffer two test indignities in a row. They won the decider 16-10 before a 32,000 Brisbane crowd, Offiah scoring a try and Eastwood three goals, and while it was never a runaway win for the Kangaroos, and the Lions put up a brave scrap, the series ended in another frustrating Ashes triumph for Great Britain's nemesis. It was also another World Cup defeat.

After swallowing the familiar bitter medicine the Lions crossed the Tasman for a two-match series against the Kiwis which, in all honesty, felt like a huge anticlimax, though the 'holiday' parts were pleasant enough. The two games were played at Palmerston North on 12 July and Auckland a week later. Both games were tight and the teams won one each. Great Britain lost the first 15-14 before an 8,000 crowd but tied the series in the second by winning 19-16 in Auckland before 7,400 spectators. Both attendances emphasised rugby league's rather secondary role in New Zealand to the iconic rugby union All Blacks, an imbalance which has slightly improved in recent years with the entry of rugby league's New Zealand Warriors, based at Auckland, to Australia's NRL.

As tour time ran out, there were to be two more memorable moments on that last Australasian trip, one light-hearted, one extremely unpleasant.

During a fine, gentle sunny day at Auckland leading up to the second test, a group of journalists decided to take a leisurely walk up a hill at the top of which was a restaurant renowned for its local cuisine and for its spectacular view over the city and out to sea.

The climb was mildly demanding, but negotiable at a steady walk with occasional pauses to take a breath and enjoy the magnificent long-distance view. At the top we enjoyed an excellent outdoor fish and fruit meal in the garden of the restaurant and then went in groups for a further languid stroll in the sun.

Ray French, Brian Batty and I formed one such group, and eventually we found a small clearing with a perfect panoramic view of Auckland - rooftops, high buildings, leafy estates and playing fields - and out to a deep blue sea bathed in sunshine. In the clearing were several large rocks, worn smooth by countless tourists' bottoms over the years. Frenchy, Batty and I sat on one rock each, and full of a good lunch and the odd glass of wine, mused about the events of the tour and the world in general, like you do.

It was Frenchy who said it after one long, quiet moment of reflection. "Look at us," he said. "The Last of the Summer Wine".

Philosophy gave way to laughter, especially when the other press lads joined us.

It should have been the perfect memory with which to end the last of my tours. But it was followed just a few days later by the start of a personal nightmare.

Not that it started off as one. In fact, quite the reverse. Along with Paul Fitzpatrick of *The Guardian* and John Whalley of the *Daily Telegraph* I had arranged for a brief stopover in Singapore on the return trip, primarily to break up what would have been an extremely long series of flights back home from New Zealand.

Although Paul and John had booked separate flights back home from Singapore the three of us would be able to spend a night on the island, sampling the delights of its world famous cuisine, plus a decent night's sleep in a good hotel.

At first all went to plan. The flights from New Zealand to Sydney, and Sydney to Singapore went well, the hotel was top class, we had an excellent Chinese meal, and retired to bed in buoyant mood looking forward to the journeys home on the morrow. I would have longer to savour the sights and sounds of the city, all day in fact, because my flight was scheduled to leave at 8.15 the following evening.

In the early hours of the morning it began to go dreadfully wrong. I awoke feeling distinctly unwell and with a nagging pain in the lower abdomen. By daybreak I had a splitting headache and the stomach pains were much worse. When I tried to get out of bed the room swam around and I slumped back on the pillow. Much as I hate troubling foreign doctors when in a strange country thousands of miles from home, I felt so awful I just had to ring reception and summon help.

A worried porter came up with stumbling English, and through my sign language and ghastly appearance, I convinced him that I needed some medical attention, or at least some pills for stomach cramps and nausea.

He went off, to be replaced by a kindly and efficient woman who introduced herself as the hotel housekeeper. She said she had sent for a doctor and he would arrive shortly. In the meantime I must stay in bed.

The doctor arrived an hour later, during which time the stomach pain seemed to get worse, I felt more and more unwell and the nightmare scenario was looming. If my condition worsened, or if I had some perniciously infectious disease, I would be shipped into a hospital isolation ward, and would not be allowed to catch the flight home at 8.15 that evening. I would be marooned alone on Singapore island with no money, for we had spent our reserves of cash the previous night.

The doctor gave me a thorough and somewhat painful going-over, prodding and poking and putting a thermometer in various places. His verdict could have been a lot worse, but was grim enough. I did not have a life-threatening or infectious disease but had a temperature and was probably suffering from a severe bout of food poisoning. He strongly recommended that I should stay in bed for at least another 24 hours and, if there was no improvement he would have me admitted to a local hospital for further tests. It was a harrowing scenario and an awful dilemma.

I felt absolutely dreadful, the stomach pains were getting worse despite the ingestion of some pills, but staying in bed in a Singapore hotel for another 24 hours was just not an option. I had no money to pay for another day in the hotel and, more importantly, my plane for England and home would leave at 8.15. There was nothing else for it. As rotten as I felt, I had to get up, struggle into my clothes, pick up my cases, and stagger out into the broiling heat of Singapore's long, world-famous shopping parades. I was in no fit state to be impressed by the city's sights and sounds.

That day in Singapore in 1992 remains one of the most miserable of my life. It was also one of the longest. The hours crawled by, there was no friendly London-style park where I could lie down on a bench or lawn, and when I tried to spread myself on a street bench passers-by glared at me as if I was a helpless drunk or drug addict. Twice a policeman moved me on like a vagrant.

But 5.15 at last arrived, the special bus took me to the airport, I went through the gates and customs lurching like a zombie, and pulled my aching bones, bursting head and croaking voice together to use up my last remnants of change ringing my good friend Kate, in Blackburn. I tried to sound as cheerful as possible, and pretended I was just tired, though Kate was not fooled. We arranged for her to pick me up nearly 24 hours later at Manchester Airport, and I dozed fitfully throughout that long, long flight. It was a grim, anticlimactic end to the last of the traditional odysseys to the South Sea islands.

15. Rovers' title

After arriving home in Blackburn, my first stop was bed, where I stayed for several days on doctor's orders. Because I have been a lifelong hypochondriac I was convinced that my final hour had come, and that I would go down in medical history as the first man to expire from a combination of brain, lungs, back and stomach disorders aggravated by corkscrewed bowel syndrome, the last being my own personal diagnosis. The doctor sent me by ambulance to Blackburn Infirmary, where chatty nurses tested all the above areas and organs and gave me a blood test. Eventually a specialist arrived to confirm the Singapore doctor's diagnosis that I seemed to have no more than a particularly virulent form of food poisoning, which was nasty but not life-threatening.

The first few weeks back home were not particularly pleasant, though it helped eventually to get out of bed and start work again. However, any improved sense of wellbeing was dampened, and the *annus* became a little more *horribilis*, when I finally got round to reading the pile of accrued correspondence and caught up with telephone calls, for the summer and autumn of 1992 would see the healthy pile of professional outlets that had kept me working seven days a week for as long as I could remember suddenly crumble. Screensport's French rugby league programmes and British Aerospace had given up the ghost and, most disappointing of all, though under the circumstances it was inevitable, my 13 years as rugby league correspondent of the Thunderer came to an end.

Standing out among the post pile was one letter headed *The Times*. It was from Tom Clarke, the genial sports editor, with whom I had always had the most pleasant of relationships though, it has to be said, at a freelance distance of around 300 miles between Blackburn and Gray's Inn Road, London.

The letter started nicely enough with Tom thanking me for the "full and excellent" coverage of the tour and for 13 years of quality reporting. Then came the sting in the tail which, to be honest, was not entirely unexpected.

In the 1980s and early 1990s *The Times* had undergone certain revolutionary changes. The Thunderer, the historic standard bearer and 'newspaper of record' of the British crown, establishment, empire and tradition, had gone from front page advertising to front page news. Its leaders, feature articles and reports, while retaining authority and literary quality, had unbuttoned their starchy formality and adopted a much more relaxed and flowing style. And there had been a radical improvement in the sports coverage caused by a huge breakthrough in printing deadlines following a bitter, but successful, battle with the restrictive practices of the trade unions.

One of the frustrations for a series of sports editors and their reporting teams and sub-editors had been the fact that the deadlines for copy, both news and sport, had been early in the evening. This meant that the late overs in cricket matches had to be rushed to press, and, crucially, evening football and rugby matches had no chance of making the morning editions. Ironically, this had made life easier for me, because if an evening game was in any way inconvenient, I had no reason to attend it.

However, there had been times when midweek matches had been missed through clashes of loyalties, particularly with my contract job, Red Rose Radio, and the players' testimonial Roadshows. On these occasions *The Times* had had to take agency copy on the games which is not the same as an individual, signed report.

The letter from Tom Clarke made it clear that this situation would not arise again. The new-look, front-page news, livelier Thunderer would henceforth, and for the first time in its long and distinguished history, have a full-time rugby league correspondent, who would be a member of the London-based staff, and would work exclusively for the paper. It was sad news, but totally understandable, and Christopher Irvine moved in seamlessly to make the job his own.

There is an old northern saying that as one door closes, another shuts. In the space of a few months a considerably chunk of my portfolio had disappeared. Nevertheless, it was hardly disaster. There was still the bedrock of the radio station, regular freelance work on Border TV's *Lookaround* and *The Union and the League* programmes, and a Manchester production agency was using me for television commercials and voiceover audio-visual productions. An honest crust or two could still be earned and the wolf was not exactly at the door. Certainly, after the hectic, almost madcap, schedule that had been the perennial norm, things would be more balanced and in the summer I could enjoy again the gentle, pastoral delights of league cricket on Saturday afternoons.

However, dramatic and unexpected developments were afoot at the radio station, and Sunday rugby league would be back. Life would be no longer frenetic, but still time-consuming.

It was to be my great good fortune that the era - the mid-1990s - when fate decreed that I would have more time to spend with the Lancashire-based radio station, was the period when Wigan rugby league club were at the pinnacle of their dominance. It also coincided with the spectacular re-emergence of Blackburn Rovers as a major force in football, culminating in a nerve-shredding final day of the 1994-95 season when Rovers snatched the Premiership title at Anfield in the tensest of finishes.

With the end of my *Times* responsibilities came freedom to follow both sides with regularity. Reporting on successful teams is much more fun than chronicling failure. It also makes for higher listening figures, particularly at away games.

In their ruthless dominance of the Challenge Cup, Wigan won the trophy a record number of eight times in a row during the seasons 1988 to 1995. Consequently, just as the Central Park fans had an annual outing to Wembley and London to look forward to, I could book the date in my diary for a Red Rose commentary, thus continuing a virtually continuous run of reports and commentaries dating back to my debut with St Helens versus Halifax nearly 40 years earlier.

The Wembley trips became a one-day event, with an early train down and the return at 7.23pm from Euston to Runcorn and Liverpool Lime Street.

On the morning train I would board the train at Runcorn and meet the Red Rose Saturday sport presenter John Gillmore, who boarded at Preston, and the inevitable cheery carriage-loads of Wigan supporters. The train was a sea of cherry and white, and it has to be said that though they could be a boisterous and raucous bunch, as all fans are, there was never a hint of bother, coming or going. Indeed, it is only fair and proper to say that in every Wembley trip, over the years, whatever the teams, the same has applied. Rugby league supporters can be as noisily enthusiastic as followers of every sport, and there have been minor and isolated outbreaks of hooliganism at league games, but I believe from personal experience that there are no better behaved fans anywhere.

They had certainly proved it at an earlier Wigan final, the 1989 beating of St Helens by 27-0, when these cheerful, understandably cocky fans could have vented considerable annoyance and frustration on me. John Gillmore enjoys recounting this particular Wembley incident, funny in retrospect, in his own collection of after-dinner stories.

London's magnificent interlocking tube system offers a variety of routes to Wembley depending on which mainline route is taken to the capital. On this particular occasion Gilly and I found ourselves changing trains at the busy Baker Street junction.

On this journey John and I had been spotted by radio sports programme listeners and older Wigan fans who recalled the *RL Action* television programmes, and a chatty relationship had built up. So, quite a large party of cherry-and-white bedecked supporters were with us on one of the many platforms going at Baker Street.

Indeed, John tells me that he heard a woman say to her party as we got off the train at Euston: "Just follow Keith Macklin. He's done the trip dozens of times. He'll know the way".

Sure enough, about 30 or 40 fans followed Gilly and me as we boarded a train to Baker Street. We marched confidently through the network of platforms and found the one which would take us to Wembley Park. Everyone, including a huge phalanx of Wiganers, poured on to the train and settled comfortably in the seats.

Then some instinct caused me to look up at the illuminated sign on the platform. Our train was the one heading south, not the one heading north to Wembley. Gilly assures me that I learned forward conspiratorially and said "John, we're on the wrong train. We're going in the wrong direction. It's the one on the opposite platform". Gilly said "But what about all these fans?" It was not a time for sentiment. We grabbed our equipment and, as the gap in the door began to close, leapt out. The gap closed behind us, and several dozen cherry-and-white fans, faces pressed in anxious bewilderment against the windows, roared off into the tunnel heading south. It was an extremely embarrassing situation in which another reputation, this time as an all-knowing, sophisticated guide collapsed in ignominy. For months, indeed years, thereafter on visits to Wigan in general and Central Park in particular I have dreaded a confrontation with Wigan fans reminding me of the day I sent them on a wild goose chase away from Wembley Stadium.

Strangely, it has never happened. Perhaps I have been forgiven, perhaps they found their way comfortably by another route. They may have even seen the joke and laughed about it, and got as much fun out of telling and retelling the tale as Gilly, now with BBC Radio Lancashire, has done down the years. I just hope I have been forgiven.

Anyway, something of a comeuppance hit us when we got to the stadium. As any broadcaster will tell you, the worst hazard of all is one's equipment, especially when it is hand-held and self-operated. I often think back nostalgically to my starting years on radio outside broadcasts with the BBC, when a producer and, more importantly, an engineer or crew would assemble the equipment, test it, and then dismantle it after the commentary, leaving the commentator to concentrate solely on the job of writing, researching, describing the game and doing interviews. Most major network BBC OBs still have this luxury, but in local radio the reporter or commentator has to carry around the equipment, assemble it, and pack it up afterwards.

The moment to be dreaded is the one when, having stuck in all the plugs, attached all the wires and switched on the mains or batteries, one of three things happens. Either you shout down the line to the studio base, but they can't hear you; or the studio staff call you, but you can't hear them, or the lines are completely dead both ways.

When we switched everything on at Wembley the worst technical problem hit us. The lines to and from the Preston studio were dead, silent and empty of sound. Gilly and I tried everything, changing batteries, changing power points, using replacement mikes, earphones and connecting cords. Nothing worked.

We got so exasperated that we finally contemplated adopting a measure not included in the technical manual: kicking the machine all round the press box, which probably would not have solved the problem, but would have made us feel a lot better.

There were a lot of crocodile tears of sympathy from our colleagues in local radio such as Clive Tyldesley, then with Radio City, and Stuart Pyke, with Radio Piccadilly, and offers of spare equipment, but nothing worked and I ended up doing reports down a telephone line. Fate had exacted retribution on behalf of the stranded Wigan fans.

Thus, in the last decade of the last century local radio assumed a central role in my professional life for the first time since the heady and adventurous opening years of the 1980s. Football came to the fore, as it had done with YTV in 1969, but this time the loyalties were split between five Lancashire clubs: Blackburn Rovers, who were my responsibility, Burnley, Preston North End, Blackpool and Wigan Athletic. Each team had its own reporter: Tom Parker with Preston, Graham Emmerson with Blackpool, Mike Tunstall with Burnley, and Steve McIlwham with Wigan.

Red Rose Gold carried sport on the AM wavelength, with pop music dominating Rock FM. In the 1990s the station's sports output reached its pinnacle. Two managing directors, first Tom Hunter and then, crucially, Michelle Surrell, gave strong support both professionally and financially to a three-man sports department of Nigel Reed, Gary Flintoff and me. It was a happy day when Michelle invited Nigel and me to lunch at the Crest Hotel and informed us that with company cash and some sponsorship we could at last give comprehensive commentary coverage to all our football teams. Previously *Saturday Sport* had been music plus match reports, now it would be full coverage.

This was exciting news. Hitherto, Red Rose Radio had been a frequent brand leader against national and local stations in official audience ratings, it had never gone head-to-head with its main local rival, Blackburn-based BBC Radio Lancashire, on Saturday afternoons. The previous Red Rose Saturday show, a mix of easy listening music and sports reports, had done reasonably well and found its own audience, but the excellent, all-round sports coverage of Radio Lancashire, and particularly its comprehensive, blanket presentation of football, had never been seriously challenged.

It would cost something like a six-figure sum to get commentary rights for all our clubs but the station management was prepared to give it a go. The decision gave Red Rose Sport access to some great games, culminating in Blackburn Rovers winning the Premiership in 1995 and entering the European competitions in two consecutive seasons. Equally importantly, it provided the sports team with the opportunity to compete for audience on equal terms with Radio Lancashire. We had the pleasure of splitting the audience down the middle in the keen, but always friendly, contest with our rivals until economic pressures and adverse programming decisions sent us back to square one.

The catalyst for Rovers success was, of course, the capture of Kenny Dalglish as manager in 1991. This coup was made possible by Blackburn's wealthiest fan, the self-made industrial magnate Jack Walker, a classic case of the old north country fable of the poor lad from working class beginnings who becomes a multi-millionaire.

Jack Walker, and his brother Fred, had taken over their father's small car body and sheet metal workshop in Blackburn and, by dint of hard work and shrewd business deals and acquisitions, built a steelworking empire which was eventually taken over at a huge price when the industry was nationalised by the government. With his millions Jack Walker, a lifelong Blackburn Rovers fan, fulfilled his lifetime's ambition by taking over the club, and pulled off a master stroke when he persuaded the great Kenny Dalglish to take over from the luckless Don Mackay. Mackay had done the best he could with limited funds and playing resources, including winning the Full Members' Cup, but could not match Dalglish's charisma and track record.

Jack Walker also bankrolled the rebuilding of tattered old Ewood Park into a 21st century Premiership stadium, and provided funds for Dalglish and his experienced sidekick Ray Harford to build a top-class side with headline-grabbing signings. Alan Shearer rejected Manchester United to come from Southampton to Ewood for a £3 million fee, and other inspired swoops in the transfer market brought Chris Sutton, Colin Hendry, Stuart Ripley, Graeme Le Saux, Tim Flowers, Henning Berg, Tim Sherwood, Jeff Kenna, Tony Gale, David Batty and Kevin Gallacher to Blackburn. With local winger Jason Wilcox, and established team members Paul Warhurst, Mark

Atkins and Ian Pearce, they formed a formidable squad. Jack Walker's vast investment paid off spectacularly under the guidance of Dalglish and Harford. Arguably the finest ever Blackburn team were Premiership runners-up in 1993-4. Then they hit the jackpot and fulfilled Jack Walker's dream by winning the Premiership the following season. These dramatic seasons coincided with the Red Rose full football coverage, and the climactic last day of the season in 1995 brought excruciating tension and then euphoria.

The final Premiership fixtures were played on a Sunday, and the two contenders for the title were the holders and perennial favourites Manchester United and Blackburn. United were at West Ham, Rovers had the daunting task of facing Liverpool at Dalglish's former stamping ground Anfield. Blackburn had to beat the Reds to ensure the title, if they failed to win, United could snatch it by winning at Upton Park.

There was a strong contingent of Rovers fans at the game but we knew that there would also be a sizeable and tense audience at home for the radio commentaries on Red Rose and Lancashire. It was a huge game for everybody, and it began well for Rovers when the prolific Alan Shearer put them ahead and the lead was held until half time. But it began to turn pear-shaped when John Barnes and Jamie Redknapp cracked in two fine goals for Liverpool. We were anxiously monitoring United's progress at West Ham and, as the games entered the final quarter, we heard that it was 1-1, and United were battering the Hammers defence for the winner that would give them the title for the third year in a row. As we listened in our earphones to the news flashes the closing minutes of the Upton Park match were like hours, an absolute agony for all of us who were willing the referee in East London to blow up at 1-1. When finally he did, and the news filtered through from hundreds of radio sets all around Anfield, there was a monumental roar from every part of the ground. The Liverpool fans joined in, ecstatic at a double triumph, Manchester United's failure and their own team's show of professionalism. The final few minutes of the game at Anfield passed in a dreamlike trance. The action on the pitch did not matter, we were gabbling into our mics about the tears streaming down Jack Walker's face and the joyous atmosphere all around the ground.

As with the lesser Full Members' Cup triumph of 1987, it was carnival night on the return journey and in the streets of Blackburn, and it was an immense thrill to feel a minor part of the celebrations that weekend.

The only downside came the following season when at last the Anfield euphoria had evaporated and Rovers entered the European Champions Cup. The previous season the team had qualified for the UEFA Cup, but had gone out ignominiously in the first round to Trelleborg, a club from a small town near Malmö in Sweden. Tom Parker and I, plus engineer Stewart Lythe, had made the fixture in Sweden, and we were looking forward to the thrill of more European trips in the 1996-97 season, although a dampener was that Kenny Dalglish had 'moved upstairs' at Ewood after winning the Premiership with Ray Harford taking over as manager.

The draw for the first group stage sent us to Rosenborg, near Trondheim in Norway, and Legia Warsaw in Poland. We should also have made the final trip to Spartak Moscow but, by then Rovers, having lost the first four matches, were already out of contention, and the company saved its money. Anyway it was a below-zero freezing cold night in Moscow and in no way did we envy those who made the trip, for some journalists were chilled to the marrow trying to write with lifeless fingers while sitting on the touchline amid packed snow on improvised benches.

The saving grace for me was the air travel, and the delightful turning back of the clock to the Leeds United European journeys, the World Cup games of the 1970s and the rugby league tours of Australasia. Briefly I could savour again the camaraderie of the flights, the pre-match meals and socialising with other broadcasters and star summarisers like Mark Lawrenson and Ian St John. Above all, there was the sense of occasion even when the games ended in anticlimax, and the pleasure of seeing the sights of sounds of Europe.

Meanwhile, although Rovers' exploits and dramatic failures inevitably led the way in the coverage, there were other memorable moments during the high peak of the Red Rose Gold football output in the 1990s. One of the special pleasures of working on local radio, as with a local newspaper, is the sense of belonging, of being part of a community, where daily work means living alongside, mixing with and chatting to people with whom life, activities and sport are common ground.

The detached impartiality of network broadcasting is an essential and necessary discipline, but local radio commentaries allow, indeed demand, loyalty to the 'hometown' club, providing, of course, one avoids going hysterically and foolishly over the top. There was a famous case of the Newcastle reporter who once closed his eyes when the opposition took a vital penalty, saying to his Geordie listeners "I daren't look".

For us at Red Rose it meant that the successes or failures, not just of Blackburn but of our other clubs, were of equal importance. We had listeners and fans in those towns. Consequently there was delight and celebration in the years up to the millennium when Preston North won promotion as Division Three champions in 1996, and as Division Two champions in 2000; when belatedly Blackpool went up from Division Three in 2001; and when Burnley achieved three promotions between 1992 and 2000. For Wigan Athletic the great seasons were still to come with the remarkable Whelan-Jewell revolution, but they, too, gave Red Rose sport something to shout about by winning the Division Three Championship in 1997, having previously won the Freight Rover Trophy, which was for lower division clubs, in 1995.

These later 1990s years were good radio days, putting the traumas of 1992 behind me. And, in late 1999, came another unexpected and amazing uplift. More of that in due course.

John McGrath celebrates a manager of the month award when
he was manager of Preston North End FC. Keith enjoyed
working with him as a co-commentator.
(Photo: *Lancashire Evening Post*)

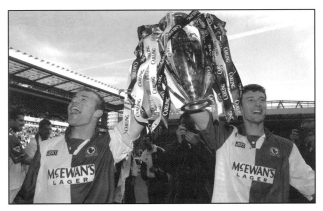

Alan Shearer and Chris Sutton celebrate Blackburn Rovers'
memorable Premier League title triumph in 1995.
(Photo: Action Images)

16. John McGrath

There used to be a poster advertising campaign for a famous bottle of brown sauce which read: "Laughter is the best sauce... We are the next best". This amusing dictum has stayed in my mind because it equates with my own philosophy. While I would never dare to question that great football sage the late Bill Shankly's stated belief that "Some people think football is a matter of life and death. It is much more serious than that," I have always welcomed the chances to lighten the stresses and tensions of sport with its light-hearted moments.

One man who encapsulated this belief was John McGrath. The magazine *Reader's Digest* had a famous regular feature named "The most unforgettable character I have met". This, for me, was John McGrath and I suspect it is true for his former team-mates, his charges when he was manager of Preston North End and for colleagues at Red Rose Radio.

McGrath was truly larger than life. A veritable brick outhouse of a man, he was a fearsome centre-half with Newcastle and Southampton who took no prisoners. As a football summariser he became a cult radio figure with his outrageous statements, excruciating jokes, and a complete inability or unwillingness to engage his brain before opening his mouth. His tragic sudden death was a devastating blow, both personally and professionally.

Big John or simply McGrath, as he was known to us at the radio station, made his name as an old-fashioned 'stopper' who could also terrify defenders when he went up for corners. Fearless himself, he knew how to intimidate opponents. Yet when the match was over the jokes would fly like Saturday night at a comedy club.

He took wicked glee in telling stories about his rumbustuous playing career. His favourite, and the one that sums up his on-field reputation, came from his Newcastle days. The manager was a St James Park legend himself, Joe Harvey.

In his pre-match team talk Joe singled out McGrath: "Big man," he said, "stick close to that centre-forward of theirs. I'm told he's very fast out of the blocks."

"Boss," said McGrath, "how fast does he limp?"

His antics in opposition penalty areas were also a source of, perhaps unworthy, personal pride. He would go up for corner kicks and as the ball came over would set off at a gallop towards the opponents' goalkeeper, roaring the fabled Wild West Red Indian war cry "Geronimo!" Many a keeper quailed at the sight and sound, and one keeper, whom we shall mercifully not name, was so petrified that he stayed on his line as the big man charged in and headed home one of his very occasional goals.

McGrath was not a malicious man and he had great respect for his fellow players, but as a radio summariser his knee-jerk, spontaneous judgements could be both funny and brutal at the same time. There was one Preston North End player, again nameless to spare his blushes, whom McGrath criticised by saying "He's a good defender, but when he passes a ball it carries a note: 'To whom it may concern'."

Sharing a commentary with John was a rollercoaster. You were never sure what he would come out with next. He would have no truck with political correctness or namby-pamby euphemisms. One evening he and Tom Parker did a commentary on Macclesfield Town versus Preston North End, and both Red Rose sports editor Nigel Reed and I were listening. Nigel was in the studio directing operations, I was at home and by the end of the game we were both close to being nervous wrecks.

Playing centre half for Macclesfield was defender Efe Sodje, who achieved minor fame by wearing a colourful bandana on the field. Not for the first time John had difficulty pronouncing this name, and, as he claimed later, Sodje's name was not clearly printed on a hand-corrected Macclesfield team sheet. Whatever the reason, every time Efe touched the ball McGrath called him "Sooty", which in view of the player's colour, could have been misinterpreted by listeners. Both Nigel and I were immediately on the telephone to Tom Parker, telling him to put the big man right, and ultimately the mispronunciation was corrected. The following day Nigel and I were bombarded by complaints and offered genuine apologies to outraged listeners, assuring them that no racial overtones were intended, which was the truth, and that the radio station offered profuse apologies. McGrath, protesting his innocence to the last, said that his error had really been quite apt, since Sodje had been playing as a sweeper.

McGrath was also a relentlessly gregarious man who could talk for England, and once he was in full garrulous flow he lost all sense of time and responsibility. When Tom Parker and I were sharing big game commentaries with John as summariser, we would sit around at road junctions or in motorway station cafés for up to an hour after the appointed rendezvous time waiting for him to turn up. One hair-raising evening on the way to Nottingham Forest's City Ground he was 90 minutes late at the motorway meeting point, and we finally dashed to our press box seats for a 7.00pm opening to the programme and plugged in frantically to get on air at 6.59. Nigel Reed in the studio lost more hair that night.

At a Saturday afternoon game, Sunderland versus Blackburn Rovers, I finished the commentary and while I went to get a Rovers interviewee John said he would see me back at the car in an hour's time. When I got back to the car there was no sign of him, which was not surprising and I switched on the radio to listen to a results programme.

Six o'clock came and went. Then seven o'clock. No sign of McGrath. Knowing that he had little sense of direction and might have gone to another car park, I twice drove slowly round the perimeter of what was than Roker Park and still saw no sign of him. I went back to our own parking place, now in semi-darkness - no John. In desperation now, because I did not want to spend the night in Sunderland searching for a large missing person I went back to the one gate which was still open, though it too was on the point of closing.

Up a flight of stairs there was a bar which still had a few late stayers. One of them told me that the Sunderland manager, Peter Reid, was still in his office down the corridor. I virtually sprinted down there, since Reidy and McGrath were old mates. I knocked, pushed open the door, and walked in. On one side of the desk was a jovial Peter Reid, glass of whisky in hand. On the other a jovial John McGrath, likewise holding a glass.

McGrath turned cheerfully round in his chair, and said with mock concern: "Keith. Where've you been? I was just about to come looking for you".

The big man spent most of his matchdays working with Tom Parker at games involving Preston, the club he had managed between 1986 and 1990. He and Tom were both heartily fond of - indeed they were addicted to - fish and chips, so much so that a lunchtime meal of their favourite delicacy was *de riguer* and just as sailors are reputed to have a girl in every port, they had a favourite chippy in every football town.

At the end of every season they would draw up a league table of the best chippies, and towards the end of the Red Rose period of full Saturday football coverage they produced their definitive top three. They were Wycombe, Torquay and Scunthorpe. The last-named got in because, in addition to being tasty, the fish and chips were served in natty pizza boxes. My own favourites, Crewe and, of course, Grimsby, were lower down the order.

On a visit to Rotherham United John and I broke ranks for the only time and paid the price. For some reason we both chose a mixed grill at a café near Millmoor. Next door was a chippy, and Tom stuck to his guns and ate there. Tom got it right, as both McGrath and I had tummy trouble that weekend. Big John loved his food. In addition to his partiality for fish and chips he enjoyed

143

cooking and frequently hosted huge barbecues of steak, burgers, sausages and onions in his garden at Middleton, near Manchester. His digestive system must have been like a cement mixer. He thought nothing of driving home from an away game late at night and having a private barbecue washed down with beer.

It needs to be said of the big man that, for all his instinctive bluntness and outspoken spontaneity, he was never brutal in his comments on his fellow professionals. He always tried to temper any criticism with humour while making a salient point. When one of the Red Rose teams went through a dreary spell of bad results he said during one particularly dull and unimaginative passage of play that the club's end of season highlights video would be entitled "One hundred best throw-ins".

No one took offence, because players, coaches and directors knew that McGrath spoke and talked at endless length, from experience. Anyway, John was such a huge man, in rugged personality as well as physical presence, that if he said it was Christmas everyone burst into a chorus of *Good King Wenceslas*. There is no doubt that the big man was a major reason for the audience-getting success of the Saturday programme.

Suddenly and dramatically it all came to a tragic end at Christmas 1998. After a pleasant Friday Christmas Day relaxing there was a full set of Saturday Boxing Day fixtures. I was due to report on Blackburn versus Aston Villa at Ewood. Tom and John were in harness at Preston's away game with Stoke. I was short of a small piece of equipment which was in Tom's possession so after an overnight meal with friends at Rainhill I arranged to rendezvous with him at the Post House Hotel at Haydock, near St Helens. In good spirits I set off on the short journey to Haydock for the pre-lunch meeting and handover of equipment.

I drove cheerfully up to the Post House, and saw Tom's car parked on the left. I pulled up behind him expecting him to leap out with his usual alacrity, for chirpy Tom enjoyed everything about football reporting days, even the ear-bashings on the journeys with the garrulous McGrath.

As I wound down the window I noticed that Tom's face was pale and drawn. I said: "What's the matter?" Tom said: "Brace yourself and take a deep breath... the big man's dead."

He then revealed, with total recall, the telephone conversation he had finished a short time earlier with sports editor Nigel Reed. He was driving to Haydock along the East Lancashire Road when his mobile rang. Nigel said: "Pull over as soon as you can I've got some bad news." A few hundred yards ahead was a petrol station, where Tom hurriedly pulled up and grabbed the phone. The conversation went like this.

Nigel: "The big man's dead."

Tom: "What, Keith's dead?" (A reference to my own six-feet-and-a-bit.)

Nigel: "No, McGrath. He collapsed from a heart attack making the Christmas dinner at home yesterday."

The word 'devastating' can be a cliché, but not on this occasion. The vastly larger-than-life McGrath had been the life and soul of Red Rose football, an enormous and inescapable presence. He could not possibly be dead.

But he was, in the most tragic of circumstances. He had prepared the Christmas turkey lunch for his wife and daughter, had gone to take it from the oven ready to carve, and had collapsed and died. It must have been a nightmarish trauma for his wife, who heard the crash and ran into the kitchen. And for those of us who had worked with him for a few short years it was an almost unbelievable shock.

Football lost all relevance and meaning for us that Boxing Day - everything did. Tom paid a heartfelt tribute to his *Little and Large* sparring partner on a telephone line to the studio, and all the reporters went in a daze to their separate matches. But we just went through the motions of reporting and then had to carry out another sad charade with Monday's matches.

There were several moments of pathos. When Tom arrived at the Britannia ground he was surrounded by a large crowd of North End supporters who had left home before the news had broken.

"Where's John McGrath? Is he here today?" they asked. When Tom told them the news they, too, could hardly believe it, and the news swept round the ground like a bushfire. Many players, managers and fans rang the radio station with tributes and memories in the days that followed, and while Red Rose football continued for another season and a half, it would never be quite the same without McGrath's hearty, uninhibited, noisy, jocular and trenchant presence. He is still missed.

****

McGrath supplied most of the humour which pleasantly seasoned our football coverage, but not all of it. We endured one or two other laughable incidents which perhaps were not too funny at the time, but lightened the humourless seriousness that increasingly pervades professional sport. Everton's Goodison Park provided one in a Toffees versus Blackburn commentary game. Again Tom Parker was a central figure and I was sharing the commentary with him. Things started going wrong from the moment we arrived. Although we had booked our seats in the press box, so had dozens of other media outlets, and even though we arrived well before the 3.00pm kick-off, the press area was obviously oversubscribed and there were no seats left.

Desperately we looked around, but in the areas where journalists were willing to make room the seats were too far away from our ISDN transmission point. After much desperate toing and froing we hit upon a solution. In a front row recess next to the central gangway there were two seats reserved for duty policemen. As kick-off neared there were no police officers, so we persuaded the press stewards, with some difficulty, to let us use them, on the proviso that if the bobbies turned up we would move at half time.

We hurried into the seats, got our equipment up and going, and our broadcast commentary went out smoothly for about 25 minutes. Then shock, horror...

The officers arrived to take their seats. While Tom continued the broadcast I pleaded with the men in blue to let us see out the remaining 20 minutes or so. To their credit, the genial Bobbies agreed. But not the stewards. Declaiming that it was written in tablets of stone, and was more than their job was worth and so forth, they descended on Tom, who stoically ignored them and carried on talking into his mic.

I have already indicated that Tom, while big in personality, is slight of stature and vertically challenged. The two burly stewards took one armpit each, yanked him upright out of his seat, his legs dangling a foot above the ground, and dumped him still talking into his mic with wires trailing behind him, in the gangway.

It was a hilarious sight which reduced the press area to a mixture of stupefaction and laughter, with Tom determinedly looking at the pitch and trying to commentate while bobbing up and down like a human yo-yo in the arms of the stewards.

Tom told me later than while he was being manhandled out of his seat, albeit gently, he could hear the chaos in the studio through his earphones, whose cables were also trailing behind. Inevitably all that thousands of Red Rose listeners could hear was a clunking, crashing and banging, the hubbub of alien human voices, and Tom's voice coming loud one minute, then quavery and distant the next. Then there was silence as the line went dead.

Presenter John and producer Nigel in the studio had no idea what had happened at Goodison. John restored calm by pronouncing the catch-all phrase in such circumstances "We appear to have lost our commentary match, so let's get another update from the golf".

With wires and equipment all over the place at Goodison and the two of us eventually perched on the edge of two seats at the back we hired a telephone from a helpful press agency and did the rest of the commentary on the blower. It seems funny now, but it was a chaotic, nerve-jangling experience at the time - one of many such ordeals that every broadcaster who has ever lived can recount.

Another hairy, but funny, moment happened to me at Chesterfield's Saltergate ground during a match against Blackpool. In those days the press box was a cramped edifice with narrow aisles and on the front row was a very dodgy seat. Fate decreed that Tom and I would do our commentary from the front row and, true to form, I got the wobbly seat. However, it held out, and I forgot about the slight discomfort as I opened the second half commentary. Suddenly there were a series of loud cracks as my seat came apart underneath me in mid-sentence. One second I was describing a Blackpool attack, the next I was painfully dumped on my pants and my head cracked against the seat behind me. Tom, resourceful as ever, grabbed the mic and carried on with the commentary, while I must have resembled that classic David Jason pratfall in *Only Fools and Horses* as I climbed sheepishly to my feet, to loud and unsympathetic laughter from fellow journalists.

Two of the most bizarre and risible incidents came from evening matches at York. Preston were the visitors in both fixtures, and both were on freezing cold nights. On the first occasion we arrived at Bootham Crescent in good time, enjoyed the excellent fish and chips from the popular and excellent emporium in a street near the ground and went back to our seats.

As we assembled our ISDN machine we discovered that, seemingly due to the freezing weather, the batteries were flat, we had no spares, and at that early time no other battery-using equipment was in the press box.

Preview time was some 20 minutes away and we could not guarantee that a fellow broadcaster would appear with a sackful of spare batteries. Just as we prepared to let the Red Rose studio know the bad news before looking for a telephone, a weird and wonderful solution came from a fairy godmother in the shape of a lady press photographer who had also arrived early.

Her solution was primitive but simple. Obviously, for the equipment to work, the stone-cold batteries needed to be warmed up. She outlined her plan, and while we felt somewhat sheepish and embarrassed, we accepted her self-sacrificial offer. It was our only faint hope. The lady, whose name wild horses will not drag from me or Tom to protect her blushes, took the batteries to the ladies' room. When she reappeared they had lost their Arctic bite and were warm to the touch. Anxiously and eagerly we put them into the machine. The lights went up. We were on air.

To quieten those readers who may be of a prurient mind, our lady rescuer had placed the freezing batteries inside her upper garments until the chill went out of them. She was the toast of Red Rose Radio that night, and Tom and I remember her affectionately.

On the second York occasion the evening was even colder, with a hint of freezing fog, and this time we had with us two sets of fully tested batteries. As we drove down the long main road towards the turning to Bootham Crescent we got caught in one of the Minster city's occasional monumental traffic crawls. At one stage during that journey our car, driven by *Lancashire Evening Post* sports writer Brian Ellis, was stationary for several minutes. Suddenly the rear passenger door opened and without any attempt at a by-your-leave someone got in and sat next to Tom.

The politically correct way to describe this man would be to say that he seemed to belong to a severely socially-disadvantaged group. His long hair, straggly beard, crumpled clothes and limbs had obviously not been in contact with soap and water for some considerable time. He was, in short, a tramp of the old school, and declared that he would like a lift into town where he would visit an unfortunate friend in hospital. When we explained that we were on our way to watch York City versus Preston North End and would be turning left fairly soon he seemed unfazed and said we could drop him off at the ground. An uncomfortable silence ensued.

On arrival at Bootham Crescent we got out of the car, locked it and bade farewell to our guest as we made our way to the fish and chip shop. On learning where we were going, our dishevelled friend said "Good, you can buy some for me. I haven't eaten for two days."

We placed our usual order, plus one more, at the counter, aware of the distinctly odd looks and uncomfortable shufflings of others in the queue when they spotted our scruffy and unhygienic companion. When we were served, understandably quite hurriedly, he accepted his portion with a muttered "Thanks" and trudged off into the bitterly cold York night. He left behind three journalists who were no wiser as to his identity or history at the end of our acquaintance than we were when he stepped into our car, but it was another oddity that broke the mould of routine.

17. Cricket

Two sports, rugby league and football, have been the bedrock of my time in broadcasting. Because of this my account of the highs and lows, pleasures and frustrations, fulfilments and disillusionments of a sporting journalist's existence has leaned heavily, if inevitably, in the direction of what used to be called winter games, before the seasons overlapped and converged.

Yet it was a hot summer's day at Old Trafford that first kindled the spark of ambition. Over the years the so-called summer game of cricket has provided an oasis of tranquillity, amid bursts of excitement, as an antidote to the frenetic pace of the other sports. That is, of course, until the emergence of novelties like one-day cricket and the frenzied slog-and-run of 20-20.

In most of the 25 years I have spent in and out of the converted Preston church that houses Red Rose Radio some of the happiest, most relaxed and therapeutic days have been spent on sunny Saturday afternoons at traditional one-day cricket in three splendid northern leagues during the few short months between the middle of May and the beginning of August. There were three months of the year in which, in the intervals between Australasian tours and World Cups and other intrusions Saturday sport on Red Rose meant for me a weekly visit to a small, compact ground to join a few hundred cricket lovers sitting on benches, or under trees, with flasks and sandwiches, applauding a team of local amateurs, joiners, policemen, postmen, teachers, as they take the field headed by a big-name, or emerging big name, professional. The Lancashire League, the Northern League and the Ribblesdale League have been, and still are in fact or in memory, as much a part of the summer scene as pie and peas, Morris dancing, brass bands, and Whit walks.

Alas, when the end of full football coverage at Red Rose Gold came just before the millennium, league cricket coverage also made way for summer afternoons of popular music. Visits to Lancashire's lovely spacious grounds such as Rishton, Ramsbottom, Oswaldtwistle Emmanuel, hilly Barnoldswick, sloping Darwen, Blackpool, St Annes and Netherfield, under the ruined castle, became precious rarities.

The matches were, and are, always competitive, whether over 50 overs, 46, or 45, and the quality of the cricket has always been good enough for world-class professionals to come from all over the globe to live among, coach, and play with some very good amateurs, some of whom would go on to greater things. A precocious youngster named Andrew Flintoff was hammering senior players and star pros all round the grounds as a 14-year-old in the Northern League, and counties throughout the Championship have drawn freely on products of league cricket down the years. Two of many who have also made it with Lancashire are Ian Austin and renowned trencherman Jack Simmons. Simmo, latterly chairman of Lancashire, preceded Flintoff in playing for his local club Enfield as a 14-year-old. And from Earby, a tiny village in the east of Lancashire the county recruited a young all-rounder named Glen Chapple, whom I had watched play for his village club in the Ribblesdale League.

Between the two world wars, and for a few years afterwards, league cricket games attracted packed crowds of several thousands to see famous professionals strut their stuff away from the test arenas, and to see if some importunate local bank clerk or truck driver could rattle their cages. Mind you, this was an adventure fraught with danger. The ferocious West Indians Roy Gilchrist, Wes Hall and Charlie Griffith who played Lancashire League in the sixties would make the ball fly and beat a tattoo on the uppity batsman's rib-cage when it was not flying past his ear like a marksman's bullet. They did not enjoy being hit, and it showed, and in one season with Bacup, Griffith took 144 wickets.

Another world famous fast bowler who struck dread into the hearts of even the bravest amateur batsmen was Dennis Lillee, one half of the fearsome Australian combination of Lillee and Jeff Thomson, who had a spell with Haslingden in 1971. Phil Lloyd, a Blackburn local historian, recalls that in his teens he played in the 'Seconds' for East Lancashire, and during one memorable week was told that the team for the coming Saturday was short-handed, and he might achieve his ambition of playing in the first XI. The snag was that the fixture was against Haslingden, and the possibility of facing Lillee gave the 16-year-old Lloyd a sleepless, nervy week at the thought of losing several front teeth so early in life. In trepidation he crept across to the clubhouse in midweek when the team sheet was put up. Half of him wanted to play and be a young, heroic debutant. The other half was trembling at the prospect. To his relief he was not on the sheet, and his debut came in calmer cricketing waters.

During the happy times when I had the privilege of reporting league cricket in the 1980s and early 1990s I recall a cocky young Australian named Shane Warne turning out for Accrington in 1991, and a tall, stylish batsman Steve Waugh - another Australian later to achieve worldwide success and fame - scoring centuries for Nelson in the 1987 season.

However, the one professional who created the biggest and most immediate impact was Allan Donald, the South African fast bowler of lightning pace and instinctive antipathy towards batsman, especially anyone, amateur or professional, who showed timidity.

When he arrived at the small town of Rishton near Blackburn to play in the Lancashire League, I took a microphone to the homely little ground to record an interview. He was helpful and talkative, gave an excellent interview, signed dozens of autographs, and then set about whipping the local lads into shape and winning the league championship.

Donald, a fast bowler who combined pace with accuracy, had some famous battles of will and flesh with Michael Atherton in South Africa versus England tests. However, against the brave, defiant but out-of-their-depth amateurs of the Lancashire League, particularly the middle and lower orders, he wrought havoc.

One near-farcical match remains in the memory. The victims were Accrington at their own Thorneyholme Road ground. Donald's opening onslaught knocked the early batsmen over like skittles in an alley and, at one stage, when the South African whirlwind had taken seven wickets for three runs, it looked as if the game would be over in less than an hour and a half. Somehow, with a few lucky snicks and blind swipes and some lusty hits against the other Rishton bowlers, the demoralised home side scrambled an easily beatable, but not humiliating score. But the sight of the dazed early batsmen trooping back to the pavilion within minutes of walking out was tragi-comedy as Rishton breezed through to another comfortable win on their way to the championship. Today the overseas professionals continue to enliven leagues up and down Britain with their personalities and skills and while crowds have inevitably diminished with the many modern counter-attractions, in particular television, attendances can still move into four figures for local derby fixtures and knockout cup matches.

In the middle of it all laughter has always had its place and that same Accrington ground was the scene of another of those red-faced moments.

It was in 1985 and the professional for Accrington on this occasion was David Lloyd, a local lad who had opened the batting for England with distinction and had played in nine tests. As I recall his 16-year-old son Graham, a batsman who was to follow David into the Lancashire side, was also playing.

Accrington were fielding when, during a quiet passage of play, I decided to go for a gentle stroll around the perimeter of the pitch in between sending the half-hourly score flashes to the radio station. On the way back I must have wandered on to the pitch itself while in a dreamy reverie accentuated by the warm sunshine.

My daydreaming was rudely interrupted by a voice roaring "Hey, you" from somewhere. When I looked for the source of the shout I saw that it came from the centre of the cricket field, where play had stopped and all the white-clad players were looking in one direction - at me.

The source of the shout was none other than 'Bumble' himself, David Lloyd. In his fruitiest Lancashire accent he barked "Gerroff our pitch". I needed no second telling, and sped red-faced back to the pavilion, running the gauntlet of grinning fans.

People have been chortling and laughing at Bumble for many years as a brilliantly funny after-dinner speaker who is a quirkily eccentric but knowledgeable television commentator. I didn't particularly enjoy the embarrassment at the time but I have seen the funny side since.

At this point another confession is necessary. The lure of Saturday afternoon league cricket was not entirely confined to the game itself. As an army is said to march on its stomach, so does the journalist require sustenance to provide inspiration. At least that is my excuse. And sustenance at an afternoon's Lancashire, Northern or Ribblesdale League cricket game meant, and still means, an appreciation of that traditional north-country delicacy, pie and peas. If one was fortunate enough to be invited to have tea with the players or the committee there would be sandwiches and a selection of cakes, but on a walk round the ground the pie-and-pea stall was an essential creature comfort for spectators. Whether the pie's filling was steak or meat and potato, according to taste, it was only complete with a total covering of mushy peas. There were no posh fol-de-rols like vegetables or cheese and onion.

Thus, for a brief spell during the late 1980s and early 1990s, Saturday afternoon became a lads' excellent day out. Friends from schooldays and childhood mates - two Alans, John, Chris, Ken and Geoff - decided that a summer's siesta on the grassy banks or seats, with pie and peas and a pint or large mug of tea, was the perfect antidote to a week of toil. On many Saturdays I had a car full heading to my own, professional choice of game, which could be anywhere from Barnoldswick to Whalley; or Haslingden, or Bacup or, a pie-and-peas favourite, Blackburn's East Lancashire. Needless to say, because I would be doing half-hour reports on the club telephone, there would be no consumption of alcohol for me, and a lot of time would be spent writing notes or consulting scorers. But the others thoroughly enjoyed themselves and I recall a baking afternoon at Whalley when two of them went to sleep on the grass. They were all sad when Red Rose Radio local cricket coverage ended.

No mention of the joys of these salad, and pie, days would be complete without mention of Lancaster Cricket Club. For it was at the spacious Lune Road Northern League ground that I achieved what must be the ultimate in hedonistic, self-indulgent pretence of being at work.

Normally the routine involved a fair measure of walking, primarily to the score box to pick up the detailed minutiae such as bowling analyses, names of fielders taking catches, number of boundaries in a batsman's 100 or 50, and any bits of potted history that might be relevant to the game. Then I would make my way to the allocated telephone in the clubhouse (which could be full of cheerfully noisy drinkers) or a helpful secretary's office.

Sometimes this meant a long trek halfway round the perimeter, or, at the scenic ground of Netherfield - the pitch up the hill from Kendal to Oxenholme - a climb up the pathway on the gentle slope leading to the ruined castle. The scoreboard at the top of this pathway gives a perfect view of the playing area and the countryside and fells beyond, but is a bit of a trek.

Lancaster created none of these physical exertions. In fact, it required no physical exertion whatsoever. The only effort required at the Lune Road ground just a mile or so up from the town centre and railway station was the 100 yards stroll from the car park to the pavilion and dressing rooms.

The warm welcome, customary at all grounds, was extended and then I was shown to the seat where I could file my reports at 30-minute intervals, be provided with information, be fed and watered with frequent cups of tea and remain almost totally undisturbed throughout.

The room was the committee meeting room, which was empty on match days as members preferred to sit in the sun on the veranda. It had its own private telephone on the well-polished table within easy arm's length. The scoreboard, well-equipped with information windows, was just to the left of the pavilion and in full view, and the scorers sent the occasional obliging runner with titbits of information.

Adjacent to the room was a corridor leading to the bar and tea room and toilet facilities. And to cap it off, a lively and friendly tea lady was assigned at regular intervals to come and recharge my cup. There was a dish of biscuits on the table and, at the tea interval, once the players had been served, a plate of small pies, sandwiches and fancy cakes was placed at my disposal. The only exertions required from me were to answer calls of nature.

While at all grounds club officials offered at least a tea interval plate and cup, and were unsparing in their helpfulness, the only other club to provide a full sit-down meal in the committee room, where one could join committee members and wives, was East Lancashire. Over and above the call of hostly duty it certainly was, and obviously I need to make it clear that, despite the sumptuous hospitality at Lancaster, my conscience forbade me to apportion to the club more than its proper allocation of coverage - tempting though.

Cricket in the short, too short, summer months did not consist entirely of league games. To my additional delight, during the *Times* years of 1979-92, I had the pleasure of covering trophy competition one-dayers, and several County Championship matches. These took me around the country, not merely to my beloved Old Trafford, but to Headingley, Middlesbrough, Worcester, Chesterfield, the vast Derby bowl, Southampton and The Oval. Border TV also used me at intervals in the 1980s and 1990s to watch Cumberland play at Netherfield, Barrow, Carlisle and Millom, where welcomes were no less effusive than at league games.

Among the personal highlights which deserve to stand alongside rugby league and football in the hall of memory is one doubly disappointing one. I was reporting for Red Rose at Lord's in 1986 when the great Clive Lloyd, a West Indies giant in every sense, and wonderfully entertaining stroke player and free hitter, played his last first class game for Lancashire in a NatWest Cup Final against Sussex. He was applauded all the way to the wicket by the spectators of both sides and by the Sussex team. Then Dermot Reeve churlishly had Lloyd leg before wicket for a duck. Afterwards one newspaper suggested that Clive was still wiping the tears from his eyes when Reeve did him. It was an unfortunate anticlimax for the big man and Lancashire especially as Sussex went on to win the game and Lancashire's one-day glory years were over.

The cricket years came as a welcome short break in the hectic rugby league and football schedules, and it is a source of considerable personal regret that the boundaries between the sports have now been blurred, if not erased, by round-the-year, and round-the-clock football competitions, club tours and friendlies. We even have the day-night frantic whirl of 20-20 cricket which I think bears as much resemblance to the real game as six-a-side indoor tournaments do to football, but which, in fairness, pulls in big crowds to see bat flung against ball. It is a depressing thought that the County Championship, once the bedrock of the game, now has to struggle to survive, often against enemies from within the game, however unwitting, who demean its importance in preparing tomorrow's test cricketers.

No matter how keen the competition, however important the match, however large or small the crowd, cricket watching is essentially a sporting rest cure from the often overheated angst of other sports.

Of course, the days are long gone when the great humorist writer P.G. Wodehouse wrote of a languid, hot, drowsy game of village cricket where the peaceful afternoon's quietude was only occasionally disturbed by "the uproar of the butterflies flapping their wings in the adjoining meadow".

Nevertheless, the relaxed, patient enjoyment of a genuine contest involving bat, ball and fielders against a backcloth of cloudless sky is still a restorative to the soul and a blessed escape from an increasingly chaotic, noisy, and cynical world. If only the questionable practice of giving a cushion of central contracts to England players could be amended to allow star players to appear more often for their counties, the Championship could then be resuscitated and made more popular, and we could avoid farcical situations such as those where Darren Gough played little or no part in a championship year with Yorkshire, and a crowd-pleaser like Lancashire's Andrew Flintoff makes only token appearances for his native county.

Keith's greatest rugby league players

Top: Alex Murphy in action for St Helens (Courtesy Alex Service).
Left: Neil Fox practicing kicking. (Courtesy Robert Gate).
Right: Ellery Hanley packing down for Great Britain against Australia
in the 1992 World Cup Final at Wembley (Photo: David Williams).

18. Back to football

If 1992 had been the *annus horribilis* of my career to date, 1999 was the *annus mirabilis*. It produced a chain of events, all stemming from a chance, casual conversation with a veteran colleague.

At the start of 1999 I was happily plying my trade primarily with rugby league reports and commentaries with local radio - both commercial and BBC - and filming on television with Border. By the end of the year I was back reporting football on ITV, and by 2001 I was doing post-match interviews for the Saturday evening and Sunday morning Premiership highlights programme hosted by Des Lynam on the full ITV Network.

The casual conversation was at a pre-season press conference. The eventful years of head-to-head commentaries between Red Rose and Radio Lancashire were over and Saturdays were not quite the same, though some match reports had continued. I said as much to Tom Tyrrell, for years the voice of Manchester United with Piccadilly Radio, and a well-established freelance. Tom said he was working for the newly launched ITV2 channel, which had a Saturday afternoon live show *Football First* on cable and digital. He said the network was looking for match reporters and suggested I got in touch. Suddenly the clock was turned back more than three decades as I dropped a line to ITV's top man in sport, Brian Barwick, who had moved over after building a big reputation with BBC Sport, and is now chief executive of the FA.

As one of nature's pragmatists, or even pessimists, I half expected a politely worded rejection slip. Instead, within days I got a reply from Brian saying that he welcomed the letter and had passed my name on to the producer of *Football First*, Mark Schofield.

A few days later I got a letter from Mark, welcoming me aboard, and immediately offering a couple of games, Stoke City versus Oxford United and Liverpool versus Watford at Anfield. It all happened within a fortnight of the half-time chat with Tom Tyrrell, and is dreamlike even in retrospect.

To coin yet another cliché, I felt I needed to pinch myself to ensure that this was not one of those wish-fulfilment dreams that evaporate dismally on waking. For the first time since 1976 I was back reporting football on ITV national network sport. The divinity that shapes our ends was working positively again. It stayed that way for four very happy and professionally satisfying years, culminating in that brief, heady return to the full ITV network where ITV would go head-to-head with *Grandstand* and *Final Score*

157

on BBC, and replace the opposition's flagship *Match of the Day* with ITV's *The Premiership*. And, to cap it all, I would round off the weekends with rugby league on GMR.

Despite the decades of accumulated experience, the apprehension I felt on that Saturday afternoon in August 1999 rivalled that of February 1956. I had settled into a comfort zone of local radio and Border television rugby league, football and the summer afternoon delights of league cricket. Now I would be back reporting on a live national television programme with the challenge of winning over not merely a new audience but also, and equally importantly, a national network sports department and producer.

And, no matter how long a career has lasted, there is always the nagging question at the back-of-the-mind, semi-neurotic but always present: will the equipment work when I switch on?

It was therefore an almost eerie feeling as I got out of my car and walked up to the spanking new Britannia Stadium in Stoke. I still felt it hard to believe that I would soon be asking for an ITV press pass at the ticket office, but it happened, I took the envelope and walked up to Stoke City's commodious new press box, shouldering the new equipment.

The next hurdle to be climbed was a major psychological one. Machines and I have never been particularly compatible and at times there seems to be a mutual hate/hate relationship. *Football First* producer Mark Schofield had sent me by motorcycle courier a different type of ISDN broadcasting unit, larger and with different configurations, and there was a new set of instructions to put into operation for the first time. Pragmatic pessimism gripped me again and I was convinced that somewhere along the line I would press the wrong button or key, or get out of sequence and hear that silence, or continuous howl, that tells you the dial-up has failed.

With quavering fingers I went through the half-dozen or so phases of button pressing from the sequence written down on the inside lid of the ISDN.

There was a pause.

Don't panic. It takes a few seconds …

Eureka - the machine lights went up and a cheery female voice at the other end chirruped "Football First". It felt like the first sight of land by Captain Bligh and the cast-adrift crew of The Bounty.

The game itself, won 2-1 by Oxford, was not exactly a sparkler, and because the programme understandably concentrated on Premiership matches I contributed only about five short reports. In one I attempted to make a joke about the Stoke mascot, a red and white hippo, being called Hippo-Pottermus, which dropped like a concrete balloon in the studio. I also recall an oddity in the match when the referee stopped Hippo-Pottermus running up and down the touchline because he was confusing him with the players and on one occasion blew up for offside.

After the final whistle the same cheery voice of the production assistant passed on a "well done" from Mark Schofield, and the car journey home was a much more buoyant and less anxious one than the journey down. I had got over the first hurdle, always the hardest one, and the next game would take me back to schoolboy days and the headed winner for Prescot School. It was Liverpool versus Watford at Anfield.

Over the years I had made a host of trips to my boyhood shrine to follow Leeds United for Yorkshire Television and Blackburn for Red Rose and to do the occasional report for *The Times*. The end of the radio Saturday sports programme had, however, seemed to pull the curtain down finally, yet the latest twist of fate had steered me back to my theatre of memories: recollections of Arsenal's Ray Kennedy and Alan Ball imperiously controlling midfield in a midweek match where Liverpool's failure to win gave Don Revie and Leeds United the League Championship in 1974; and of the anxious wait for the final whistle to blow at West Ham when the ultra-professional Liverpool had beaten Blackburn 2-1 and could have snuffed out Rovers' and Jack Walker's dream in 1995.

Now I was back again and it was a great feeling, even if the nervousness was there again about handling the new, bulkier ISDN with its new configurations and instructions. Fortunately the system worked again, Liverpool were surprisingly beaten 1-0 by Watford, Tommy Mooney scoring, and the only real problem was the familiar but cramped press box. Liverpool are one of the world's great clubs in every conceivable sense, but for radio people with cumbersome equipment to assemble it can be a bit of a nightmare, at times resembling an overcrowded lift.

It was most certainly a nightmare at a later ITV game at Anfield. The match was against Charlton - by now the programme title was *The Goal Rush* and I was settled as part of the ITV reporting team. It was a pleasantly sunny day and all was right with the world - that is, until I made my way up to the press box to find the radio area full to overflowing, with not a seat anywhere, and the bench crowded with sardine-packed ISDNs. This was an unexpected setback and when I sought out Ian Cotton, the Anfield head of press and PR he sympathised but pointed out that no press pass had been asked for by ITV. That was the start of a sequence of events that ranks with anything I have experienced in terms of sustained mental stress over three and a half hours.

When I informed Mark Schofield of the situation by telephone to the studio he asked to speak to Ian Cotton in his office and, after what I imagine was a frank exchange of views a compromise was reached, though it was hardly a comfortable one for me. By now the whole press box was full, with not a square inch of space to be seen. There was nowhere to sit and nowhere to plug in my machine. To the rescue came Tom Tyrrell who had first introduced me to ITV2, and Ian Cotton. It was agreed with Tom, who was working for Today FM in Ireland, that before the game, at half-time and at full-time he would do his pieces, then close down and dial up *The Goal Rush*, and let me do my reports, before redialling Today FM. It was a kindly fraternal gesture, happily quite common among radio reporters, but one big problem remained: where was I going to sit?

Ian Cotton, after much thought, came up with a bizarre lifeline. In doing so, he bent club policy, probably for the first and only time, and for that I will be forever grateful. I would be allowed to watch the game at the entrance to the players' tunnel, on the pitch side, a holy of holies, and when I needed to do my preview, half-time and full-time pieces I could dash upstairs. Tom would then unplug and redial, I would do a quick 45 seconds or so and then I would dash down again to the tunnel with yet another helpful human being, a pitch side steward, providing a safe passage and escort.

By the end of the afternoon I was close to being a physical and nervous wreck. The game, which Liverpool won 3-0 if I remember rightly, passed in a breathless and confused blur and ITV got their reports, even if they were slightly rushed and truncated ones.

It was yet another Anfield occasion to store in memory, though on the debit side, and my thanks go to all those who baled me out. Happily, the problem in communication between programme and club was sorted out and later visits went smoothly.

The only other game which provided acute discomfort, this time mainly of the physical kind, was ironically at Stoke's Britannia Stadium where I had made my comeback debut.

This time it was a weather problem. It was one of those depths-of-winter games between November and February when advance weather forecasts are anxiously scanned, fixtures go down like ninepins after morning inspections and the only games reasonably safe are at grounds with underground heating.

Snow had fallen overnight in the north and midlands, but the weather information, and radio lists of postponed fixtures, indicated that the Stoke game was still on. So I set off early from Blackburn and got on to a snowy motorway which was down to two lanes and even one lane at times, because of packed snow.

Progress was slow but steady until just past Crewe. Then the snowfalls came back and got heavier, and the traffic ground to a crawl and occasional halt. I telephoned the studio, explained the situation, and got the encouraging message "Get there when you can".

The clock was flying round, the snow was coming down steadily and I waited for the radio sports bulletins to add Stoke to the postponed fixtures. But no, the ground staff had apparently worked minor miracles, and the match was on. So I ploughed on, literally, through snow and ice.

I turned the final corner to the Britannia Stadium in a queue of white-coated vehicles at 2.55pm. Cars were parked, or dumped, all over the place, and there was no point in trying to get to an official car park. I found a space down a lane about half a mile from the ground, jumped out of the car, grabbed the equipment, went through the motions of locking the car and trudged, skidding frequently, up to the ground. It is a spacious press box at the Britannia, but it is also pretty high up, and I was half-frozen when I dialled up and got through to the studio. Fortunately, no goals had been scored and I probably had not been missed.

The game, and the result, eludes my memory, but not the journey home after the game. By the time I had wrapped up and got out of the stadium the shades of night had fallen fast, the wind was biting and I slipped and skidded down to the country lane and my snowbound car.

As you will certainly have gathered, I was feeling extremely cold, extremely low-spirited and extremely sorry for myself. But worse was to come. The car lock was part frozen, and took about 15 minutes to let me in. Then, when I shivered into the driving seat and looked to the left I saw that the passenger seat window was wide open and letting in a fearsome blast of icy air. So I pressed the automatic button to close it. It was frozen stiff, and would not budge.

There was nothing else for it. I would have to drive nearly 100 miles home on a bitterly cold night with the freezing wind blasting through the open window. I had an overcoat and cap on, the heater mercifully was working, but neither was a match for the remorseless wind, and when, nearly two hours later, I arrived home I was convinced that I was in the fatal last stages of hypothermia.

So perhaps I may be forgiven if my memories of games at Stoke - the nervous second debut for ITV and the night I nearly died of hypothermia - are not, pardon the pun, of the warmest. Perhaps I should arrange to do a match in mid-May to exorcise the memory.

Other memories from the three and a bit seasons with *The Goal Rush* on ITV1 are infinitely more comfortable and easier to store. With Yorkshire Television and Red Rose the assignments had of necessity been regionalised. With the ITV network I could theoretically go anywhere, although on one rare weekend when there were few league fixtures available Mark Schofield decided not to send me to Torquay because it seemed a long way to travel, and he wanted to spare me the journey.

There were several dramatic games, and dramatic moments; those times when being a reporter takes on special significance over and above the simple 30-second retailing of facts. There was the occasion at Goodison Park when Paolo Di Canio, then playing with West Ham, displayed a remarkable and unexpected streak of the kind of sportsmanship that is now presumed to be dead or moribund in today's ruthlessly professional sporting climate.

Some way into the second half with both sides pushing for victory, West Ham launched an attack down their right hand side. Paul Gerrard, the Everton goalkeeper, dashed to the edge of his area, and was injured as he collided with a Hammers attacker. As Gerrard lay prone outside the area, the ball was crossed and Di Canio had a simple chance in front of goal. But he had obviously seen Gerrard's plight, and deliberately caught the ball.

It was a rare and remarkable gesture, though what you might expect from a player who won a FIFA Fair Play Award in 2001. Whether it endeared him to his team-mates and travelling West Ham fans is open to conjecture, but it may have helped cleanse Di Canio's reputation after his notorious push on referee Paul Alcock when he was playing for Sheffield Wednesday.

One of the minor hazards of live broadcasting almost cost me dearly in a match between Middlesbrough and Leeds United. I can still shudder at the thought of how close I came to being caught with the proverbial trousers down.

In order to be able to do half-time and full-time reports, and even the occasional update, with factual accuracy, it is necessary to scribble down key events like scoring movements, near and bad misses and individual moments of brilliance. This means a few seconds, sometimes a little more, in which one's eyes are detached from the play to make the note, and you have to choose the right time to do this. An injury, a ticking-off from the referee, or a desultory passage of play all present opportunities to jot a note or two. Having just finished an update for *The Goal Rush* I decided to freshen up the notes while very little seemed to be happening on the pitch.

Almost in a trance of concentration I heard the voice of studio presenter Angus Scott in my headphones. He was saying, in crisp, dramatic tones, something like this: "He's been sent off already this season... and now, after that suspension, he's done it again ..."

As I wondered who Angus was referring to I looked up. Just below me Alan Smith, then of Leeds United, was walking down the players' tunnel... "Let's get the details of his latest misdemeanour from Keith Macklin at The Riverside."

Help! What had Smithy done while I was scribbling my note? The deity came to my aid again. As Angus spoke the last few words of the cue I looked at the pitch and there on the ground, writhing in pain, was Boro's Gareth Southgate.

Somehow, without pausing or waffling, I managed to frame a coherent sentence: "Yes Angus, Alan Smith is off again. And as he walks down the tunnel just below me his victim of another rash tackle, Gareth Southgate, is writhing about on the Riverside turf in the centre of the pitch". I gave the latest score as a cue back to the studio and Angus and the panel of experts gave their verdicts on the latest Alan Smith rush of blood.

It was a very, very close call. The thought of having to admit that I hadn't seen it, or being heard off microphone asking press box colleagues a panicky "What happened?" still brings me out in a sweat, for it is the type of clanger that sticks in a listener's memory, and gets no plaudits from an annoyed producer.

Such instances are common, and I have yet to meet colleagues who cannot recall moments when they wanted the earth to open up and swallow them. Thankfully, they can be laughed at with the passage of time. Another potentially embarrassing on-air moment was much less harmful, but nonetheless provided a studio hiatus. It was at Manchester City's Maine Road ground, and during a quiet spell in the second half a colleague in the front row made an extremely funny remark, so funny that I have completely forgotten its context. However, journalists in the vicinity, myself included, burst into howls of laughter, which drowned the fact that *The Goal Rush* presenter had decided to cue me, unexpectedly, out of turn. When the studio turned up my microphone all they heard was a loud roar of communal laughter, led by my own raucous basso profundo. It startled everyone in the studio, indeed it made the sound engineer jump.

The director quickly pulled out and I heard a voice say: "There's obviously something funny going on at Maine Road. We'll find out later". Rather shamefacedly, I sent my off-microphone apologies down to the production and sound rooms and tried to offer an explanation. Shortly afterwards I was cued again for a report, with the presenter apologising for the earlier burst of mirth, and I thought the matter was forgotten. However, Mark Schofield rang the following week to ask if he and the rest of the staff could share the joke but, as always it fell flat as a pancake on retelling.

Occasionally - thankfully very occasionally - mistakes happen which affect other innocent parties and these are a cause of considerable embarrassment. One that I unwittingly perpetrated was at another Everton game at Goodison. The match reports seemed to go well and, after recording an interview with David Moyes in the ground floor television room, I returned to my seat in the press box to unplug the equipment and drive home. A lot of wires and plugs are involved and much winding of coils, but at last there were just two things left to do - pull out the three-point electrical supply plug for the ISDN machine and pack up. The plugs are underneath the press box benches so I did the usual scrabbling movement down below and stood up, plug in hand. Suddenly I heard anxious shouting from the row in front. There was Frank Stapleton, one of many famous players turned reporter and summariser, waving his arms about manically and shouting "Hello... hello... hello. The line's gone dead".

It was obviously not my plug and lead I was holding. Quick as the proverbial flash I stooped and pressed the plug into the point it had just vacated. As Frank shouted with relief down the line to his producer "Someone must have cut me off", I decided not to do the cowardly thing, though it was a huge temptation, to decamp upstairs to the anonymity of the press room. I waited until he had finished, made a grovelling and shamefaced apology and, to his credit Frank waved the apologies aside and said "We've all done it". This is true, but it is still embarrassing to be the culprit.

Mind you, it's probably worse to be on the receiving end. My mind goes back a decade or two to a rugby league match I was covering for local radio. I think it was Widnes versus Halifax and playing for Widnes that day was Robin Whitfield, later to become a first-grade referee.

The game was a closely fought one and it came to a climax that is every reporter's dream. Widnes levelled the scores with a try in the last seconds and the attempted conversion from the left touchline, which would win the game if successful, would be the last action. The studio presenter cued me in and in a right lather of excitement I set it up: "This crucial last kick of the game from Whitfield... all the home fans are holding their breath", and so on and so forth. Then, suddenly and horribly, the line went dead. As Whitfield's kick sailed through the posts the listeners at home heard nothing, just radio silence. What an anticlimax. When I looked around in disappointment and anger I saw the shame-filled face of John Stringer, former Leigh RLFC secretary, then doing a spot of reporting. In the excitement of that last minute his feet had threshed about under the table, pulling out my plug. As Frank Stapleton said so many years later at Goodison: "We've all done it".

But to return to the early millennium years with ITV, an all too short period of time in which four years sped by as if they were a single season. It was great to be back on Saturday network television alongside general sport with Red Rose in midweek and Sunday afternoons of rugby league with BBC GMR, but the fun was destined not to last.

For a while the expensive ITV venture opened up several television channels with extensive football coverage in live action and in features. These covered not only the Premiership but, also the lower divisions, who were promised considerable sums of money for the rights to film matches and record interviews.

The honeymoon did not last long. ITV, amid legal wrangling, threats of court action, and considerable ill-feeling, pulled out of the deals with lower division clubs, causing financial distress to many clubs who had budgeted and spent their promised television money. Saturday afternoon's *The Goal Rush* had held up reasonably well against the powerful opposition from BBC's *Grandstand* and Sky's comprehensive coverage and the well-entrenched and smoothly professional *Final Score* also on BBC. *The Premiership* on Saturday nights struggled to get audiences in the early evening, but got a tidy share later in the evening with a show which lost little in comparison with the BBC's *Match of the Day,* which it replaced.

However, the shows were draining ITV coffers and at Christmas 2003 *The Goal Rush* was summarily axed, later to be followed by its senior partner *The Premiership* as the BBC reclaimed the flagship highlights programme. It was a shattering blow for Mark Schofield who had created and built up the afternoon programme, and for all of us working on it. We had expected at least to see out the 2003-4 season. Instead we were gone with the last of the Christmas turkey.

It was a huge blow and personal disappointment, but recriminations were pointless. Life is like that, and always will be, and it was certainly not the end of the world. Indeed, there was still plenty going on in the bedrock world of radio. Sundays were happily occupied with rugby league, and in the north-west football world the Red Rose teams were providing their followers and the media with some cliffhanging moments, some happy others, alas, deflatingly unhappy.

Wigan Athletic provided the most up-and-down roller-coaster ride with the most joyous of landings. The club which had gone out of existence as Wigan Borough in 1930 had come back into the Football League in 1978 to lead a humdrum hand-to-mouth existence in the lower divisions. This all changed when the sports-mad owner of JJB Sports, Dave Whelan, took over the club, along with Wigan Warriors rugby league and Orrell rugby union clubs, and lured the ebullient and straight-talking scouser Paul Jewell to the JJB Stadium as manager in 2001.

When Whelan declared shortly after the appointment of Jewell that the Latics would work their way up to the promised land of the Premiership within three to four years people marvelled or laughed at his seemingly cockeyed optimism. But in May 2005 I had the thrill of reporting from the JJB Stadium on a dream and a prophecy come true. Wigan beat Steve Coppell's Reading 3-1 and leapt the final hurdle into the Premiership. There were ecstatic scenes on and around the JJB as the football club, so long under the shadow of Wigan rugby league club's dominance, carved out their own niche at long last. Dave Whelan's ebullient interview called it "The greatest day in Wigan Athletic's history".

The following year a little more icing on that considerable Latics cake was a first major trophy final appearance in the Carling Cup, though it ended in a 4-0 defeat by Manchester United.

Blackburn Rovers, under Graeme Souness, gave their loyal supporters something to shout about at the climax of the 2002 season. Rovers had suffered the indignity of relegation and a season in Division One before Souness took them back to the top flight. They were total underdogs to Glenn Hoddle's Tottenham Hotspur in the Football League Cup Final at Cardiff, but with talisman of success Mark Hughes in the side they shocked Spurs, and opinion outside Blackburn, with a 2-1 win before 72,500 at the Millennium Stadium. Less fortunate have been Preston North End, who have been destined for the role of bridesmaids four times after working their way into the play-offs and losing to Bolton and West Ham after reaching the final match.

Along the Fylde Coast at Blackpool, the Tangerines kept spirits alive as long-absent supporters came out of holes in the ground in their thousands to see them win two Football League Trophy finals under Steve McMahon in the early post-millennium years. Then, in 2007, came an achievement that dwarfed these minor triumphs, of which more later.

All these successes, near-successes and gallant failures made reporting a bitter-sweet experience. However, from an unlikely source came a true Cinderella story, almost rivalling in football terms the recent film about James J. Braddock, the boxer who came back from the depths to win the World Heavyweight Boxing Championship in the 1930s.

More than 20 years ago there was a popular and wickedly funny television commercial featuring two small boys wearing Liverpool FC jerseys and speaking in scouse accents. One was drinking milk, the subject of the commercial, while the other was drinking fizzy pop. The lad proudly quaffing milk said "Ian Rush says people who don't drink milk end up playing for Accrington Stanley". It was a cruel, if funny, barb against the club from the small Lancashire town who had gone bankrupt and quit the Football League midway through the 1961-62 season.

In 2005 Accrington Stanley laid that television joke to rest, and others of a similar ilk, when the revived club, managed by John Coleman, fought its way through the football pyramid, topped the Nationwide Conference and came back into the League. Rock FM and Magic 999 had a big football story to tell, and we reported those ecstatic closing games of the season. It was like the good Saturdays of the 1990s again.

A vast amount of the credit for this remarkable Accy resurrection must go to Eric Whalley, yet another self-made Lancashire businessman. While not possessing the vast wealth and huge business substructure of his Blackburn neighbour, the late Jack Walker, Eric poured his own money, time, organisational ability and physical effort - working together with a small but loyal staff - into transforming an impoverished club playing in lower semi-pro leagues before sparse attendances into a Football League Division Two side again.

On a warm, bright summer's day in August 2006 I had the pleasure of talking to Eric Whalley about his hopes for the new beginning and the new season at the tiny ground - crowd limit just over 5,000 – which was situated down a lane just off a major road outside Accrington. In a typically forthright interview he revealed that Stanley needed home crowds of around 2,000 to break even. A worldwide fan club buying memorabilia would help keep the club afloat as would a six-figure pay off from Blackpool for the sell-on of striker Brett Ormerod to Southampton. Stanley drew a plum Carling Cup home tie against Nottingham Forest, won it, and then were drawn at Watford, losing, agonisingly, 6-5 in a penalty shoot-out.

For a time the team seemed to be making an immediate impact on Division Two, but the loss of influential players to bigger clubs and a mid-season slump had them hanging on grimly against relegation in the closing weeks of the season. But they finally clinched safety with a last-gasp home win against Paul Ince's Macclesfield, and ensured at least one more season in the Football League.

The year 2007 saw mixed fortunes for the clubs within radio microphone range, with the balance happily on the positive side in both rugby league and football. In the BBC Radio Merseyside and Manchester areas of the XIII-a-side code St Helens again set the benchmarks, Wigan, despite having a mixed season including a four points deduction for salary cap breaches, got the top six, and Widnes, my home and base for 22 years were challenging at the top of National League One.

I also had the pleasure, via Radio Cumbria, of paying a nostalgic return visit to dear, battered old Craven Park at Barrow, the springboard of my broadcasting career in 1956. It was good to turn the clock back and see the Division 2 club continue its determined efforts to bring back the good days under the enthusiastic coaching of local man Paul Crarey, a former player.

In football the Red Rose clubs provided a great conclusion to the season, and managerial interviews were filled with optimism instead of tailing away into anticlimax. Sadly, Preston North End's Paul Simpson drew the short straw, as the Lilywhites, after a storming start to the season, missed out on the play-offs on the last day of the season. Wigan, too, had a low-key ending as they narrowly escaped relegation and their normally ebullient and resilient manager Paul Jewell resigned.

Elsewhere, there were celebrations. Blackburn Rovers, after an indifferent injury hit start to the season, came back splendidly under the shrewd and purposeful management of Mark Hughes. A late unbeaten run took them into the Intertoto Cup, which some affect to despise, but which led Rovers back into the UEFA Cup.

Joy was unconfined at Blackpool, where the Tangerines, so long in the doldrums and the shadows of Matthews and Mortensen and the heroics of 1953, were boosted by a big injection of Latvian cash from magnate Valery Belokon and swept on an irresistible tide under manager Simon Grayson to a Wembley victory over Yeovil in the play-offs and a return to the second tier of English football for the first time since 1981. In brutally stark contrast the struggling Division 2 rugby league club Blackpool Panthers slumped to the bottom of the table.

If Grayson was overjoyed, his Wembley celebrations were humorously overshadowed by the antics of the manager of the football team in Blackpool's neighbouring and rival Lancashire resort Morecambe. They entered the Football League for the first time in their history by beating Exeter City, and their chirpy Irish manager Sammy McIlroy stole the show with an act of pure pantomime and comedy.

When Morecambe's winning goal flew into the net late in the game the former Manchester United inside forward and Northern Ireland manager could not restrain himself. Like an exuberant schoolboy he raced on to the pitch to hug a celebrating Shrimps player, and the momentum saw him swing round and round and tumble acrobatically to the ground. He immediately bounced up like a rubber ball, only to be knocked down by another Morecambe player rushing to join the celebrations. Again the animated rubber ball that was Sammy McIlroy rolled and bounced up, still waving his arms. Charlie Chaplin could not have bettered it, it is pure slapstick, and it is a television moment for the comedy archives.

Finally, in cricket Lancashire challenged for their first County Championship title for over 70 years, but lost out on the last day of the season, falling short by 25 runs in a dramatic day long run chase against Surrey at The Oval.

****

Amid the professional swings and roundabouts of the early years of the 21st century there was one deep personal sadness. In February 2005 our younger daughter Tracy, victim from early childhood of a slow but remorseless degenerative condition that eventually left her totally paralysed with the mind of a child, died overnight in a Widnes nursing home whose staff had worked round the clock to make her last days as comfortable as humanly possible. The previous evening, when her mother and I left Tracy after visiting, she had said goodbye with the only two means of communication left to her: her eyes and her smile.

We have placed a bench and a plaque to her memory in the gardens of her favourite spot, Norton Priory, across the bridge near Runcorn, and we go there often and sit for a while.

Left:
Keith after being
presented with his degree
certificate from the
University of Lancashire in

Below:
The grandchildren, Daniel
and Elizabeth.

19. Reflections on rugby league

While the last decade of the 20th century and the first decade of the 21st brought renewed activity in football coverage, and a few summers of cricket to provide an essential counterbalance, there was vigorous and dramatic movement on the rugby league front. I was able to watch and report at all levels of the sport with four radio stations, Red Rose, Radio Leeds, GMR now Radio Manchester, and West Yorkshire Classic Gold in Bradford.

The launch of summer rugby and Super League in 1996 was a seismic explosion within the game, irreversibly changing the century-old traditional patterns, practices and habits despite initial doubts, debates and pockets of resistance. Some older supporters steeped in 100 years of Northern Union and Rugby Football League winter fixtures, where standing in caps, scarves and overcoats on rainy, windswept, icy and occasionally snow-covered terraces from November to February was the norm, opposed the move to summer rugby. They did so out of a mixture of physical hardiness, ingrained tradition, and the unshakeable belief that rugby league was a winter sport played between August and May, with the Challenge Cup at Wembley at the end of the season the crowning glory. Summer months were for summer sports like cricket, golf and tennis, and for taking annual holidays while looking forward to the pre-season friendlies and the restart in August. Anyway, they suggested, the players would surely collapse with exhaustion or dehydration on baking hot days.

These were honestly held views, but the counter-arguments, and particularly the massive financial input of initially BSkyB, then Sky, swept opposition aside. One particularly irresistible argument in favour of summer rugby, alongside the fact that not everybody found that standing on freezing terraces created the right atmosphere, was that fewer games, if any, would be postponed through foul weather, frost and snow.

Super League did not catch on without teething troubles and some bitter opposition from all traditionalists and supporters of clubs who were left out of the favoured mix. There were grumbles about the fact that matches were played on Friday, Saturday and Sunday evenings, and often at weird and wonderful starting times between 6.05pm and 8.05pm depending on Sky programming schedules. There were occasional late morning and lunchtime kick-offs too, and fans would have to consult Teletext, radio and newspapers to find out exactly when matches would start.

From the comfortable certainties of Sunday afternoon, with matches slotted neatly between normal Sabbath activities, time-honoured match-going routines were thrown haywire, and rugby league as 'the family sport' changed its shape as top clubs like St Helens, Wigan, Bradford and Leeds opted for regular Friday night slots with the certainty of television games and income.

Human beings are, however, resilient creatures and it has to be admitted that the Friday to Sunday weekend has taken off. Attendances, which stuttered originally to reach pre-Super League norms, now fill venues like Hull's KC Stadium, Wigan's JJB Stadium, Headingley and Bradford even when matches are on television and receiving the excellent presentation, direction and commentary treatment provided by Sky. This has grown in quality year by year, though with, in my opinion, some tendency to over-decorate the cake, a subject for later discussion.

Yet this very success of Super League has produced a downside, one that I have been able to witness at first hand. This has been the steady and inexorable undernourishment bordering on starvation of the lower division teams outside the Super League cartel. Admittedly, when Super League was launched, clubs outside the initial frame received reasonably generous one-off funding and relegated clubs receive so-called parachute payments. But so many clubs were either deep in debt, or spent the money unwisely that the cash has disappeared like water down a plughole.

In recent years, the popularity and growth of television rugby league and television funding and sponsorship from the well-packaged Super League weekend programming has meant that the rich have got richer and the poor have got poorer. It would be churlish and futile to cavil about the former, but it is also right to regret the latter. For the game of rugby league will surely shrink and decay in its own heartland, the north of England, if clubs are allowed to go into liquidation while others cream off the fruits from handsome television payments and the lucrative sponsorships and spin-offs that go with Super League status. These have bankrolled some successful clubs into the luxuries of full-time professionalism and sophisticated development of new and existing stadia.

All this is marvellous news if the long-term aim of the Rugby Football League is the establishment of an isolated 12 or 14 team Super League, undisturbed by intrusions from promotion and relegation systems. However, if the broader picture, as it surely should, remains one of consolidation and expansion, then clubs outside Super League, most of them in proud, self-contained towns with strong community spirit, need to feel part of the overall picture, not mere hangers-on kept in existence by directors putting in their own cash, plus hard-working and often overworked staff and volunteers.

In the 2007 *Rugby League Annual Review* David Hinchliffe, former MP for Wakefield, an avid rugby league fan and lifelong supporter of Wakefield Trinity, had some trenchant opinions to offer on promotion and relegation in an article titled *"Closed Shop – Super League and the Soul of the Game".*

He says: "...the prospect of a Super League closed shop in the very near future seems to me... to be against the best traditions and philosophy of the game."

David adds that he can understand the Super League clubs' self-centred point of view that relegation causes "short-term thinking within the clubs concerned, whose sole objective is to avoid going down". But afterwards he states that "the fear of relegation... is a consequence of the game's collective failure to champion the relevance, importance and quality of the lower leagues."

David's article then enters ground already strongly asserted in this chapter: "We have had some full-time squads within National League One, and I believe the game should be aiming to create an environment within that League where it would be possible for all competing clubs to move in that direction... Pulling up the drawbridge and leaving National League clubs to sink or swim simply isn't the answer."

On this question of promotion and relegation David is again on the same bandwagon as me. He states that "the drama ...is surely integral to attracting media and public interest in any sport" and makes the salient and crucial point that when neighbours Wakefield and Castleford met in the final league fixture of 2006 to decide who stayed up and who went down the gates were closed on more than 11,000 spectators, and many more watched on television (and on nearby rooftops). This sort of cliff-hanger finish to a season could not happen without promotion and relegation, a system, by the way, which has always been an integral part of association football.

It may well be claimed that the RFL cannot be expected to pour good money after bad and constantly bale out insolvent clubs. Yet a more equitable share of television and other major funding plus more input into marketing of the National Leagues might save the life of several once-successful clubs and avoid terminal meltdown of rugby league in some communities, while Super League thrives and prospers. Rugby league will never unseat football or rugby union in popularity in certain major cities throughout the north-east, midlands and south. And to allow this splendid game, the most consistently exciting of all sports, to wither away in its heartland of Lancashire, Yorkshire and Cumbria would diminish the sport rather than strengthen it. We could end up with a competition with a top six monotonously competing for trophies while the bottom six fill out the fixtures, and Super League could become as tediously predictable as Scotland's Premier League, dominated annually by Celtic and Rangers.

Against this background local radio station live commentaries in particular, and local evening and daily papers with previews, team news and reports have kept the National Leagues alive where regional and national television and newspapers would have left them dead or dying. Some national newspapers ignore the results at weekends and on Monday mornings; others tuck them away in the 'other weekend results' section. Yet some of the most exciting and keenly contested matches games I have seen in recent years have been at grounds like Barrow, Doncaster, Hull KR, Oldham, Rochdale, Swinton and Whitehaven. And where would former top teams and trophy winners in Castleford, Featherstone, Halifax, Hull KR, Leigh, Widnes and Workington Town be now if only Super League existed?

These traditionally deep-rooted and once famous clubs have found a life-giving source of publicity through the Sunday afternoon live transmissions of commentaries and reports on community and area-based radio stations. The BBC blazed the trail in the 1970s and new independent stations rallied effectively to the flag, only to falter and fade out of the picture in recent years when cost-saving and financial viability became more important than public service broadcasting, which has always been the remit of the BBC anyway.

The role which local, as opposed to network, radio has played in keeping alive the XIII-a-side game in the lower divisions was discussed in an article in the monthly *Rugby League World* by Mike Latham. Among the trailblazers when the BBC had the radio field to themselves before 1972 were Radio Leeds and Radio Merseyside in 1967, with Blackburn and Manchester following close behind in 1972. One of the pioneers in XIII-a-side coverage was John Helm who, like me has also combined both rugby league and association football in a long career in both radio and television. In those early days John recalls a working day when he would start at 9am with one of the cumbersome old tape recorders and drive round to do match preview interviews at Leeds, Bradford, Halifax, Wakefield, Batley and Dewsbury, often meeting the part-time coaches and players at their places of work. Then, at the weekend, all the matches would be covered by reporters who included Peter Ward, Tim Heley, Jack Wainwright and Harry Gration, with Ron Hill, a prominent player himself, later joining the team to become lead commentator.

When John Helm's career took him to Yorkshire Television John Boyd put in a long stint as anchorman and until comparatively recently Radio Leeds has provided saturation reporter and commentator coverage of all the teams in the station's geographical area, though, alas, some cutbacks have been made.

A similar pattern emerged on the west sided of the Pennines with Radio Merseyside and then Radio Manchester. From the 1970s onwards Merseyside had the late Gerry Burrows, Ray French and me up front, and I have had the privilege of joining Ray, Alan Rooney and Steve Roberts from time to time as they feature St Helens, Warrington, Widnes and Wigan. In earlier years Merseyside also followed the many lives and manifestations of the now defunct club that was called numerous names, including Liverpool City, Huyton, Runcorn and Prescot.

Manchester has carried the torch for a host of teams in a big population area. They share coverage with Merseyside at Warrington, Wigan, Widnes and St Helens, and have to themselves Salford, Leigh, Oldham, Rochdale and Swinton. It is a huge remit but well covered by a team led by Jack Dearden, though here, too, there are rumours of cutbacks.

BBC stations Humberside and Cumbria, with fewer clubs to cover, deserve particularly high praise for filling their weekend schedules with hours of rugby league programming. In Cumbria the pattern of using former players as commentators made local household names of Ron Morgan and Ivor Kelland, though sadly these stalwarts are no longer with us. Cumbria's coverage is all the more praiseworthy for the fact that they have no Super League club representation.

Radio Manchester's Jack Dearden believes and affirms strongly that local radio has, in his own favourite phrase "kept the faith", particularly with struggling lower division clubs when the game was slumping in popularity in the late 1970s and early 1980s. Jack knows all about keeping the faith. His own favourite club, Oldham Roughyeds, failed to win a game in 2006, yet both he, and Radio Manchester, continued to give them regular airtime.

Recent years have seen the emergence of new commercial stations which have joined their BBC rivals in giving excellent coverage of the game at all levels, but have often pulled out after promising starts, and left the field clear for the BBC while retaining interviews and news items.

The twin stations Rock FM and Magic 999 do not provide a match reporting service, much to my own personal regret, but regular press conference interviews at Wigan Warriors are used both on the wavelengths and on their website. Similarly BBC Radio Lancashire, while eschewing actual match reporting, has a rugby league magazine programme in midweek.

All these local radio outlets together provide a large network of coverage - not merely of the glamorous, high-profile and self-centred world of Super League - but where publicity is needed most as an essential aid to survival. Without them the future of the National Leagues would be bleak indeed.

After all the years in which local radio kept the flag flying for live match coverage outside Super League, television has only recently come to life with a prize-winning programme *Rugby League Raw*, which covered the closing stages of the promotion play-offs in a manner which, though extremely professional, concentrated as much on the dramas behind the action, expletives and all, as on the action itself. Many saw it as earthy, gripping viewing; whether it improved attendances at National League grounds throughout the following season is open to genuine debate.

It would be unjust to ignore other occasional life-saving crumbs, and drip-feeds from on high that have helped many lower division clubs stay barely alive. These include the sponsored trophy competition which has acted as a curtain-raiser at the beginning of recent seasons, though the sums of money have been miniscule compared with the millions poured into Super League.

In a welcome new development Sky TV has launched regular Thursday live coverage of the National Leagues, which could help boost empty or dwindling coffers. Again, however, the fees offered for staging games are not astronomical or likely to turn rags into riches. They are nevertheless welcome to clubs existing often from week to week. These include clubs like Oldham, who less than a decade ago were in Super League, but who nearly went bust in 2006, and would have done so but for the sterling input of chairman Chris Hamilton and his fellow directors, and some unexpected benevolence from the Inland Revenue in the matter of debt enforcement. Many other First and Second Division clubs could easily tell a similar tale, notably Halifax, who came very close to extinction last season after budgeting shortfalls.

Ironically, while National League clubs struggle to make ends meet, all is by no means lost on the expansion front. The number of clubs playing in the 2007 Rugby League Conference in its 10th season reached a record total of 88, and a glance down the list of registered teams gives rise not merely to optimism but also to wide-eyed wonderment. Some of the towns and districts embracing the once parochial northern game would have been greeted with sheer disbelief less than a generation ago. Leagues exist from Scotland throughout England and into Wales, with National League Three becoming re-named Rugby League Conference National, and a welcome financial boost was provided by the sponsorship of United Co-operatives.

It seems to stretch credulity that teams now playing rugby league, albeit at the lowest, evolving level of the pyramid, include names like Moray Eels, Port Talbot Steelers, Leicester Phoenix, Bristol Sonics, North Wales Coasters, Broadstairs Bulldogs, Whitley Bay Barbarians and Somerset Vikings. Some of the 88 may not survive, but the fact that they exist at all is a huge tribute to the pioneering work of a host of enthusiastic newcomers at playing and organising levels.

Nor, in talking about continuing survival and success stories, should the strength of the traditional northern amateur game be overlooked. Despite stormy interludes when the leaders of the professional game and their BARLA counterparts locked horns and splits appeared in the ranks, the amateur game thrives in the Cumbria, Lancashire and Yorkshire heartlands of the game, with highly competitive multi-divisional leagues, promotion and relegation and magnificently dedicated officials at all levels. The roots of rugby league remain healthy. Super League goes from strength to strength. More's the pity then, that in the middle, the National Leagues struggle, although their attendances in 2007 did show an increase.

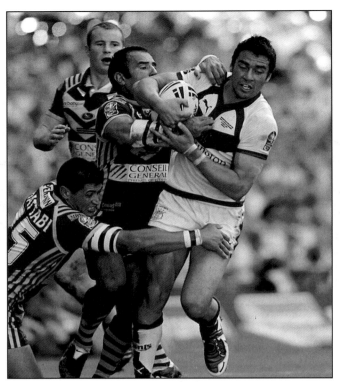

Ade Gardner fights off three Catalans defenders in the 2007
Challenge Cup Final, the big match's return to Wembley.
(Photo: David Williams).

Keith's ISDN machine – an essential piece of equipment
for a radio broadcaster. (Photo: Peter Lush)

20. Looking back...

Looking back over half a century or more carries with it an inevitable danger - the risk that a hazy, rose-tinted glow of nostalgia will lull the mind away from reality in comparing present with past, and create a misguided sentimentality.

I have tried to avoid falling into this trap because people, attitudes, styles, manners and mores change continually, sometimes for the better and sometimes for the worse, and the world of sport goes with the flow.

When I did my first nervous rugby league commentary in 1956 teams were playing on pitches and in stadia which were already more than half a century old. Before the advent of regular television coverage the XIII-a-side game was ignored outside its northern enclave, and despised in entrenched rugby union circles for its cloth-capped professionalism. Those players who dared switch codes for filthy lucre became outcasts and sporting lepers, particularly in Wales, where even favourite sons of the principality's union sides risked total ostracism before and after their treachery.

Within rugby league's northern boundaries big crowds attended the most attractive fixtures, with up to 47,000 watching Wigan versus St Helens derbies at Central Park. Once a year the populace of London realised that rugby league existed as crowds which eventually reached 95,000 swarmed to Wembley Stadium. A few columns of grudging space were found in national and London-based newspapers, and British Movietone News would show a couple of minutes of highlights in the cinema with a plumy voiceover. Anyone who predicted that by the millennium there would be full-time professionalism and vast amounts of live television coverage would have been directed to the nearest lunatic asylum or psychiatrist.

Players, even top internationals, were part-timers, with the luckier ones, such as star imports from Australasia and Wales, given well-paid sinecure jobs by club directors which allowed them unlimited time off for training and playing. The less lucky worked a full week in a factory, office or coal mine, trained in the evenings, and got a match fee sometimes as low as £5 whose value may have topped up the weekly wage packet but would be laughed out of court as pocket money by today's top professionals. A small win bonus would also help the housekeeping budget, but in no way contributed to a luxury lifestyle.

The standing joke in the then busy Lancashire, Yorkshire and Cumbrian coalfields was that any club coach or director whose team was below strength for a Saturday fixture would go to the nearest pithead, wait for a cageful of burly miners to come up from the day shift, and sign them on. The funny thing is that there was more than a smidgen of truth about the joke.

At most clubs daytime training was out because it meant players, and usually the coach, having to miss a shift, or a half day's work in the factory or office. At some clubs a week's training would consist of a couple of evenings of ball work, followed by half a dozen laps of the pitch, and for the less conscientious a pint or two at the local.

Many of what were euphemistically called 'medical rooms' were little more than small huts with basic, and by today's standards, primitive equipment. Players frequently played through the pain barrier after a rub-down and an injection or two, and in later life this caught up with them in the form of arthritis or a related complaint. I well remember, as many older Leeds players and supporters will, a huge man named Arthur Clues who came from Australia as a back-row forward and became one of the most fearsome and respected enforcers in the game. No one threw a punch at 'Cluesy' and survived to tell the tale. Indeed, when French forward Edouard Ponsinet in a France versus Other Nationalities international match caught him off guard at a high kick-off and laid him out, Arthur waited for the return game at Headingley, eyeballed Ponsinet at the kick-off and told him in no uncertain terms what was going to happen. Edouard did not wait for the retribution. Ponsinet turned and fled from the pitch, up and along the terraces and sought refuge in a locked French dressing room. According to Arthur they later became great friends and visited each others' homes.

In later years Arthur was a summariser with me at many broadcast commentaries and it was sad to see him hobble up and down the steps to the radio box. His knees were gone, riddled with arthritis, and those mighty arms little better. Nor was he the only former player before or since to face this painful situation in middle and later life.

Nowadays, and thankfully so, Super League clubs and many in the lower echelons have large and sophisticated fitness centres and medical treatment rooms, spacious, well-lit and ventilated, containing state-of-the-art equipment and staffed by experts in medical care and fitness training. Players are subjected to rigorous testing before being pronounced fit to play after injury or illness. No wonder today's top players seem to have the speed of Derby winners and the stamina and endurance of Olympic marathon runners.

Therefore, because of these facts of sporting life and several other reasons, it is futile to draw comparisons between the game and its players in earlier years and in the 21st century. Many a pub debate centres round arguments about great players and teams of yesteryear and those of today. The outstanding performers of the past, from Harold Wagstaff, Albert Rosenfeld, Johnny Ring, Martin Hodgson and Alf Ellaby through Billy Ivison, Brian Bevan, Lionel Cooper and on to Alec Murphy, Billy Boston, Neil Fox, Lewis Jones Eric Ashton, Vince Karalius and many more were just as talented, tough and skilful as this generation's crowd idols in Shaun Edwards, Ellery Hanley, Martin Offiah, Mike and Andy Gregory, Paul Sculthorpe, Andy Farrell and their peers. Yesterday's legends were they to be magically restored to today's game, would adapt their natural skills and fitness levels and would shine just as brightly.

However, one effect of the lightning speed of today's game is that there is little room for yesteryear's so-called 'ball player' who made up for lack of pace with a combination of low cunning and sleight of hand. Billy Ivison, Steve 'Knocker' Norton, Brian McTigue, John Whiteley, Vince Karalius, Mike Stephenson and their ilk were not the fastest of forwards but could produce a delayed pass, an outrageous dummy or a last-second offload from behind the tackler which opened up gaps in the tightest of defences, and in the days when the emphasis on sound defence was at least equal to that placed on attacking flair this type of forward could break many a torrid stalemate.

To bring a lighter note to this topic I recall Albert Blan, skipper of the fluent Swinton side which won back-to-back championships in their early sixties heyday at dear old Station Road. While the most spectacular contributions came from the superbly quick three-quarter line of John Speed, Bobby Fleet (how aptly named these two were), Alan Buckley and Johnny Stopford, the architect of so many tries was Albert Blan. He was not the fastest of players, indeed quite the reverse. Albert was so slow that when he came from behind a scrum, would-be tacklers would collide before he even reached them. Other defenders would hold back, waiting to see if he would kick, feint to pass, pass to the right, pass to the left, or suddenly accelerate, which to Albert amounted to breaking into a brisk walk.

There is an apocryphal joke about him that I must attribute to Mick Morgan's after-dinner repertoire. During the second half of a game at Station Road a tortoise amused the spectators by plodding gently up the touchline. Suddenly Blanny gave the tortoise a kick which sent the poor creature up into the stands. Shocked team-mates and opposition players rushed across to rebuke him for an act of wanton cruelty to a harmless creature. "Well," said Albert. "The b****y thing's been following me around all afternoon".

181

It was a joke, but not too far from the truth about the type of forward for whom speed alone was not the essence. It is a moot point whether there can be room in today's game for such a player, for there is no doubt that a combination of high fitness levels, full-time professionalism, advanced coaching techniques and attack-favouring law changes like the six-tackle rule and the 10-metre separation between defence and attack after a tackle puts constant emphasis on speed of thought and movement.

One result of this is the rise in the number of tries scored as the result of kicks on the fifth or final tackle. Defences are always vulnerable to the high, hanging cross-kick, or the quick, awkwardly bouncing grubber, occasionally touched down by a speedy back who is marginally offside and whose early anticipation can beat the watchful eye of the referee or the television cameras.

There are other laws which swing the emphasis towards attack and one in particular is, to my mind, counterproductive, because it is completely anti-competitive in its impact on a game. It is the kick-off after a score, which sees the conceding side kick back to the scorers. My apologies to those who have heard this view several times from this quarter, but I have yet to hear anyone give a convincing justification for it. In recent years several scores of more than 70 points and more than 100 in at least one minor Challenge Cup tie have made farces of matches - great fun for the wining side, but humiliating for the losers and not the kind of game or result that pulls in the crowds.

Instead of producing a game of continuing ebb and flow in a truly competitive manner this law can enable a side which is temporarily on top to come back again and again against rattled opponents and put themselves virtually out of sight on the scoreboard. Its worst influence is that many a tight game, most noticeably in Super League, can last no more than 77 or 78 minutes, because the team which has just taken the lead can use up the remaining time taking the conversion kick, and then exercising the age-old tactic of 'tucking it up the jersey' for five tackles before hammering it deep and tackling out the remaining seconds. If the kick-off were from scoring side to conceding side there would still be time for a comeback and a thrilling finish, rather than anticlimax.

Another law favouring attack whose wisdom eludes me is that which allows the completion of six tackles to the attacking side when an attacker gets over the line but is held up by a splendid or desperate last-ditch tackle. It seems ludicrously unfair that such great defence should be rewarded by the ball being handed back to the opposition for the remaining tackles to try again in an attempt to have a second bite of the cherry.

One of the broader issues and problems already touched upon affects not merely rugby league but also association football. This is the growing prospect that, as the annually successful clubs become richer and more successful, the also-rans will become poorer, and supporters increasingly more disillusioned. Dave Whelan, who owns both Wigan Warriors and Wigan Athletic, has called for a salary cap in the round ball game similar to that operating in rugby league in the perhaps highly optimistic hope that this might somehow rein in the cartel of Manchester United, Chelsea, Arsenal and Liverpool annually carving up the trophies between them. Other big names in football, while not directly supporting the Whelan salary-cap scheme, echoed his fears about endless dominance slowly killing the game in a *Daily Mail* feature headed "New Firm: New Danger", a reference to the tedious Old Firm Celtic - Rangers stranglehold in Scotland. Among those names were managers Howard Wilkinson, Neil Warnock, Stuart Pearce and Aidy Boothroyd.

A trenchant, and scathingly witty, article in the *Daily Telegraph* by columnist Tony Francis concentrated on the current dominance of Manchester United and Chelsea. Francis said: "The English game is a duopoly masquerading as a competition... the top end patently couldn't care less about the rest. It hasn't dawned on them that United, Chelsea, Liverpool and Arsenal will have to play among themselves before long. There'll be nobody else around."

If we substitute the names St Helens, Leeds, Bradford and Wigan for the four top football clubs we have the same potentially menacing phenomenon slowly taking shape in rugby league. No doubt the very welcome Sky TV gravy train will be running for some years yet, but how long before clubs outside the top four - six if you throw in spirited but token challenges from the likes of Warrington and Hull FC - lose heart.

There has to be an acknowledgement that at the top end of the rugby league pyramid crowds are healthy and television and radio coverage plentiful, professional and enthusiastic, even if there are lengthening shadows elsewhere. And it goes without saying that I have enjoyed more than half a century of privileged broadcasting, and beg leave to offer a few observations about the life and art, if it dares call itself an art, of sports commentary, which, like the games it has described, has undergone changes and faced new challenges.

In rugby league a whole new terminology has emerged, much of it due to the influence of Australian coaches and players. Whereas, not too long ago, players used to pass the ball to each other, now they are more likely to offload it, though this term seems to mean a pass from within a tackle rather than in the open. We also have interchanges for substitutes.

Also irritating is the practice of referring to a drop goal as a field goal, which makes no sense, because a drop goal describes exactly what happens, the player dropping the ball to his feet before placing it through the posts, whereas a field goal is meaningless in that all goals are kicked from within the field of play.

An element of mathematics has come into the vocabulary with players 'running the angles'; there is a new word for describing good tactical thinking as 'smart', and an amusing statistical word is 'busts', which apparently means tackle-breaking rather than a sculpture. They all add new texture to the coaches' armoury.

Football commentators have also had to expand and modernise their dictionaries of useful words and phrases, even more dramatically than their rugby league opposite numbers, thanks to the drastic changes in team formations and patterns of play. Sir Alf Ramsey is credited with being the founder of new-style football with his World Cup-winning side of 1966, the so-called 'Wingless Wonders'. Before then, and certainly until well after the Second World War, teams played with a goalkeeper, two full backs, three half backs, and five forwards, most of whom had specialised roles.

The full-backs and centre-halves were primarily defenders, the wing-halves helped out in defence, but were the link between defence and attack. The inside-forwards supplied the wingers and centre forward, and the winger's primary role was to provide the centres and crosses for the goal scorers. Players knew their place, and didn't roam around the field looking for the ball.

For reporters and particularly commentators, identification was much easier, with 2 and 3 being the full-backs, 4, 5 and 6 the half-backs, and 7 to 11 the forwards from right to left. In fact it was written in stone that your main goalscorer, the centre-forward, wore the number 9 shirt, and number 5 was a burly centre-half. Number 9 was synonymous with Dixie Dean, Jackie Milburn, Tommy Lawton and all the great target men, and while such as Alan Shearer have maintained the tradition, squad numbers have now blurred the issue of identification all over the field, with hurried reference to team sheets and programmes to quickly name who the number 32 is that is coming on for number 15. This problem applies also to Super League, though happily the traditional 1 to 13 or 1 to 17 with substitutes still largely applies in the National Leagues.

Another significant development in football has been the emergence of an entirely new position, an all-purpose player called the midfielder, who has single-handedly made the roles of wing-halves, wingers and inside-forwards redundant, and can also fill in at full-back where required. There are attacking midfielders, defensive midfielders, right-sided midfielders, central midfielders, and left-sided midfielders.

When a year or two ago I mentioned the term 'winger' to a famous former international player who was then managing a Premiership club he tartly replied: "There are no wingers in today's game". It made me wonder what roles Stuart Ripley and Jason Wilcox had played in Blackburn Rovers' Premiership winning side of 1994-95, providing the supply line for the great Shearer-Sutton partnership. And what term would be applied to such as George Best, Stanley Matthews, Tom Finney, Duncan McKenzie, Frank Worthington and other ball-playing wizards if they were around today? What role has the seemingly ageless Ryan Giggs played in 15 years of Manchester United success? And does Ronaldo really get all those goals from midfield?

Midfielders? Jim Royle of TV's *Royle Family* would have a short, sharp answer to that one. But the term is here to stay, and commentators have had to adapt to it and live with it.

Knowledge of mathematical formulae has become essential for today's football commentator with the evolution of tactical formations. These can be 3-4-3, 3-5-2, 3-5-1, 4-4-2, or 4-3-3, which makes them sound like the wheel structures of old-fashioned steam locomotives as collected by train spotters. There is also a new and subtle position, that of 'sitting in the hole behind the front two' which conjures up all kinds of comic images. Fortunately these days there is always an expert former player summariser around to help out.

There is undoubtedly the belief that such technical guidance is of help to viewers or listeners, though I imagine most would be content to have the action described, the scorers identified and the score given. Ultimately too, it would be expected that the winning side would be the one with the better players, rather than the more impressive mathematical formation.

There have been changes in styles of play; changes, most certainly for the better in stadium architecture and spectator comfort, though the latter seems to come at an increasingly exorbitant price for the family fan. And certainly there have been huge changes in all professional sports in the pay and lifestyles of the players, altering changes in the relationship between themselves, the media and fans. Before the Second World War, in the 1950s and well into the 1960s players' contracts and wages were worth only a fraction of the astronomical sums demanded at today's top level. Rugby league players were part-timers, football players - stars and journeymen alike - were on a maximum wage of £20 a week until 1961, and rugby union players were, theoretically

185

amateurs, though with generous expenses and, allegedly, something called 'boot money'.

Reporters and commentators were given open access to clubs and players, and struck up many friendships and easy-going relationships which created mutual trust. This still exists, thankfully, in rugby league, the most open and family friendly of all sports. I cannot speak of rugby union since I see so little of it, but football at the highest Premiership levels, has become exclusive and secretive. Players are shielded from the media, except via strictly regulated press conferences, and the new breed of multimillionaire players, complete with security-guarded mansions, flash jewellery, watches and top-of-the-range cars are virtually unapproachable behind designer sunglasses and i-pods.

Fortunately, during a long stint on local radio in Lancashire, I have found that the friendly family theme still applies at Blackburn, Wigan, Preston, Blackpool and Accrington football clubs, and certainly at all rugby league clubs, but there is no longer the freedom for accredited journalists to amble in and out of grounds and training centres to have a friendly chat with whoever might be around. The new breed of press officers, who have the unenviable task of pleasing both club managers and the media corps, walk a thankless tightrope, and, minor irritants apart, do it well.

Other factors in football reporting not envisaged half a century ago, affect both commentators and supporters. Local identity, even national identity, has disappeared from programme team lists. And shouting for the Reds or the Blues away from home sounds silly when the away strip is black or yellow, thanks to the requirements of the merchandising department.

Another sphere of change - a much more personal as well as professional one - is in what is politely referred to as journalistic dress code. When, as a nervous and tentative sprog reporter fresh from national service, I walked into the *Warrington Guardian* offices in Sankey Street and met the editor Reg Thompson, he completed his interrogation with a stern injunction: "Always come to work dressed as if at any moment you might be sent out to interview the Prime Minister or the Archbishop of Canterbury. First impressions are very important if you want to get a good story".

Times and attitudes may have changed considerably since the 1950s, and so-called dress codes have relaxed but the grain of truth in that advice has, for better or worse, stayed with me perhaps to the point of pedantry - though not to the point where I would follow the example of Stuart Hibberd, the once famous senior BBC newsreader of the 1930s, who wore evening dress to read the main evening news bulletin on radio.

It is obviously not a view which is universally shared and it would be ludicrous to take part in a television outside broadcast on a beach on a baking summer's day clad in full evening dress or sober suit and tie. Nevertheless the wheel seems to have turned full circle nowadays, and nowhere more than in that former bastion of traditional values and correctness, the BBC. Before I seem to have backed myself into a solitary corner I can quote a reader's letter published in the *Daily Mail* in April 2007. The letter was from Pat Stewart of New Romney in Kent, and was brief, to the point, and pertinent to this discussion:

"Ties coming back into fashion? That doesn't seem to be the case on the BBC. Most of the reporters look as though they're dressed to sell the *Big Issue*." Anyone disposed to quarrel with this comment at the time of writing who has access in particular to the continuous *News 24* would see ample endorsement of the viewpoint. Call it a pedantic conditioned reflex if you like, but I myself have winced at the sight of reporters covering bomb outrages, civil wars, murder investigations, floods and other natural disasters and major criminal trials looking as if they have just had a stroll on the beach or left a pint or gin and tonic on the bar to rush out and do a quick piece. The tieless and jacketless look demeans, to me, the serious weight of the story.

It is much the same in sport. BBC *Match of the Day* and Wimbledon presenters have abandoned suit and tie to adopt the open-neck, self-consciously laid-back and casual look, though John McEnroe, who seemed to have been arm-twisted to adopt Pat Cash's designer-casual mode, looks comfortable again in suit and tie. At both national and regional level some presenters look as if they've just got out of bed and haven't had time to comb their hair.

Gary Lineker, Alan Hansen and Mark Lawrenson do adopt a smart suit and tie to present FA Cup and major European match coverage, but the overall presentation ethos of the BBC's output hints strongly at a dress-down policy, perhaps from top brass edict.

It needs to be said that the dress question has nothing to do with the intrinsic quality of the broadcasting output, and the professional knowledge and on-air skills of all the major networks are on a par in their presentations. Nevertheless, the sartorial battle lines have undoubtedly been drawn.

Consequently, in May 2007 I was pleasantly surprised to see that, at the World Snooker Championship Final at The Crucible in Sheffield the admirable all-rounder Ray Stubbs - a former colleague at Radio Merseyside in his formative years - and star summarisers Steve Davis and John Parrott, who had adopted the prevailing shirt-sleeve order throughout the tournament, gave a true sense of occasion by wearing dinner jackets and bow ties. It took me back to the 1960s and 1970s, when Davis, Parrott, and other champions in John Pulman, John Spencer, Terry Griffiths and Ray Reardon were in their pomp. Every player in the tournament then wore dress suit and tie at the table, and snooker was the best-dressed sport outside backgammon at a Victorian gentlemen's club.

No doubt there is a vigorous modern counter-argument in favour of the casual look, suggesting that the bulk of the television audience will probably be wearing it. However, there is little doubt in my mind that, consciously or subconsciously, viewers see their sporting pundits as figures of knowledge and authority, not just other blokes sounding off on the adjoining bar stools, and expect them to dress accordingly. No one ever saw David Coleman or Harry Carpenter in open-neck shirt or spiky hair during the impressive television sports heyday of *Grandstand* and *Sportsnight*.

The contrast is noticeable in studio and outside broadcast front-of-camera presentation, with Sky and ITV opting for smart, and the BBC opting for smart casual and occasionally dress-down.

Richard Keys and Andy Gray at games, and Jeff Stelling and company on *Saturday Sport* do it for football, though Matt le Tissier remains compulsively tieless. In rugby league Eddie Hemmings, Mike Stephenson, Phil Clarke and colleagues lend the dapper touch against the laid back casual look of the summarisers with Clare Balding on BBC's Challenge Cup games.

In rugby union there are the same contrasting styles with Simon Lazenby, Dewi Morris, Scott Quinnell and Simon Barnes adopting the trim jacket and tie look against the trendy casual of John Inverdale, Jeremy Guscott and Jonathan Davies on BBC and Jim Rosenthal and company on ITV's Rugby Union World Cup coverage.

Test cricket is now a no-contest area, with Sky's monopoly giving the channel a controversial uncontested run, unfair in my view to terrestrial viewers. But here again David Gower, Sir Ian Botham, Mike Atherton, Nasser Hussain, David Lloyd and international guests set standards both sartorially and in authority which would be hard to improve.

Obviously for me Reg Thompson's 1951 guideline on professional dress etiquette has gone deep enough to stand the test of time and shifting social attitudes, perhaps stubbornly so. Maybe some thorough research will be undertaken among a wide representative sample of viewers and listeners to come up with some kind of opinion pattern. Or perhaps the differing dress codes are irrelevant provided acceptable and objective judgements and common sense are seen and heard coming out of screen and radio.

It needs to be reiterated that today's television coverage of sport, despite individually perceived blemishes, is on all channels light years ahead of the formative early days of the 1950s, 1960s and 1970s. Much of the credit must go to Sky and, for example, the latest visual aid in rugby of a graphic diagram of the goalposts from the view of the goalkicker is brilliantly informative.

The need, or compulsion, to modernise and change is as rampant behind the cameras as it is in front, and as someone for whom technicalities have always been a closed book and no-go area I have the greatest admiration and respect for the technicians and production staff who actually put programmes on air. Sky in particular, with their massive battery of strategically placed cameras, but also BBC and ITV, have made huge and welcome strides in on-air action presentation.

That said, I wonder, as a viewer and listener, whether the search for progress, advancement in technology and experimentation in format have not in certain instances gone too far, with innovation for its own sake rather than for improvement. One such development, now the norm on Sky TV's coverage of Super League, and BBC Challenge Cup games, is the practice of putting a live microphone on the referee during matches. The idea behind it is presumably to ensure that when a puzzling, contentious or difficult ruling is made the viewers, and the commentators, hear the referee's explanation. This is sound thinking, though the crowds on terraces and in grandstands manage quite well without it.

However, when the referee's microphone remains switched on throughout, and the official's voice is coming through loud and clear, there is frequently a clash between the commentary and the bellowed orders of the man-in-the-middle, with commentary often drowned. A compromise would be to bring up the referee's mic only when one of the really debatable decisions is made.

Another widespread bone of contention is the video referee. It is the subject most talked and argued about, in other sports as well as in rugby league. The majority verdict is that it is an excellent idea, especially when the validity of a try is being questioned, and its presence in Super League has certainly helped the referee to make the correct ruling on most of the occasions when it has been called for. Its success in rugby may yet pave the way for limited use of the video referee in football goal-line debates.

There is, however, an unfortunate side effect, one which was actually seized upon in print by a rugby union observer, BBC sports presenter John Inverdale, in a *Daily Telegraph* column. Inverdale made the point - one to which I and perhaps many others readily subscribe - that the video referee was introduced to assist the referee when there is genuine and often considerable doubt as to a try's validity. Yet many referees seem to regard it as a prop or pair of crutches on which to lean. As Inverdale's article stated, the video ref is often called upon when it is "blindingly obvious" that a try has been scored; and in addition it often seems to take minutes and dozens of replays from every conceivable angle before the inevitable decision is arrived at. How on earth great middlemen like Charlie Appleton, Eric Clay, Billy Thompson and Fred Lindop lived and won respect without it I do not know, although they did not have to contend with endless replays and saturation television coverage. One referee and two touch judges are surely enough for all except the most controversial cases.

Having already, as a viewer, acknowledged the huge strides made in technical equipment, production and presentation since what a mischievous colleague described as "the horse-drawn days" of television and radio, I have just one more gripe. And this is the opening and particularly closing title sequences of some, but not all, sports programmes. These used to contain coherent, crisp, relevant and informative highlights, and with long-running shows like *Grandstand*, *Match of the Day*, and events like Wimbledon, test cricket, show jumping, snooker and dear old *Ski Sunday*, they were accompanied by tuneful, catchy signature music which was so instantly recognisable that anyone who heard the pleasant, hummable tune knew exactly which programme it belonged to. The tunes became so familiar and popular that they were published on disc and tape compilations and sold commercially. BBC Radio's *Sports Report* still has such a cheerful, bouncy, individual signature tune, and listeners know exactly when it is five o'clock on Saturday.

Nowadays, particularly with closing action sequences, we are more likely to get exercises in technical wizardry from producers, editors and sound mixers who seem more anxious to show off their state-of-the-art visual conjuring tricks, backed by the latest grindingly tuneless rock group, than to inform and satisfyingly round off a highlights and title sequence. The action replay images of goals, tries, and tennis shots, are distorted, and fly past the eyes in a manic blur; the credits flash on and off the screen at an unreadably fast speed (a disease rampant throughout most television programmes), and the half-second images are backed by rock music tracks. The whole exercise looks and sounds like a series of pop videos designed for teenagers with the attention span of gnats. Clever? Undoubtedly. Helpful? A matter of opinion.

With traditional normal speed closing credits, however sharply edited, it is possible to have missed a game, and arrived home just in time to grab them, and still work out the score and what happened. With the new look, helter-skelter whirl of shots it is much harder, although the last shot usually features the winner. Credit where it's due; the excellent BBC closing coverage of Wimbledon 2007 - a montage of shots with the classic ballad *Let there be love* - was spot on.

21. And finally

Vast changes have been made in Britain's social, industrial and domestic life during the decades since the end of the Second World War, and particularly since I made my first beginner's entry into broadcasting in 1956. There have been big changes, too, in sport, with football, once dubbed 'the beautiful game' becoming a multibillion pound global industry rather than a mere sporting exercise. It was once played for fun as well as for pittance wages; nowadays it is a very serious business, with the fun element removed by the relentless search for success and its attendant riches and fame.

Rugby league has become, through vast and professional television exposure, a major sport in its own right, capable at the highest levels of Super League and test matches of pulling huge crowds and providing, in the considered opinion of this observer, the finest and most consistent sporting entertainment to be found anywhere in the world.

Consequently, as with football, a new breed of XIII-a-side player has evolved, a full-time professional whose speed, strength and athleticism have consigned the pit shaft, cloth-cap and clogs image to history. They, too, are financially well rewarded, though their salaries are nowhere near the ridiculous amounts paid to top footballers.

But not everything has changed in my own half-century in broadcasting. In the 1960s I lived in a bungalow overlooking the last hole and clubhouse of Widnes Golf Club, and retrieved many hundreds of balls from the garden. On one memorable occasion my mother-in-law visiting from Barrow was quietly communing with natural digestive functions in the smallest room in the house when a golf ball hit and shattered the window and sent her screaming with shock, surprise and considerable loss of dignity into the bedroom. When I went outside to discover the cause of the commotion, at the fence I encountered a cross-faced lady golfer who greeted me with the words: "Damn. That shot ruined a very good round."

The bungalow, golf course and the 19th hole are still there although now there seem to be more trees to shield the bungalow from low-flying golf balls. There is still the short walk down Lowerhouse Lane to the new state-of-the-art stadium on the site of what was homely, working class Naughton Park. It was there that I cut my rugby league reporting teeth on the long-defunct *Widnes Guardian* - offshoot of the Warrington paper - watching the Chemics, or the 'Comics' as my disgruntled neighbours dubbed them when they had their frequent spells of non-success. Further afield the walk to the Saints' Knowsley Road ground down Dunriding Lane from the Bird I' Th' 'And pub is still the same, as is the old time-expired, but warmly familiar stadium.

There is still the left turn off Cardigan Road, Leeds, down to the Headingley gates... and the old press box is still there at Craven Park, Barrow, though it is now decrepit and disused on an old ground still redolent with memories of Willie Horne, Jimmy Lewthwaite and Phil Jackson playing before crowds of 10,000.

The Willows at Salford is also on its last legs before the move to Barton, but it still holds memories of Gus Risman, David Watkins, Keith Fielding, Mike Coulman and Ron Hill. I still bang my head on the low crossbeams walking along the back row of the old stand at what to me will always be Hilton Park at Leigh, and Castleford still play at Wheldon Road, even if the craze for daft nicknames of teams and grounds has grotesquely titled it The Jungle.

Wonderfully, the train trip to a Wembley Challenge Cup Final was back, this time packed with Saints fans looking for another cup victory, and Wigan and Warrington fans rooting for the Catalans. Good-humouredly, of course, with a Wigan party from the amateur side Shevington Sharks all wearing black berets and blue and white hooped shirts, with strings of garlic and onions round their necks.

This 2007 return to a new Wembley provided a welter of mixed emotions. It was a great feeling to share again the occasion which, even in the era of the Australasian style Super League Grand Final, will always represent for me the summit of rugby league in terms of tradition, anticipation and atmosphere.

However, as in most of life's big occasions there were overlapping highs and lows in what was undoubtedly a visual and aural explosion of spectacle, colour and noise.

Old Wembley had become timeworn and obsolete, yet it had a personality and character of its own, an atmosphere of relaxed camaraderie and cheerfulness in the mass walk up Wembley Way during which fans accepted as part of the event the stalls purveying burgers, frankfurters and hot and cold drinks at scandalous, rip-off prices, and the clutter of detritus in the old entrance passages.

As yet, new Wembley is an imposing fortress which dominates the skyline. I found it more awe-inspiring than welcoming. Its state-of-the-art tiers of seats loom so high into the sky that even the thought of sitting in the back row of the topmost tier can induce an attack of vertigo. It is the 21st century version of Rome's historic Coliseum.

For the media, the route to the admittedly magnificent press, radio and television facilities is like going through customs at Heathrow airport. In today's terrorist-ridden times, the security

192

measures are ruthlessly efficient, for which we must be thankful. Identification documents most be shown, including driving licence, national insurance number and media role proof; then the divesting of all metal objects from pockets, a frisking, and the opening up of the broadcasting equipment in the search for explosives; then came the wearing of various tags, including one round the wrist.

It has to be said that the facilities are magnificent. Extremely helpful security officials offer individual guidance to one's allotted seat, where the RFL's efficient press corps provide programmes, general information and teamsheets. Individual television monitors follow the BBC coverage of the game which also appears on the Stadium's giant screens for all to see.

Nor should nostalgia be allowed to cloud the fact that the new Wembley, like all the world's best and most modern venues, provides fantastic replacements for the former rundown and inadequate comfort facilities. There are 30 escalators and 26 lifts, wide concourses, 2,618 toilets, four restaurants and bars with pumps that can dispense four pints in 16 seconds. And the stadium is so designed that all the maximum 90,000 spectators has a clear view of the pitch.

Now to the ceremonies before the game: I was delighted to read in the programme that this included magnificent echoes of the past. There was the school students' curtain raiser, a parade of Lance Todd Trophy winners, the band of the Royal Marines marching in full regalia, the Marines' commando display, and a substantial musical contribution from the London Welsh male voice choir and the Icelandic classical tenor, Cortes. On paper it looked perfect, yet even this impressive mix had its share of amusing problems.

The schedule in the half hour before kick-off was so tight that at one stage there were Cortes, the male voice choir and the Marines band sandwiched between the two sets of players running about for their pre-match warm up. Meanwhile, up in the stands the fans chanted their players' names and practised their ditties. I think that the musicians must have felt that they had wandered onto the set of the climax of a Mel Brooks movie, or the finale of Chipperfields Circus.

It all came right in the end with the magnificent ensemble rendering of the great hymn *Abide with me*, and the game itself, while no classic, saw Saints eventually win comfortably after a lively Catalans start. All this before a magnificent attendance of 84,241, which dwarfed every other crowd, football and rugby union included, of the weekend, and emphasised that rugby league can still pull in the crowds and produce a show fit to grace Wembley and any stadium in the world.

Despite the spectacular advance in the quality and popularity of the sport, and the continuing pleasure I get when reporting games at every level, I still indulge in bouts of nostalgia. I can understand what the tragically short-lived poet Francis Thompson, a great fan of Lancashire cricket at Old Trafford in the late 19th century, meant when, sick and exiled in London, he penned the line: "The field is full of shades". He was referring particularly to Albert Hornby and Richard Barlow, the Lancashire heroes of his boyhood as they came back to life in memory and imagination.

But on the fields of my memory they are not really shades. I can visualise them clearly, as if it was the day before yesterday. Old Wembley provides so many: Willie Horne of Barrow and Alan Prescott of Saints leading their teams to victory in the late 1950s; Tom van Vollenhoven and centre Ken Large inter-passing from near their own line for the spectacular van Vollenhoven try that killed off Wigan on a baking hot day in 1961; and the utter heartbreak of Don Fox when he slipped in the swamp in front of the Leeds posts and missed the simple conversion that would have given Wakefield Trinity the Cup in the 1968 'Watersplash final'. I was writing a note about Fox's "dramatic late winner in Wembley's flooded arena" when I looked up and saw the Leeds forward Mick Clark jumping six feet in the air with joyous disbelief behind the posts. On live television there was Eddie Waring's simple, brilliant, timeless summary as tearful disconsolate Don trudged away: "He's missed it... poor lad".

Just one or two more 'shades' among so many. There was a rubbery-legged, semi-conscious Hull hooker Tommy Harris concussed and legless, being unwillingly dragged off the field by Hull coaching staff after literally running and tackling himself senseless in a pathetically brave attempt to stem the Wakefield tide in the one-sided 38-5 beating in the 1960 final. He was unaware that the press had awarded him the Lance Todd Trophy as man-of-the-match.

Then there was Wigan forward Norman Cherrington's headlong dash and missile dive across Wembley's turf in 1958 to slam Ike Southward into touch as the Workington winger was going in at the corner for what could have been the winning try, and Halifax's John Pendlebury's near-miraculous Wembley match-saving tackle over the line on St Helens' Mark Elia, when he punched the ball out of his grasp inches from the touchdown in 1987.

I also remember being a Brit in Sydney on that magical Saturday night when Mal Reilly's Lions shocked the cocky Australians on their own midden in 1988.

And in football, I recall the tears of joy streaming uncontrollably down Jack Walker's face as the whistle went at Anfield in 1995 and Blackburn Rovers had pipped the red-hot favourites Manchester United to the Premiership title...

These were memorable, unforgettable moments. But it would be wrong and foolish of me to pretend that the journalistic and broadcasting life is a continuous peak of visual adventure, excitement and human drama.

In between the highs and the lows there are times, familiar to everyone who has ever plied the trade, of humdrum boredom, disappointments, near-humiliation when you get it wrong, sleepless nights, and long, tedious journeys.

There were the weekends of worry and self-criticism when a goalscorer or key player has been wrongly identified, on air, even if only for a second, but long enough on radio or television for the producer to cut back to the studio before you can make the correction.

Then there was asking a first, contentious question at a press conference to a losing manager or coach and realising too late that you have just put your head in a sore and angry lion's mouth; or leaving an evening football game at Ipswich, Norwich or Southampton after waiting an hour in a freezing grandstand for a post-match interview with a manager, knowing that a four, five or six-hour journey home will get you to bed, at the earliest, around 4 or 5am. And then you hit fog at Crewe.

There were times when you were so neurotic about leaving behind the ISDN box of equipment on a long away trip that at various motorway stations you'd stop the car and rush round to the boot to check for the second or third time that the box was still there. Then you would arrive at the ground and open it to find a small but essential piece was missing.

Then there is the personal and private downside inescapable in a job of erratic hours and widespread locations. Travel and overnight stays make a stable, normal home life or family existence virtually impossible, particularly, as I found out when I was at my busiest, 50 out of 52 weeks involved some work on every day of the week.

Family and friends too often have had to accept rare and token days off and even rarer holidays, putting a huge strain on relationships, and regrettably my own marriage was a casualty. Thankfully, Sheila and I have remained friends and we retained close contact with our daughters, and friends have shown their value by remaining loyal especially in the bad times.

Contact with my younger brother Brian has been particularly sporadic, though always amicable, and Brian has recently reminded me that he, unlike me, has actually played rugby league at a professional level. His career lasted precisely 26 minutes. As a six-foot, wiry centre he got a trial with Liverpool City in 1960 at the Knotty Ash ground. The match was Liverpool City 'A' versus Oldham 'A', and since Brian had asked that no member of the family should be at the match, we gathered at my parents' home in Rainhill to await his return from what we hoped would be an outstanding debut.

Eventually, some time after 6pm an ambulance arrived at the front door and out stepped a pale-looking but attempting-to-be-cheerful Brian with his arm in plaster and a sling. A heavy tackle and fall in the 26th minute had broken his collarbone and his brief career in rugby league was over. Not for the first time did I reflect that reporting on the game was by far the safer option.

I was always close to my mother, but my father was the one who spent most time with me until his death in 1981. He was like an overgrown schoolboy in his delight in 'going to the match'. Wherever and whenever possible he travelled with me to games, loving the atmosphere and enjoying what he saw as the privilege of being welcomed into the always hospitable inner sanctums of rugby league social clubs and boardrooms. He supported first Warrington and then Widnes, an odd combination of loyalties, but had a quirky and unusual aversion to St Helens, the club where he had taken me for my XIII-a-side watching baptism in 1938.

I questioned him about this, and he explained that in the wire mill at Prescot cable works, where he was a fitter, everyone was a Saints fan, talked about nothing else and ribbed him about his friendship with Warringtonian Dick Carter.

His abhorrence of Saints, obviously not shared by me, showed itself in a chat we had the evening before I was to report on a St Helens versus Warrington derby at Knowsley Road. He said that he hoped my report would recount the fact that after the match there were two deep craters behind the St Helens posts where Warrington's prolific Brian Bevan had slammed down the ball for tries!

He was ever the humorist, my dad. I missed him terribly for a long time after he died, and during the months after his death would still pick up a spare programme to take home to him before realisation set in.

It is inevitable nowadays that certain questions crop up frequently regarding my past, present and future. Retirement? Not among the options as long as my voice and enthusiasm last, and I can still piece sentences together to a producer's satisfaction. Broadcasting and writing remain, more than ever, pleasurable fulfilment rather than a chore.

I envy those who move happily into retirement knowing that they can spend more time in the garden or the allotment, on the bowling green or the golf course, touring the country or the world, and generally fulfilling hopes and ambitions for which work gave them no time. To my shame, while I love beautiful gardens, I have been known to propel the blades of a lawnmower over its electric cable, and have also dug up a whole row of freshly planted sweet peas in the belief that they were a virulent form of weed.

Nor does DIY appeal. If there was one of those reality television shows for the world's most impractical man I would win the contest hands down. Computers are merely work tools, and cars are no more than beasts of burden which have overtaken horses. Relaxation for me is a book, a crossword puzzle, a classical concert, or a visit to the theatre, but only as an occasional break from the day job.

Another frequently asked question is: of all the sports I have covered, which is my favourite? The honest answer is that the variety, moving from one sport to another often within 24 hours, is the real thrill and pleasure. I enjoy watching all sports. But if a single straight answer is required it comes down to a choice between the big three of cricket, football and rugby league, the three games I still have the privilege of reporting.

Cricket, once the unchallenged summer sport, now has to compete with ever-lengthening football seasons and summer rugby, and has introduced so many Test series and one-day tournaments that county cricket, the bedrock of the game, has been shunted into a siding, denuded of test players.

Football, my first love as a schoolboy, and the source of my biggest schooldays' achievement, has provided me with the privilege of watching many exciting games and the opportunity to broadcast World Cups, club international tours and FA Cup Finals. I saw Tommy Lawton and Billy Liddell, Tom Finney and Stanley Matthews in their twilight years, George Best in his brief, dazzling prime, followed Leeds United to victory in the FA Cup, and Blackburn Rovers to the Premiership. Players undoubtedly are fitter and have more technical skills, but the so-called beautiful game once renowned for the simplicity of its laws, has seen the evolution at the highest level of complex team structures and tactics which often produce stalemates and low-scoring games rather than end-to-end excitement. A perfect, or imperfect, example of this was the turgid 2007 FA Cup Final between the country's top two clubs, Chelsea and Manchester United. Here was an anticipated showcase event which, taking away Drogba's goal, actually made watching paint dry, a hen sit or a glacier move seem like exhilarating experiences. Football at all levels from Premiership, Championship and the lower divisions through to the non-League pyramid still produces occasional exciting, competitive games but is in danger of becoming too predictable.

Players at top Premiership clubs have lost touch with the supporters whose vastly overpriced season tickets help provide them with hugely inflated salaries. It is a far cry from the 1950s when underpaid, maximum-wage stars like Sir Tom Finney and Nat Lofthouse caught the bus down to training and matches and chatted amicably with fans on the way and outside the ground. Today the top players drive top-of-the-range luxury cars, and are protected by a battery of stewards. While it is conceded that these huge £75,000-plus weekly salaries are due to the workings of the economic law of supply and demand, to many outside the game it must seem ridiculous that a man kicking a football about for 90 minutes can be paid more in a week than a junior doctor, nurse or policeman earn in a year, largely due to ruthlessly greedy agents.

So football, which I have always, naively perhaps, regarded as a sport to be enjoyed on and off the field, is now increasingly a global big business fuelling corporate and private greed; a target for international investors where the game and its players are merely marketable commodities.

There are still clubs, mostly below Premiership level, and certainly in Red Rose radio territory, where the hometown, family atmosphere still exists, and players are part of the community, but their number is diminishing in the struggle to survive and compete.

The last comment might well apply, as has been discussed earlier in these pages, to rugby league and the newly wealthy Super League in relation to the lower divisions. Top players are now full-time professionals, many from Australasia, but economic circumstances, the League's salary cap, the absence in smaller towns of football-type 60,000 and 70,000 crowds for league games, and the unavailability of Monopoly-money sponsorships has kept the lid on salary explosions. Rugby League is still a family sport, with friendly and approachable players, officials and staff, from its headquarters outwards, and a game where any player who has a tendency to get uppity or swollen-headed learns painful and salutary lessons on the field of play. From a reporter's point of view it is a journalist's dream once mutual trust is established.

I have left to the last the real and major reason for the choice of rugby league as my favourite. And that is, I suppose, the ultimate test of a spectator sport, its entertainment value. Every first class sport offers its great contests and moments, but for me the XIII-a-side game provides more excitement, tension and entertainment per minute of play than any other major team sport.

There are no tedious and contrived 0-0 draws; no breaks for rain or bad light; no repetitive kicking to touch, untidy rolling mauls and pushovers, punctuated by the continuous peep of the referee's whistle. Rugby league flows, with the emphasis on attack, perhaps overly so under current laws and rules, with speedy handling and frequent spectacular tries. The game offers no scope for divers or injury cheats, and whatever may happen at schoolboy matches, senior referees, even when they make the occasional appalling gaffe, stand no risk of being manhandled.

I'd like to answer just one more regular, hardy annual query. Who do I think is the best-ever XIII-a-side player? This is so tough a call to be virtually impossible to answer. It could be any member of the League's Hall of Fame, or every fan's personal choice. After much soul-searching it comes down to three. The first is the best-ever scrum half: rule-bending imp Alex Murphy, who could win a game single-handed with one lightning break. The second is Neil Fox, prolific all-round points scorer and a true sportsman in every sense of the word. The last is my one-time nemesis but a complete performer and leader Ellery Hanley. I cannot choose between them.

The question I often ask myself is whether, knowing all the pitfalls and vagaries of the journalistic life, I would choose it again if some magical time machine were to take me back to boyhood and schooldays.

Would it have been more comfortable, less tense and edgy, more family friendly had I opted for a life as a psychiatrist, librarian or an English teacher?

Would I still want the seven-day week, the long hours and long journeys, the post-match waits for a potentially testy manager, the uncertainty of freelance life with its feasts and famines, contracts gained and contracts lost?

Would I really want to live through all that again?

If only...

Index of names

N.B. This index does not include members of Keith's family where they are referred to by first names only.